To Israel, with Love

A Journey of Discovery

Second Edition

To Israel, with Love

A Journey of Discovery
– History, Mystery, Travel, and Relationships –

Second Edition

With a Foreword by Dr. Norman Neaves

CAROLYN B. LEONARD

A guide to the unexplained mysteries and histories
of the holy land according to the Bible and other references;
where to go, what to see, when to go, what to learn and why;
how to get the most out of your trip
whether traveling in person or vicariously. Revised, updated, fully indexed, and
illustrated, including maps and charts.

© 2016, 2018 by Carolyn B. Leonard, rev 12/1/2020
All rights reserved. First edition 2016. Second edition 2020.
Hardback ISBN 13: 978-1883852-18-4
Softcover ISBN 13: 978-1883852-09-2
E-book ISBN 13: 978-883852-10-8
Library of Congress control number 2018902864
Manufactured in the United States of America
5678910

No part of this publication may be reproduced, distributed, or transmitted in any form or by any means, without prior written permission from the publisher, except by a reviewer who may quote passages in review. Although the author and publisher have exhaustively researched all sources to ensure the accuracy and completeness of the information contained in this book, we assume no responsibility for errors, inaccuracies, omissions, or any other inconsistency herein. Some names have been changed to protect their privacy. Any slights against people or organizations are unintentional.

To Israel, With Love by Carolyn B. Leonard, Color 8x10
Buffalo Industries, LLC

Epigraph and Preface

Quote from the foreword of *Innocents Abroad* by Mark Twain (Samuel Clemens) in 1867:

This book is a record of a pleasure trip. If this compilation were a record of a solemn scientific expedition, it would have that scholarly look and impressive incomprehensibility that seems to stick with proper tomes of that kind. This is more like a record of a picnic, except it does have a certain purpose which is to suggest to the reader how he would be likely to see this country and what he might learn and remember if he looked at Israel with his own eyes instead of mine. I think I have looked with somewhat impartial eyes, and have written honestly, whether wisely or not.

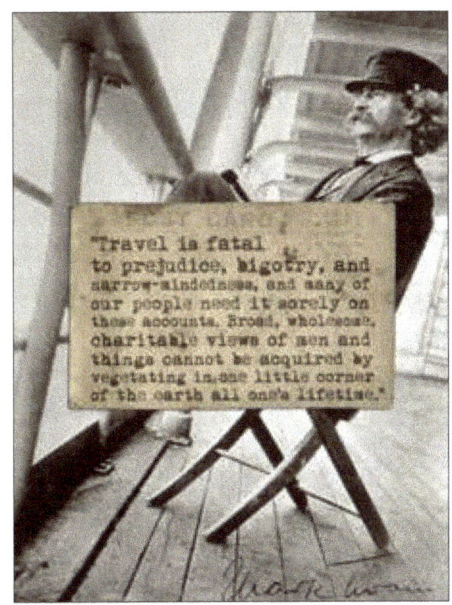

FIGURE 1: MARK TWAIN

I could not find any book that prepared me for this trip. I promised myself I would write one simple enough for anyone to understand; a guide that would explain unexplained mysteries and collect all the various names for a place so it could be charted on a map.

I tried to write objectively, but I am a Christian. I was born, raised, and remain in the Bible belt, so my perspective may reveal unintended bias. **I am not trying to convert anyone, just presenting the facts as I see them, and letting the reader make their own conclusions.**

Since this book is about travel and not intended to be scholarly, I won't burden the pages with sources and footnotes. My sources are general and ordinary with a complete bibliography at the end, and I do include Bible references at times. The acronyms for different Bible versions are in the "Bibliography by Title" section at the back.

This nonfiction book is fully illustrated with more than two hundred photos, mostly by the author, and includes many maps of the area. More than a travelogue featuring biblical events showing where each took place more than two thousand years ago, this book describes what it might be like to visit that place now. It is my hope this journal will in some small way provide information to make such a trip more rewarding for you, and that future readers will treasure the book as a historical record of travel in the late twentieth century and early twenty-first.

I hope *To Israel, with Love* will be read and used by people of many countries, faiths and levels of knowledge, so I want to be sure the playing field is level.

It took twenty years, two trips to Israel, tons of research, and now here it is. If you have ever dreamed of visiting this incredible country, this book is for you.

Best wishes,

Carolyn B. Leonard, 2020

What other readers say about *To Israel, With Love:*

Rev. Richard Greenlee of Oklahoma City, OK; Baptist Minister: *This is one of the best books on Israel I have ever read in almost fifty years of preaching and teaching. Anyone planning on going to Israel should read this book before they go. I recommend it to anyone leading a tour group to that country.*

Sally Jadlow of Overland Park, KS; author of eight books, ordained chaplain, speaker, member Kansas Authors Club, board member of Christian Writers Network: To Israel with Love *is a very informative guide to the person who is going to Israel—or to the person who wants to, but knows they will never get there.*

Rosemary Hardage, native of Independence, MO; Bible scholar, mother, tennis captain, State Capitol Senate encoder, former editor of *The Geological Survey*: To Israel, With Love *is chock full of advice and interesting details about specific places to see—a wealth of information for anyone planning a trip. It's written in an easy to follow format, mapping out the author's ten-day journey and listing each site visited as the trip unfolded.*

Sarah Yauk of Buffalo, OK; farmer, mother, public school educator and administrator: *I was worried about planning a trip to Israel, but now I am really excited and can't wait to go.*

Raymona Anderson of Bentonville, AR; author, travel writer, retired newspaper editor, and prize-winning author of state and national competitions: *I'd never visited the holy land until I read Carolyn B. Leonard's* To Israel, With Love. *This work gave me insights I'd hope to experience if I went in person. She does so in a storyteller voice and provides illustrations that draw the reader even closer.*

Anonymous Amazon customer: *In the tradition of V.S. Naipul, Carolyn Leonard brings us* To Israel, With Love. *For anyone seeking a guidebook to Israel as a preparatory guide, Leonard has written "that book." Dually, she brings us in Naipul's tradition, a literary guide with historical insight rendered as that of a historian of this ancient Land. Leonard's book prepares you for travel to this region and fills you in on history, culture and locale. Even if you don't travel and you are an avowed homebody, this is a fascinating read and a book I could not put down.*

Dr. Norman Neaves, Senior Minister Emeritus, *Church of the Servant, Oklahoma City, OK: Israel is a land you see with your heart and not just with your eyes, a land you embrace with your whole being and not just another interesting place that you visit. Carolyn Leonard has been able to capture that deeper sense of one's time there so it becomes a pilgrimage of the human soul, and an experience you will never forget as long as you live. Truly, it can transform your life.*

Table of Contents

Epigraph and Preface .... *v*
Foreword by Dr. Norman Neaves .... *xi*

1. **DAY OF LEARNING** 1
   Monday: El Al, Many Religions, Bibles, Qumran, and Shrine of the Book.

2. **DAY OF ABRAHAM** 23
   Tuesday: Tel Aviv, Mezuzahs, Abraham's family, Jews, Rachel's Tomb.

3. **DAY OF KING HEROD** 39
   Wednesday: Caesarea, Megiddo, Herodium, Haifa, Rome, and the Kibbutz on the Galilee.

4. **DAY OF JESUS** 73
   Thursday: Nazareth, Capernaum, Galilee, Jordan River, Golan, West Bank, Mount of Beatitudes.

5. **DAY OF KING SAUL** 91
   Friday: Beit She'an, Jericho, Wadi Qelt, Gideon's Spring, Saul & David, Stones of Israel.

6. **DAY OF KING DAVID** 11
   Saturday/Shabbat: Jebus, David's Palace, Tomb of Absalom, Engedi, Masada, Dead Sea.

7. **DAY OF KING SOLOMON** 141
   Sunday: Jerusalem, Solomon's Palace, Babylon, Bethlehem, Shepherd's Fields, Wedding.

8. **DAY OF JERUSALEM** 167
   Monday: The Gates of Jerusalem, The Western Wall, Zedediah's Cave, Hezekiah's Tunnel, Dome of the Rock, Model City, & Independence Day.

9. **DAY OF TRIAL** 203
   Tuesday: Last Supper, Tomb of Kings, Constantine & Queen Helena, Holy Relics, Church of Sepulcher, Golgotha & Garden Tomb.

10. **DAY OF MOSES** 229
    Wednesday: Yad Vashem, Joseph, Moses, Egypt, Passover and the Moral of the Story.

Bibliography by title and author 247
Dedication to the first tour group 254
Index of illustrations 255
Alphabetical index 259
About the author 265
Other Books by the author 266

Knock and it shall be opened …

Ask and it will be given to you; seek and you will find; knock and the door will be opened to you.
(Matthew 7:7 NIV)

AUTHOR'S PRIVATE COLLECTION

FIGURE 3: A DOOR IN THE WADI QELT MONASTERY

Israel in Jesus's time, was then called Judea, Judah, Galilee

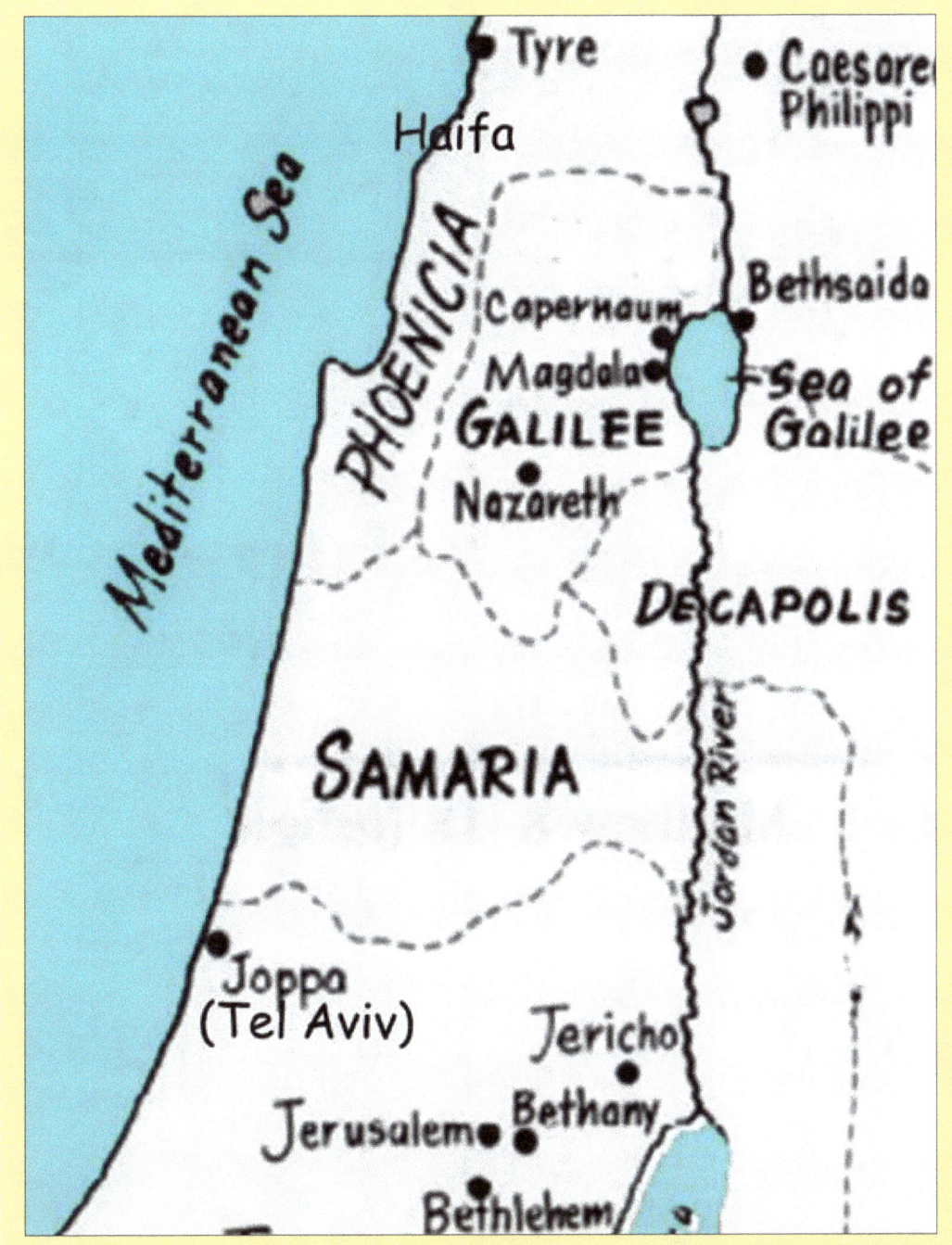

FIGURE 2: MAP OF ISRAEL IN JESUS'S TIME
The primary locations mentioned in the New Testament are shown. Some roads existed at that time, but many roads were not safe to travel.

FIGURE 4: JON SAYS COME ALONG AND JOIN OUR ADVENTURE!

AUTHOR'S PRIVATE COLLECTION

Foreword

Excerpt from an issue of <u>Thrust</u>,
publication of The United Methodist Church of the Servant, Oklahoma City.

The Power of Something Small and Seemingly Ordinary

By Dr. Norman Neaves

FIGURE 5: DR. NORMAN NEAVES

This might come as a surprise to you, but actually I never had any desire whatsoever to go to the holy land and visit those places in which our faith began—not until, that is, Kipp and I went for the first time.

I guess I thought it would be very commercialized. And I guess, too, I wondered why anyone in their right mind would want to go off to that part of the world where so much tension between the Jews and the Arabs exists. And maybe also I thought that I could read about those events and places and people in my own Bible and get everything I need in my own journey of faith. So why go?

When the offer came to go with a group of ministers and do a film, I decided that maybe I just ought to do it for curiosity's sake. Why not? I don't have anything to lose, I said to myself. And so Kipp and I went, not really expecting to get all that much out of the experience but thinking that we could at least say we'd been there.

Neither one of us was prepared for what we saw and what happened inside of each of our lives the very first morning we began touring. We arrived late in the afternoon at Ben Gurion Airport in Tel Aviv and didn't get to our hotel room in Jerusalem until nightfall. By the time we had dinner at the Hilton and got settled in our room, it was just about time to go to bed. After all, we had flown for some twelve hours over the Atlantic from New York City and we were quite tired indeed.

About 8:00 the next morning, we boarded the little tour bus and headed over to Mt. Scopus, which is very near where we were staying. And when we all got there and got off of the bus, we went to the edge of the mountain and looked to the south. And I can't even begin to describe the emotions that began welling up inside of me in the next five minutes or so. I mean, it was like the very heart and core of the whole world itself was lying right there in front of us. The Kidron Valley was running along all the way down below the mountain upon which we were standing, all the way to the south where it began a part of yet another valley.

We could turn our heads and our eyes no more than an inch or two to the left and there was the Mount of Olives upon which the transfiguration of Jesus occurred (and many other special events as well!).

And simply letting our eyes come down the side of the Mount of Olives and into the Kidron Valley, one could see off in the distance the Garden of Gethsemane itself—just as clear and identifiable as it could be.

Turning our heads ever so slightly to the right, was the Antonio Fortress where Jesus stood trial before Pontius Pilate and was sentenced to die. The Temple Mount was right there also, the place where King Solomon built his great temple and beneath which many feel the **Ark of the Covenant** is deeply buried to this day. Off in the distance, ever so slightly to the right just a little bit more, one could see from Mount Scopus, Golgotha "the place of the skull" as the Bible calls it—where our Lord died on that Good Friday two thousand years ago.

I looked over to Kipp and she to me—and both of us had tears in our eyes. Why? I don't know. I can't explain it. It's something one must experience in order to understand and appreciate what happened. But I can't imagine very many people, especially believers, who would not have happen within them exactly what happened in us. I must confess that it is about as emotional of an experience as I have ever had in my life.

As the early morning wind blew upon the mount and I kept looking at all that lay before me, I found myself standing in utter amazement that so much of the history of the world has been shaped by events that took place in that one single space over a relatively short period of time. I mean, that very place on the face of the earth is where Judaism began … and then Christianity … and then Islam some six hundred years later.

Think of it, three of the world's five major religions all began in that very spot! On the one hand, it's such a very common and ordinary spot, too. But for all of its commonness and in all of its ordinariness, it is the place where three of the world's greatest religions were born.

I didn't feel like saying anything as I stood there. Neither did Kipp. Neither did most of the others in our little group. It was much like folks feel when they walk up to the edge of the Grand Canyon for the very first time. It is so awesome, so incredible and so unbelievable, you are flooded with deep emotions and you just don't have words to express what you are experiencing. So, you go quiet and you let the silence express the depth that you are feeling.

When we came back, we were different people than when we left just a week before.

Sincerely,

Dr. Norman Neaves

Alpha—The beginning

AUTHOR'S PRIVATE COLLECTION

FIGURE 6: A CITY ON A HILL

Genesis 12:1–3 CEV: After the death of Abram's father, God told him:
Leave your country, your family, and your relatives and go to the land that I will show you. I will bless you and make your descendants into a great nation. You will become famous and be a blessing to others. I will bless those who bless you, but I will put a curse on anyone who puts a curse on you. Everyone on earth will be blessed because of you.

Quick Index to Maps and Charts:

Item	Chapter	Page
Abraham's journey map	2	28
Abraham's wives and sons	2	29
Abraham's genealogy chart	2	31
Acronyms for Bible Versions	back matter	247
Ark of the Covenant (illustration)	8	187
Church of Sepulchre	9	219
David's palace map	7	147
David's divided kingdom map	6	125
Dome of Rock, cross section chart	8	185
Herod's family chart	3	46
ISRAEL MAPS		
in Jesus Time map	front matter	ix
in AD 30 map	4	245
Topographic map	back matter	244
Greenline 1949, 1967 Boundary map	back matter	89
Jacob's descendant's chart	2	33
JERUSALEM in AD 635 & gates map	7	166
Model City of Jerusalem	8	200
Jerusalem to Babylon map	7	151
Jewish & Bible history charts	back matter	246
Roman Empire map	2	45
Solomon's Temple layout	7	141
Solomon's Temple illustration	7	146, 147
Temple mount elevation	8	177
Twelve tribes of Israel chart	2	34

ONE

DAY OF LEARNING

Monday: El Al, Many Religions, Bibles, Qumran, and Shrine of the Book

DAY ONE: There was no possibility of eating before departure. Butterflies of excitement, fluffy yellow pom-poms, piles of suitcases, and sleepy faces await us at the airport. International flights require an earlier check-in than other flights, so we leave home by 4:30 a.m. for red-eye takeoff. At the airport, Dr. Norman and Kipp Neaves, pin on our name badges and another veteran traveler surprises us by tying fluffy yellow yarn pom-poms on our baggage. I wish I had thought to bring something to share.

We are allowed only one suitcase and one carry-on bag, but that adds up to a pile of forty-four checked bags in a carousel loaded with hundreds of others. We know we must quickly locate our suitcases at every stop, match them to bag checks for security officers, and carry them away. Now we absent-mindedly notice the pom-poms, not yet appreciating how valuable those easily identified yellow balls will be at every loading and unloading event.

We look around at our group members, most of whom we had met at least once in the trip prep classes, but none of whom we know very well. Our group ranges in age from Jeanna, a young adult of twenty, to Herb and Lois celebrating their golden wedding anniversary. We struggle to remember which names go with each face and feel grateful for nametags.

I can't help wondering if the longing to see this faraway land, this desire so long denied, is as intense in each heart as my own. I'd almost given up my dream to visit Israel. I planned the journey in another life, another town, another group, but then took all my savings and sent my sixteen-year-old daughter instead. Perhaps it is right this realization was not possible at a younger age, because I could not have appreciated the privilege so much as now.

Our tour guide said Jerusalem, like Israel in general, is a year-round destination but the very best months are late March through April and October through November when prices are lower and the weather is good. Jerusalem becomes quite arid in the hot, rainless summer months. We picked late April for our first trip and late July in the second. Both those months proved way too hot for enjoyment.

Also, the brochure may say "Ten days in Israel" but you will spend two of those days in the air.

Finally, the preliminaries are over, we hear our boarding call and make our way down the gateway onto the aircraft and into our seats. Bright rays of sunshine ricochet off the silver wings of our American Airlines jet as we lift off from Oklahoma City's Will Rogers World Airport for our four-hour ride to New York's LaGuardia.

Once settled, I find some crackers, string cheese, and trail mix snacks in my carry-on bag. That proved lucky because we will not be served anything for what seemed like hours. I did have something to share after all, though not nearly enough for everyone.

Tip: Pack snacks in your carry-on. Bring something to share.

This leg of the trip flies past quickly. Very soon, the flight attendant announces we are near LaGuardia. The air is clear, and we enjoy a good view of the "Big Apple" as the plane circles for landing. We excitedly identified familiar landmarks such as the new One World Observatory and the United Nations building.

DANGER HAS NO BOUNDARIES: Perhaps you worry about news reports of armed conflicts in Israel? Remembering the 1993 and 2001 bombings at the World Trade Center's twin towers above New York's lower Manhattan, we recognize the dangers of travel, particularly to the Middle East. We are aware of our own country's risks, but there are no bans on traveling here.

In the first attack, a terrorist bomb ripped through the Trade Center, killing six people and injuring more than a thousand others. Eventually, there would be arrests of a group of Islamic fundamentalists, followers of a storefront preacher with seething contempt for Western modernity; anger over US policy; a long and mostly uneventful trial.

At that time, we could not know of the terrible disaster that would befall our city, the bombing on April 19, 1995, of the Murrah Federal Building, resulting in one hundred sixty-eight deaths and more than five hundred people injured. That Oklahoma City bombing was said to be the act of an American terrorist seeking revenge for the US Government authorized destruction of the radical Branch-Davidian compound near Waco, Texas, and the deaths of members of that religious cult.

By a strange coincidence, we learned of the Waco event on the same day we visited the Masada Fortress near Jerusalem. At Masada in the year AD 70, in a strangely similar incident, more than a thousand Jewish zealot rebels—men, women, and children—committed suicide rather than be taken captive by the Romans. More details of that story will come in Chapter Six when we visit Masada.

The World Trade Center complex in New York housed our nation's most massive office towers. On September 11, 2001, nineteen militants associated with the Islamic extremist group al-Qaeda hijacked four airliners and carried out suicide attacks against targets in the United States. Two of the planes smashed into the towers of the World Trade Center in New York City. A third plane hit the Pentagon just outside Washington, DC, and the fourth crashed in a field in Pennsylvania. Often referred to as 9/11 or nine-one-one, the attacks resulted in extensive death and destruction, triggering major US initiatives to combat terrorism and defining the presidency of George W. Bush. More than three thousand people died in the attacks, including at least four hundred police officers and firefighters. Yet just before that moment, life was normal. People maintained a flurry of activity coming out and going in. How unbelievable that those towers would topple from another Mid-Eastern terrorist attack.

Perhaps there is not so much difference in safety in our two countries?

Our pilot brought the jet to a gentle landing. Once on the ground at LaGuardia, we claimed our baggage. We quickly jumped on a shuttle to Kennedy International Airport for our connection with El

Al (Israel) Airlines. Our entourage faced quite a challenge with El Al officials, known for their tight security.

TIME FOR A CHALLENGE: So far, El Al has never had a plane sabotaged, and they intend to keep it that way. All ticket holders are interrogated and cross-examined to ensure they are not connected with any terrorist organization.

Security is no joking matter to the Israeli airline, so the tedious process drags on. "Hang in there," Dr. Neaves encouraged us. "I hear that El Al once delayed a flight for seven hours because of a rumor they had a stowaway mouse."

As the El Al people carried out their endless individual interviews and cross-examinations, we joked about what may have happened to the runaway rodent. Eventually, everyone passed El Al's test except for three people. Jon and I were shocked to learn we were two of the suspects!

Another passenger, Dr. Glass, might not be allowed to board the plane either. His passport showed an expiration date within six months of the flight. Although he had received an extension of time from US custom authorities, El Al's security people said he would have to stay behind.

AUTHOR'S PRIVATE COLLECTION

FIGURE 1: TIME FOR A CHALLENGE
Israel's El Al is said to have the most rigorous airline security of all countries.

*Tip: Be sure your passport has more than six months before expiration.

The doctor and his wife conferred with Dr. and Mrs. Neaves, assembling a plan for Neil to ride another airline and catch up with us later in Israel. No one wanted to leave him behind; our group had begun to bond. It was a time of uneasiness. An airline supervisor arrived. They conferred, studied the situation, and finally stamped approval on his ticket. We all breathed a sigh of relief.

Israel's El Al is said to have the most rigorous airline security of all countries. The X-ray machines used in airports can detect guns and other metal objects, but their screens cannot show plastic explosives. Passenger interrogations and careful manual searches of luggage continue efficiently. El Al demonstrates real security can be had only at a considerable expense of money and time.

As for Jon and me, our problem was ID. Recently married, our luggage tags said Mr. and Mrs., but my passport and driver's license were in my former name. Those Israeli officials were troubled why the labels did not match. They had not heard of a married woman retaining her previous name. They did not understand at all. We were dismayed to think after all our planning and studying, saving pennies and building anticipation—we could be left behind.

Wait, I said, as they moved our suitcases out of the loading stack. We could phone the Oklahoma County Clerk to verify our marriage license. The officials put their heads together. Finally, they loaded our suitcases back on the cart. Keeping my name was a good idea legally and professionally, but the different monikers have caused us some unexpected problems, and this was only the first.

Tip: Be sure you have your passport and legal names all in order, and your suitcases tagged to match if you want to fly El Al without a hitch.

FINALLY, UP IN THE AIR: Once all our people passed inspection, we received assigned boarding passes. Seating was alphabetical, and since our passports were in different legal names, the newly-joined were about to be newly-separated. Luckily, we talked fellow group members and even strangers into trading seats so the honeymooners could sit together. One man joked he was happy to trade with us because he and his wife had been married so many years, they now preferred sitting with other people. I never told his wife he said that and won't name him now.

We had been on transatlantic flights before but never paid much attention to arrangements. This description will sound primitive to a traveler in twenty years. The cabin was like a floating hotel. Four engine jet transports, designed for long nonstop passenger flights can fly nonstop six thousand miles or more at an altitude of thirty to forty-five thousand feet beginning with almost fifty thousand gallons of fuel. Our Boeing 747 had twelve washrooms and six galleys for five hundred passengers. However, the toilets are as small as on any domestic jetliner. We recently read about a woman who gave birth in an airline water closet, and it is a mystery how that could happen when you can barely find enough room to turn around and sit down. We never saw the front first-class section or the second cabin business class because stewards practice complete segregation, keeping high-priced ticket holders curtained off. We could and did stroll down aisles of three other sections. Coach class areas had two seats on the right by windows and three seats on the left by windows. The center stretched seven seats across with an aisle on each side. The airline may have changed the seating arrangement since then. Jon traded his aisle seat to long-legged Owen while I gave my window seat to Neil, so we could sit together for this long flight. We wound up about four rows back in the center of the middle section, every seat occupied, shoehorned in, knees knocking against seatbacks, zero inches to spare. Not the most comfortable way to travel, but we were so happy about our destination we weren't about to complain.

Once the pilot turned off the "fasten seatbelt" light after takeoff, we were able to recline the padded seatbacks a microscopic bit. Seasoned long-distance travelers had dropped hints we might find vacant seats and could move after liftoff. With every place occupied in our section, we had no hope of finding a way to recline during the long ride. We knew it would be a very long night.

The airline's folding baby cribs filled the front of each section, every bassinet occupied during the long Atlantic Ocean crossing. Even though the children behaved very well, with so many youngsters in our section, we began to wonder if we had been assigned to ride as nannies and nursery workers.

I felt fortunate to be seated next to Susan, an attractive young attorney in our group, with knowledge of Hebrew history. Susan pointed out the variety of clothing styles worn by people on the flight that expressed many different forms of Jewish customs.

BOYS IN BLACK SUITS: Young men and boys wore severe black suits, hats, and shoes. Many covered their heads with a small black skullcap on the back of their heads called a *Yarmulke*. Prayer shawl fringes often peeked out below their jackets. Some of the young boys displayed a long curl of hair in front of each ear. Susan explained the long coil is a tradition of the *Hasidic* Jews, an orthodox and devout conservative group.

I struggle to recall things learned over the years about the history of this area. While doubtful anyone has written or will write an objective and definitive summary accepted by everyone, perhaps this document will provide a good introduction.

Even finding a single suitable name to call the land of the Bible is the first issue. Each title—Palestine, Judea, Israel, Holy Land—presents issues from the first century AD continuing through the twenty-first century. Over time, many empires have ruled the country, which has been known by many different names.

Here are the basics covered in classes before our trip:

- ✓ Briefly: The land variously called Israel, Judea and Palestine is small (about the size of New Jersey, or ten thousand square miles) at the eastern end of the Mediterranean Sea squeezed between Egypt, Turkey, Jordan, and Syria. During the country's long history, population and ownership varied greatly.

- ✓ The Israelites migrated to the Palestine area from Egypt about 2000 BC, although they did not call the country Palestine then. After a period of exile in Egypt, they returned.

- ✓ A tent-like structure called the tabernacle served as their first sanctuary, where they offered their sacrifices in the wilderness.

- ✓ Under King David, the Hebrews set up their kingdom with its capital and a tabernacle at The City of David (lower Jerusalem).

- ✓ King David's son and successor, King Solomon, built the first temple on the rock protrusion of Mount Moriah (in Jerusalem). Solomon incorporated the portable tent/tabernacle and its sacred vessels into the temple, where he placed the holy Ark.

- ✓ After the death of King Solomon, the Palestine area became a divided kingdom of two hostile countries, Israel (the northern kingdom) and Judah/ Judea, in the south. Judea outlasted their

FIGURE 2: BOYS IN BLACK SUITS
Young Hasidic men and boys dressed in severe black suits, hats, and shoes, sometimes with a long curl in front of each ear and prayer shawl fringes hanging below their jackets.

rival, perhaps because of the strength of their capital in Jerusalem. Then the Babylonians overran Jerusalem and destroyed Solomon's temple. That city collapsed, and the Ark disappeared. The combined area is now all encompassed in the country of Israel. We will pursue the mystery of the missing Ark of the Covenant on this trip.

OFFERING FERVENT PRAYERS: Periodically one of the Jewish men would move near the front of the section. They pray fervently, their bodies moving in a rhythmic bobbing motion. Others pray vigorously where they are seated. "The more orthodox Jews pray even more fervently at the wailing wall in Jerusalem," Susan whispered, as their bobbing motion at times increased in intensity to a convulsive jerk.

We noted several Jewish women wearing full wigs, in strict obedience to the Old Testament Bible verse encouraging a woman to keep her head covered in the presence of men other than her husband. This wiggy thing was a new idea to me. Why would artificial hair provide better coverage than your own? I recently learned that *Hasidic* rabbis require women to shave their heads to ensure that not a single hair remains. These orthodox women cover their bald heads with beautiful wigs (*sheitels*) or a headscarf (*shmatteh*).

After standing and praying for a time, one man bent over one of the baby cribs to gently and lovingly pat the tiny, sleeping child before returning to his seat. We were glad to see the men sharing the work of caring for the babies and entertaining the children on the flight. I'm sure their wives were thankful too, with or without perfect hair covering their heads.

Israel is a country of many faiths, challenging to sort out and understand. Muslims, Crusaders, Romans, Christians, Mamelukes, Pagans, and perhaps more.

FIGURE 3: RELIGIONS
Islam, Hinduism, Christianity, Judaism, Taoism, Buddhism.

ROMANS: In those days, all roads led to Rome. The Roman Empire surrounded the Mediterranean Sea and included the country we know as Israel. The word Roman included all persons who possessed Roman citizenship, regardless of language, race, culture, or place of birth. For example, Paul was a Jew from Tarsus in Cilicia (modern Turkey, north of Palestine), but he was also a Roman citizen. The ancient Roman religion involved many gods, and they thought these gods controlled different parts of the world. Roman citizens worshipped their emperors.

MUSLIMS AND ISLAM: Muslims are followers of Muhammed, the Prophet of Islam. They call themselves Muslims, and that is how they are known commonly, but the Arabic spelling is Moslem. Muhammed was born in Mecca in southwestern Arabia (Saudi Arabia), and he founded the religion of Islam in the AD 600s. Muslims believe Muhammed was the last messenger of God, completing the teachings of such earlier prophets as Abraham, Moses, and Jesus. Muhammed believed Jews and Christians would accept him as a prophet. When they did not fall at his feet, he drove them from Mecca. Then Muhammed abandoned many of the Jewish traditions he had previously followed. The five pillars of Islam are:

1. confession of faith;
2. prayer five times daily;
3. fasting during the daylight hours of Ramadan;
4. almsgiving; and
5. making a pilgrimage to Mecca.

Located in western Saudi Arabia, Mecca is the holiest city in Islam, the birthplace of Muhammed and spiritual center of Islam. Non-Muslims are strictly forbidden to enter the city. Islam prescribes the behavior for individuals and society, codifying law, family relations, business etiquette, dress, food, personal hygiene, and much more. Jonah, from the Israeli tribe of Benjamin, is the only one of the twelve minor prophets of the Hebrew Bible mentioned by name in the Koran (*Qur'an*). In Muslim tradition, Jonah's narrative is remarkably similar to the Hebrew Bible story. A gigantic fish came and swallowed him, and Jonah remained in the belly of the fish, repenting, and glorifying God.

MUSLIM WOMEN: Among their essential values is a family-centered way of life, including a protected role for women and clear limits on their participation in public life. In the presence of adult males outside of their immediate family, Muslim women beyond the age of puberty must always wear a *hijab* (pronounced he-job), or a veil that covers the head and chest. Westerners often see the *hijab* as a tool utilized by men to control and silence women. The *burqa* (also spelled burka) garment covers women most completely; either only the eyes are visible, or nothing at all. Some Muslims believe the *hijab* for women should be compulsory as part of sharia, i.e., Muslim law. Sharia law is quite harsh and radical on women. In traditional societies, Muslims believe open social relations between the sexes result in the breakdown of family life. Contact between men and women, therefore, is rigidly controlled in traditional Muslim society.

PAGANS: Pagans profess polytheistic religion; they worship many gods. The deity Baal is one of the most prominent of the pagan gods, and the most familiar to Christians. Most Romans were pagan, and some scholars believe the little statues of the Virgin Mary and the crucified Christ figures in Roman Catholic churches could tie back to the Roman background of worshipping multiple idols, although this is quite disputable.

CRUSADERS: Crusaders claimed to worship Jesus, but today's Christians would blush at disclosures of some crusader history. The dictionary definition of the Crusades is a series of religious wars between Christians and Muslims started primarily to secure control of holy sites considered sacred by both groups. In all, eight major crusade expeditions occurred between 1096 and 1291. The bloody, violent, and often ruthless conflicts propelled European Christians' status, making them significant players in the fight for land in the Middle East. Members of the expeditions sewed the symbol of the cross on their tunics.

Although crusaders supposedly came to liberate Christian holy places, many did not follow the teachings of Jesus carefully; in fact, the most horrible inhumanities committed over the ages happened in the name of religion. Those so-called "holy wars" lasted nearly two hundred years. Crusader churches were robust in Israel for a time but gradually died out.

MELISENDE, QUEEN OF JERUSALEM: Melisende (1105–1161) reigned as Queen of Jerusalem in AD 1131 for twenty years, then she served as regent for her thirteen-year-old son from 1153 until her death. The Church of the Sepulchre hosted her coronation. Melisende's father, King Baldwin II, a crusader knight of Jerusalem and her mother, the Armenian princess Morphia of Melitene, sat on the throne until then. Baldwin arranged for his daughter's marriage to Count Fulk V, of Anjou.

The First Crusade took place before Melisende's birth in the spring of AD 1097 when more than one hundred thousand crusaders joined forces on the eastern side of the Bosphorus. The combined army fought its way along the coast of the Mediterranean, reaching the gates of Jerusalem in June of 1099. Fighting continued until blood ran through Solomon's Temple. The knights reported they waded in blood up to their knees and bridle reins. The crusaders took Jerusalem from the Fatimid Caliphate, opening the way for the Kingdom of Jerusalem to be the most potent Crusader State in the Middle Ages.

At the death of her father, Melisende and the Count became co-rulers. The coronation would have been a significant public event designed to cement in the minds of everyone who witnessed it the beginning of a new period of divinely sanctioned rule. Representatives came from Antioch, Tripoli, and Edessa, including bishops, abbots, and all the other churchmen of the realm.

QUEEN MELISANDE'S PRAYER BOOK, THE BRITISH LIBRARY

FIGURE 4: PRAYER BOOK.
One of the treasures left from Queen Melisende's reign in Jerusalem is her prayer book, created by the monks of the Church of Holy Sepulchre, probably around AD 1140. The queen, a supporter of the crusades, is pictured on the following page.

Jerusalem must have been overflowing with visitors staying with friends, fellow religious groups, or in the many hostels. Count Fulk and Princess Melisende, assisted by servants, were dressed in the royal palace in special robes, beautifully embroidered dalmatics—wide-sleeved tunics, open at the sides and topped with stoles. They would mount their festooned horses and join the royal guard for a procession from the Temple Mount to the Church of the Sepulchre for the coronation.

FIGURE 5: QUEEN MELISENDE
Melisende, Queen of Jerusalem, at her coronation in AD 1131 in the Church of the Sepulchre.

Queen Melisende ruled Jerusalem defending the crusader states against Muslim attacks and supporting art and architecture in the Holy Land. As one of Melisande's accomplishments, she established a convent and leper colony. She named her sister Yvetta as mother superior. The queen chose Bethany for the colony because it was the biblical home of Mary, Martha, and Lazarus, who were great friends of Jesus Christ. The principal historian of that era, William of Tyre, said that throughout her lifetime Melisende continually bestowed gifts upon this convent at Bethany and her most loved sister.

MAMELUKES /MAMLUKS: Mamelukes, actually Turkish slaves purchased as children by the Arab rulers, converted to Islam and trained to be warriors, fierce men, excellent marksmen, and amazing horsemen. As ordained by their owners, they became powerful Muslim soldiers. In the year AD 1250, these Muslim soldiers assumed control of the Egyptian sultanate, ruling an empire that stretched from Egypt to Syria and included the holy cities of Mecca and Medina (both now in Saudi Arabia) as well as Palestine and Judea. Mamelukes destroyed synagogues and required the Jews to wear an easily seen yellow turban. They also forced many Jews and others to convert to Islam on fear of death. When Ottoman Turks defeated the Mamelukes in AD 1516, they brought in an era of rebuilding.

SULEIMAN THE MAGNIFICENT: Turkish ruler Suleiman the Magnificent rebuilt the walls of Jerusalem and placed public fountains throughout the city. The Turks ruled the entire Middle East from Constantinople (now Istanbul) for the next four hundred years. The area known as Judea or Palestine became part of the Ottoman Empire's Syrian province with Damascus as its local, administrative capital. During the Ottoman period, the Jews, together with most other communities of the empire, enjoyed a certain level of prosperity. After Suleiman's death, the Ottoman rulers neglected Jerusalem. We will learn more about the Turk's reign when we visit Jerusalem on Day Six.

HISTORY OF THE WRITTEN WORD: We will be visiting many places referred to in both the Old and New Testaments. We will be visiting the caves at Qumran, where the Essene sect spent their lives copying scriptures. The Essenes were active from a hundred years before Christ's birth to a hundred years after. They lived in monastic settlements in the desert, close to the Dead Sea.

THE BIBLE AS HISTORY: Utilizing the Bible as a historical document will help in understanding the history of the country. The first attempts at writing probably came about in Mesopotamia out of a practical need to keep records. Those early attempts were mostly scratches used for counting items. The following history of the Bible is important, but if you are not interested, you have my permission to skip over a few pages to learn about the scrolls found a few years ago at Qumran, where we will be visiting on Day Two.

Thinking about the Bible as history reminded me of one morning when I stopped to pick up a young girl who especially loved going to church with us. She met me at the gate to say her Dad would not allow her to go with us anymore because we were not a real Christian church.

"Why would he say that?"

"Because your pastor does not use the King James Bible," she replied.

Most people know there are many different versions of our familiar Bible. First, it is not just one book, and second, there are many translations. We perceive the writing was not in English originally. The Bible is a library of books written and translated at different times of history by many people. As you walk through the religion section of any major bookstore, you will see a fantastic array of different Bible versions. The broad selection of translations—and the seemingly endless ways you see them packaged—is without historical precedent. For many people, the variety of Bibles is bewildering, if not frustrating.

Interpreters and translators always have a difficult job. We know there are many different translations and versions of our "Good Book." Occasionally translators may have unintentionally misinterpreted some words. Translating is not an exact science. A single word from another language can often be rendered in several ways, creating an opportunity to choose the wrong meaning. Anyone can verify who has tried to learn a new language—even pig Latin.

STUDYING THE WRITINGS OF JOSEPHUS: Probably the most valuable resource available for this study would be the writings of Josephus, a well-educated first-century Romano-Jewish scholar, and historian. He served as the Jewish commander of rebel troops in Galilee. Contemporary with Jesus, Josephus was born to a wealthy family in Jerusalem while the country was still part of the Roman Empire. His father was of priestly descent and his mother claimed royal ancestry.

Not a Christ-follower but a Jew, Josephus recorded Jewish history in an invaluable eye-witness account. He initially fought against the Romans during the First Jewish-Roman War as head of Jewish forces in Galilee, until surrendering in AD 67 to Roman forces led by Vespasian. Josephus defected to the Roman side, and Vespasian granted him Roman citizenship. After Vespasian became emperor in AD 69, he gave Josephus his freedom, at which time Josephus assumed the emperor's family name of Flavius. He became an advisor and friend of Vespasian's son Titus, serving as his translator when Titus led the Siege of Jerusalem, which resulted in the city's destruction and the looting and destruction of Herod's Temple.

Josephus knew about Jesus and the early Christians. He knew Jesus's teaching attracted people outside the nation of Israel. Josephus describes what life was like at that time and reminds us Palestine was a politically volatile place in Jesus's day. The works of Josephus include material about individuals, groups, customs, and geographical locations. His written words provide significant sources of our understanding of Jewish life and history during the first century.

HOW WE GOT THE HEBREW BIBLE: My reference says the books constituting the Hebrew Bible developed over roughly a millennium. The oldest texts come from the eleventh or tenth centuries BC, other documents somewhat later. The edited works are collections of various sources intricately and carefully woven together. Since the nineteenth century, most scholars agree the Pentateuch, the first five books, consist of four sources woven together sometime in the sixth century BC. In addition to the Protestant Bible with which I am most familiar, I will also refer to other writings to remain somewhat objective.

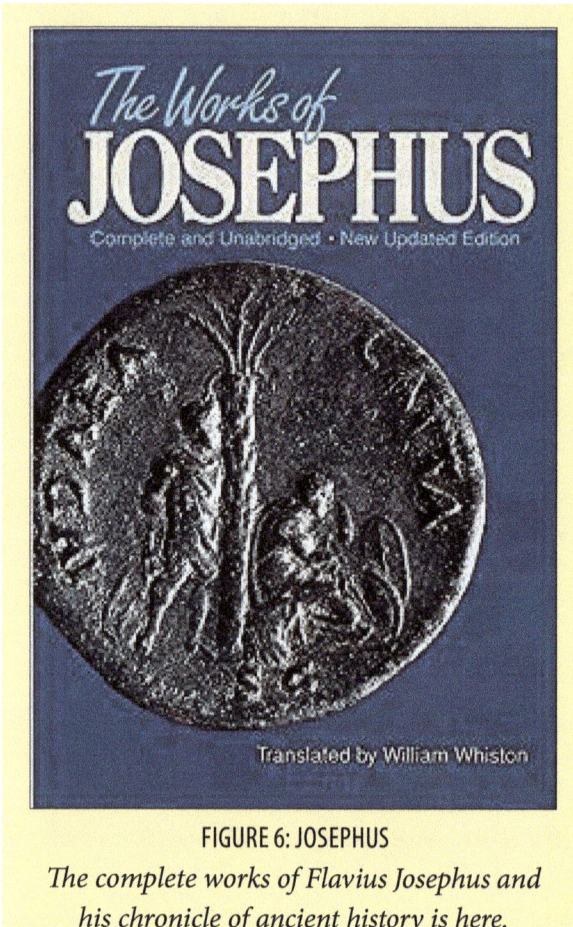

FIGURE 6: JOSEPHUS
The complete works of Flavius Josephus and his chronicle of ancient history is here. Translated by William Whiston.

The Museum of the Bible in Washington, DC, opened to the public in 2017. This place documents the narrative, history, and impact of the Bible. Billed as a museum for the world's most famous book, the one at the center of three religions and two millennia of conflict.

The five-hundred-million-dollar museum is funded by the Green family, evangelical billionaires who own the Hobby Lobby arts-and-crafts chain. We recently viewed Passages: Treasures of the Bible, a recent special mini-exhibit for contributors to the Water4 nonprofit campaign to provide clean water to needy countries. Steve Green's private collection of biblical artifacts produced the display on the history of water. In the exhibit, we saw scraps of parchment with ink from the third-century and an eighteenth-century Torah scroll, in ancient Hebrew with ink on gvil parchment. The scroll lay open to Exodus 15. The most unusual item showed a hollow cuneiform barrel of clay inscribed in Akkadian from almost four thousand years ago, 1780 BC. Parchment scrolls were used by the Israelites before the codex or bound book with parchment pages was invented by the Romans around the 1st century AD.

The Jews have stringent rules about religious writing. Torah (the Law) may only be written on gvil or klaf which is quite uncommon, and no wonder it is rare. The hide has three layers, and the top layer just below the hair is called gvil. Like their unique dietary laws, the skin parchment preparation uses a very specific kosher (kashrut) process requiring particular attention for the holiness of the Torah.

FIGURE 7: TORAH SCROLL
An eighteenth-century Torah scroll in Hebrew is open to Exodus 15. The item, in ink on gvil parchment, is from the Steve Green private collection in the Washington DC, Museum of the Bible.

Hebrew guides, knowing the tanning process, define the preparation. Only a kosher animal species hide is acceptable. Mammals, birds, fish, and even some locusts are kosher only if they meet the exacting criteria in the Bible and rabbinic law.

"Recording these Hebrew stories and copying the texts became an important part of life in most monasteries," Susan added. Each monk would make his necessary tools, goose or swan feathers, which the monks had to dry and harden before use. Using a sharp edge tool, the scribe carefully cut the tip of the feather shaft into the proper shape. Each feather tip required constant reshaping during use.

"What did they use for ink?" I asked her.

They dipped the quills into pots or horns filled with dark liquid. The most common ink was carbon-based, made from charcoal or soot mixed with plant gum or sap. A monk might even make his parchment if that monastery raised kosher animals; otherwise, they purchased the skin from a supplier.

FIGURE 8: QUILLS
Early writing tools.

Leather sheets for recording were first rubbed with pumice and smoothed with chalk to keep the ink from running.

AND THEN CAME THE BIBLE: Let's jump ahead a few centuries from those first writings to our two-part Protestant Bible.

The first part, called the Old Testament by Christians, consists of the Jewish people's sacred writings. Written originally by Moses in Hebrew, his native language, Jewish people still follow this first part of our Bible, although they arrange their books differently. Every Old Testament book comes from the ancient Hebrew text.

Catholics and Protestants unite in their acceptance of the twenty-seven books of the New Testament but are not in agreement concerning Old Testament books.

APOCRYPHAL BOOKS OF THE BIBLE: When one picks up a copy of a Catholic Bible, he sees there are several additional books included in its Old Testament section. These other books are generally known as the Apocrypha.

The Septuagint, still used in the Greek Orthodox Church, is a Greek version of the Jewish Old Testament. Many Jews were losing their Hebrew language, so the Greek translation came about. The Septuagint includes the thirty-nine standard books of the Old Testament as well as some Apocryphal books such as Judith, Tobit, Baruch, Sirach (or Ecclesiasticus), Wisdom of Solomon, First and Second Maccabees, the two Books of Esdras, additions to the Book of Esther, additions to the Book of Daniel, and the Prayer of Manasseh. We recently picked up another intriguing Apocryphal book named Jasher.

These books of the Apocrypha were composed in Hebrew or Greek after 300 BC. They were finished too late to be included in the Hebrew books officially accepted as Holy Scripture. They are considered useful but are not always regarded as scripture. All original Hebrew manuscripts making up the thirty-nine books of the Old Testament are believed completed by 500 BC. Think of that, five hundred years before the birth of our Christ.

AND THEN THE NEW: The second part of our Bible, the New Testament first composed in Greek, records the story of Jesus and the beginnings of Christianity. One reference says the first five books of the Hebrew Bible (the Jewish Pentateuch or Torah) were translated into Greek about 250 BC, finally opening the Bible to the non-Jewish world. Once Hebrew scrolls became translated to Greek in the fourteenth century, knowledge of the Bible spread throughout Europe. Every place the Bible reached, scribes copied it many times over. Each copy became an arduous undertaking with every word written down painstakingly by hand, hard to imagine.

In the Middle Ages, roughly the fifth century to the 1400s, most ordinary people were unable to read; therefore, Bibles became highly illustrated so illiterate worshipers could understand. Books were expensive, and few worshipers could afford to purchase a copy. Scribes, artists, parchment makers, and bookbinders excelled at producing works of art, like religious icons, murals, and later stained-glass window designs depicting biblical references. That is why we will see so many biblical icons and stained-glass images in the ancient churches.

TRANSLATORS BRAVELY PRINTED BIBLES: Being a Bible translator was a dangerous job in the early days. The first translators were not well received. Their lives were often cut quite short in horrific ways.

- ✓ John Wycliff, opposing papal authority, produced the first handwritten versions of the entire Bible about AD 1380. Wycliff translated from Latin into English, which sometimes obscured the meaning. Catholic officials declared Wycliff's translation corrupt and full of heresy. After he died of a stroke, the Catholics declared him a heretic. Later they exhumed his body and burned the bones, then dumped his ashes into the River Swift, a tributary of the Avon.

- ✓ After another seventy-five years, Johann Gutenberg, a German, grew brave and courageous enough to print the first Bible in Latin in AD 1455. Gutenberg died a dozen years later, and they buried him in the Franciscan church at Mainz, his contributions largely unknown.

- ✓ Next, Martin Luther translated the words from Latin into everyday German. At one point, the Roman Emperor declared Luther an outlaw, banning his literature, excommunicating him from the Roman Catholic Church, and requiring his arrest. He posted notices saying: "We want him to be apprehended and punished as a notorious heretic."

- ✓ Gutenberg's desire for people to feel closer to God led him to translate the Bible into the language of the people, radically changing the relationship between church leaders and their followers. The Roman warrant also made it a crime for anyone in Germany to give Luther food or shelter. The Emperor authorized anyone to kill Luther without legal consequences.

FIGURE 9: GUTENBERG
Johann Gutenberg and his printing press.

- ✓ William Tyndale believed that people in England should be able to read religious books, especially the Bible, in their language. He began to translate the book to English from the original Greek and Hebrew. The Emperor considered such work heresy. Tyndale published the first-ever mechanically printed New Testament in the English language in 1526, but he had to escape from England, then part of the Roman Empire, to do it. The Emperor condemned Tyndale to death by strangulation, after which they burned his body at the stake.

THE WICKED BIBLE: Something unusual happened in a 1631 printing called the "Wicked Bible." A printer's error caused the destruction of a thousand Bibles. The word "not" left out of the 7th commandment caused a verse to read, "Thou shalt commit adultery." England's King Charles I, an Anglican, was not amused by the mistake and ordered the printer killed. Neither freedom of speech nor religion were allowed back then.

Dangerous occupation that, translating the Bible!

WIKIPEDIA.COM
FIGURE 10: QUEEN MARY TUDOR
Queen Mary Tudor, daughter of King Henry VIII and his first wife, Queen Catherine of Aragon.

"THE HOLY LAND" WAS CONTROLLED BY ROMAN RULE: For most of history, the country we call Israel was part of the Roman Empire, as were the lands we now know as England and Great Britain. An appointed Roman procurator presided, controlling all political, military, and fiscal affairs.

KINGS, QUEENS, AND THE CHURCH CONFLICT: Rome controlled England through the state church, Roman Catholic. During the reign of the Tudors (ca. AD 1500), the church went through a difficult time. King Henry VIII (1491-1547) wanted a divorce from his wife Catherine of Aragon, mother of his daughter, Mary. The Catholic Pope refused to grant the divorce because the Holy Roman Emperor Charles V opposed it. The Emperor just happened to be Queen Catherine's nephew.

The King wanted to marry Anne Boleyn, who had been a lady-in-waiting to Catherine. So, in 1533, King Henry broke with the Catholics, formed the Anglican Church with the King (himself) as head, and married the now pregnant Anne Boleyn in a secret ceremony. He ordered the Catholic monasteries torn down, treasuries confiscated, and their records burned; religious art and artworks such as chalices, crucifixes, stained glass art destroyed. The new Anglican Church of England, with Henry as head, took over parish churches with all their wealth. After King Henry's maneuvering to make his second marriage legal, Anne delivered a girl, Elizabeth, instead of a boy. Henry could not forgive her.

Three years later, Anne still had not produced a male heir, so Henry had her beheaded on trumped-up charges.

He immediately prepared to marry his third wife, Jane Seymour, a cousin and lady-in-waiting to Anne Boleyn. Jane also failed to produce the required son. Henry wanted a male heir so intensely he went on to marry a total of six wives. He divorced two, beheaded two, one died in childbirth and the sixth outlived him.

At Henry's death, his oldest child, Mary, became the monarch.

BLOODY MARY PROVES A HARSH RULER: Henry's oldest daughter and heir Mary Tudor (1516-1558) daughter of Catherine of Aragon, eventually became queen after Henry's death. She was Catholic. According to contemporary accounts, Mary was vivacious, beautiful, intelligent, eloquent, and tall. She returned the country to Catholicism and earned the name Bloody Mary for her harsh persecution of Protestants.

As Queen, Mary ordered Anglican bishops Hugh Latimer and Nicholas Ridley burned at the stake as well as Thomas Cranmer, the Archbishop of Canterbury. Death by fire was probably the most excruciating form of execution.

She reinstated the Catholic Mass in 1553 and returned the Pope's authority the following year. The title of Head of the Church, which her father Henry VIII had taken, now passed back to the pope. Mary's wedding to Prince Philip of Spain took place in Winchester Cathedral. By the marriage, Mary became Queen of Naples and titular Queen of Jerusalem. Reports said she was "extraordinarily in love" with her husband. Mary suffered a false pregnancy and Philip left England to go back to Spain. Mary was heartbroken and fell into a deep depression. She became inconsolable at his departure. Childless, Mary died at age 42 during an influenza epidemic in 1558, to be succeeded by her half-sister Elizabeth I.

THE VIRGIN QUEEN CHANGES THINGS: Henry's second daughter, Elizabeth I (1533-1603), daughter of Ann Boleyn, became queen after her sister's death in 1558. Elizabeth was Protestant, not Catholic, and life for her subjects changed again. The "Virgin Queen" Elizabeth ordered a copy of the whole Bible placed in every parish church. The Geneva Bible, dedicated to Queen Elizabeth, came about in 1560, and the Bishops' Bible eight years later, but both lost prominence to the authorized King James version in

WIKIPEDIA.COM
FIGURE 11: QUEEN ELIZABETH I
Elizabeth I, the "Virgin Queen," daughter of King Henry VIII and his second wife, Queen Anne Boleyn.

1611. Bringing back Tyndale's translation, the familiar King James Bible appeared in beautiful rhythm, although priests were only permitted a copy to read aloud during church services.

Often considered England's greatest monarch, Elizabeth became head of the (Anglican) Church of England, portraying herself as the "mother of the Church," and she ruled almost forty-five years.

During her lifetime, Elizabeth received twenty-six different marriage proposals. She accepted none. Many courtiers of England, as well as foreign princes, flirted with her and professed their love. She encouraged them and even flirted with them, yet she never committed to them.

Her ladies-in-waiting were not allowed to marry without her permission, which she rarely granted. Her sister Mary's persecution of Protestants had done much damage to Catholicism in England, and the number of Protestants in the country was steadily increasing. Although Elizabeth adhered to the Catholic faith during her sister's reign, the "virgin queen" was committed to her childhood Protestant conviction.

Elizabeth's changes included allowing priests to marry, banning icons and images in the church, and removing the requirement for Anglican priests to wear gowns.

MARY, QUEEN OF SCOTS: Another Queen Mary—not Elizabeth's sister but her cousin Mary Stuart, Queen of Scots—was found guilty of plotting to assassinate Elizabeth and was subsequently executed. This Mary descended from King Henry's sister Margaret, so the girls were first cousins. Elizabeth's relationship with Mary Stuart, Queen of Scots, dominated English and Scottish politics for twenty years. Elizabeth hesitated to order Mary's execution despite unrelenting pressure from parliament and her councilors to carry out the sentence. However, on 1 February 1587, she finally signed the death warrant. Poor Mary Stuart was not beheaded with a single strike. The first blow missed her neck and struck the back of her head. The second blow severed the neck, except for a ligament which the executioner cut through using the axe. The final humiliation for Mary, Queen of Scots, was the public revelation that she wore a wig. Afterward, the executioner held Mary's wigless head aloft and declared, "God save the Queen."

AND NOW, FINALLY: Our Bible is now translated in whole or in part into more than fifteen hundred languages and is the most widely distributed book in the world. We can read it ourselves whenever and wherever we wish. *The Living Bible*, published by Tyndale House Publishers in 1971 is a paraphrase in today's English language of the Old and New Testaments. This version and the even newer *New Living Bible* go into detail where necessary for a clear understanding by the modern reader. Some claim the *New American Standard Bible* is the most accurate translation in English. The *Zondervan NIV Study Bible (New International Version)* is also popular.

THE DEAD SEA SCROLLS: On the day we visit Qumran, we learn about the Essene sect who lived near the Dead Sea in splendid isolation, and the scrolls they spent their lives creating and preserving in the desert. Israel's Qumran National Park manages this archaeological site in the West Bank. We will walk through ruins of this monastic settlement and, more importantly, observe caves that hid the famous Dead Sea Scrolls.

AUTHOR'S PRIVATE COLLECTION

FIGURE 12: LIFE AMONG THE ESSENES
The ancient scrolls were found in caves around the settlement of Qumran, near the Dead Sea.

LIFE AMONG THE ESSENES: The Essenes, a cult with an austere lifestyle, composed these parchment rolls, mostly containing prayers and Bible scriptures. The ruins of the walled monastery of Qumran show evidence these people were immaculate, taking several "purification" baths (*mikveh*) each day. Members associated ritual cleanliness with spiritual purity. Several biblical regulations required full immersion in water to regain ritual purity after any impure incidents occurred—which could include eating the meat of an animal dead of natural causes or having touched a dead body. According to their religious rites, a convert must immerse in a *mikveh*. The rules require the special pool connected to a natural spring or a well of naturally occurring water, such as rainwater. The Romans destroyed

Qumran, so on our visit we only see ruins of a twisting aqueduct, evidence of a series of bathing pools within the walls, and legendary brown cliffs laced with caves.

FINDING AN ANCIENT SCROLL IN AN UNLIKELY PLACE: The two-thousand-year-old parchment rolls appeared in a series of eleven caves around the settlement of Qumran. This find included what some scholars believe to be the earliest known manuscripts of parts of the Bible, as well as some non-biblical writings. Huge openings on the brown cliffs' sheer face reveal many grottos and caves where two Palestinian shepherd boys found the scrolls by accident in 1947. Some of the boys' goats wandered into one of the caves and failed to come back out.

AUTHOR'S PRIVATE COLLECTION

FIGURE 13: THE SHRINE OF THE BOOK
Two shepherd boys found the scroll jars by accident in 1947.

The boys "spooked," so they started throwing rocks into the caves to scare out the animals. The sound of breaking pottery frightened the young fellows at first, but curiosity eventually overcame their fear. They discovered documents preserved in earthenware jars; some buried under bat dung. Not realizing the value of their find, they used some of the items for fire starters, others to repair their sandals. Later, the shepherds sold priceless pieces of parchment to antique dealers for a few shekels. For several years the sheepskins turned up in surprising places. The story of the shepherd boys and the scrolls finally came to light. In time the ancient papers arrived at the Shrine of the Book, a wing of the remarkable Israel Museum in western Jerusalem.

Today, Israel still claims ownership of the scrolls; it exhibits them around the world and is even conducting work to digitize the collection. Palestinians claim that their 1967 acquisition was little more than theft and have called for the return of the manuscripts.

THE SHRINE OF THE BOOK: We will see an exhibit of the Dead Sea

Scrolls in the unusually shaped building that adjoins the Israel Museum in Jerusalem. This special place, the Shrine of the Book, displays them. The picturesque architecture catches attention immediately. The structure is placed two-thirds below the ground, topped by a white dome, and all reflected in a surrounding pool of water.

Inside the museum, we are amazed at a scroll displayed on a wooden rod designed to look like a scroll from a synagogue. A recent newspaper article says researchers recently deciphered a new fragment of the parchment with information about a Jewish king known as King Jonathan and the complete text of the Old Testament book of Isaiah. Israel Museum's Shrine of the Book holds the best-preserved and most complete Dead Sea Scrolls ever discovered. The parchments are too fragile to be on display permanently, so they employ a rotation system. After an item exhibits for a few months, the equipment temporarily moves the artifact to a special storeroom where it can "rest."

Visitors view an arrangement of two to four pages with a mockup of the codex while originals remain stored in a safe place. This exhibition at Shrine of the Book complex represents a journey through a history of writing, tracing the Hebrew people's evolution through their Bible stories. Generations of scribes and scholars dedicated themselves to copying the Hebrew Bible, which evolved into our current Bible versions.

Those who cherished the Hebrew Bible did anything to protect it from harm, at times even enduring martyrdom for its sake.

ENJOYING OUR NON-SLEEPOVER IN THE AIR: Gradually, we relax and even manage to doze a little on that all-night marathon ride. Sleeping was not an easy task. Stewards darken the cabin during night hours, but in our cramped coach class quarters, you must remain upright, and a short nap is about all you can manage. There is no sleeping car like on early domestic trains. In time, cramped legs and aching bodies leave you withered and lifeless the next day. You must disturb several others around you to reach the aisle if you become overpowered by a need to relieve yourself. Once you reach the facilities, you will inevitably find a waiting line at the door, particularly after several hours in the air. You should get up and walk every few hours to prevent blood clots (DVT).

Don't let anything discourage you from signing up for the journey. It is all worth it and we plan to do it again. Next time we will know better what to expect—and now so will you.

Tip: you may want to bring motion sickness pills and some sleep aids.

YOU MIGHT BE SLEEPLESS, BUT YOU WON'T BE BORED: The twelve-hour flight never became tedious or boring because all the scenes and experiences were new and strange. Each seat offered adjustable volume earphones and a choice of music or a movie. Some people did sleep, but most were too excited to close an eye for more than a few moments. The country may seem telescoped, yet biblical stories will make more sense once we see the layout of Israel for ourselves.

FEASTING ON AN ISRAELI BREAKFAST IN THE AIR: Except for a few lunches, the tour cost usually covers all expenses including taxes, entrance fees, gratuities, medical insurance, and even a phone card or cell phone, so you won't have to worry about foreign money amounts. You probably only need money

FIGURE 14: BREAKFAST IN ISRAEL
About an hour before we landed in Israel, the stewards served a typical healthy Israeli breakfast. No bacon and eggs, but vegetables, fish, and salads.

for incidentals such as snacks and drinks, lunches and souvenirs.

They tell us American dollars are welcome almost everywhere, but sometimes better bargains are in the local currency, which you can purchase at the airport, bank, or hotel. Be sure to keep the receipt so you can convert any remaining currency back into US dollars later. For larger purchases using a major credit card, let your card company know the countries you will be visiting.

*Tip: Take at least $25 in dollar bills for tips and remove all unnecessary credit cards from your wallet before you leave home. Notify your credit card company of your travel plans.

TWO

DAY OF ABRAHAM

Tuesday: Tel Aviv, Mezuzahs, Abraham's family, Jews, Rachel's Tomb

DAY TWO: While our families at home are turning off alarm clocks and getting ready to start their workday, it is evening in Israel. We've lost twelve hours of our life, but we are not alarmed as we prepare to deplane the El Al aircraft. A gentle landing, and then we scurry into the wild confusion of immigration procedures at Ben Gurion airport near Tel Aviv, Israel. A welcome surprise awaits us. Digging out claim checks and collecting our luggage from the massive stack at the carousel proved painless.

From the crowded baggage claim area, we hear the Israeli security guards' thick accent all down the line, *"Let the yellow-ball-people go through!"*

We lugged our suitcases with their bright yellow tassels through the gate without showing claim checks, saying silent thanks to our travel companion for providing those tassels. On a schedule like ours, each moment saved is a gift of time. We also realize every item left at home lightens our burden. Even with wheels and pull handles, my suitcase and carry-on already feel very heavy.

*Tip: Pack as lightly as possible, and then remove a few more items before you leave home.

MEETING THE GUIDES AND LEARNING THE LANGUAGE: Our tour guide, *whom we shall call* Daniel Aaron and his wife Anne, meet us with a bus and introduce our tour driver, Mr. Elie, whose skill will become increasingly important to us this week. Aaron teaches us our first Hebrew words on the drive to our hotel: *Boker tov*, "Morning Good." Like Spanish, Hebrew puts the words in reverse order to our English. *Please note–I do not speak or write Hebrew, so these spellings are phonetic with "o"s pronounced long. Another word we must know is "*Todah*," Thank you. "*Todah Robot*," thank you very much, and "*Tove Todah*," Good, thank you. We already know "*Shalom*" an all-encompassing term for hello, good-bye, and I love you. "*Metsue yon*," very good. "*Yo fee*" is beautiful.

Daniel Aaron, a practicing Orthodox Jew, possesses an in-depth knowledge of both the Old and New Testaments. We soon agree he must be the best tour guide in Israel. Aaron gave us his definition of Pilgrim: "climbing on your feet." He said we would earn our Pilgrim certificates by climbing all over Israel on our feet. We soon learn that is true. Every day we walk on tired, aching (but happy) feet.

Tip: Be sure you wear comfortable walking shoes every day.

OUR GUIDE'S WELCOME INCLUDES A WARNING: Part of Aaron's welcome speech to us is ominous. *"This is an important warning,"* he said. *"You are in terrible danger. My wife calls it the Israeli bug. As soon as you get home, you start saving money to come back again."* We found that warning to be valid, also.

NOW, FINALLY, A VIEW OF THE LAND: On the way from Ben Gurion airport to our hotel in Tel Aviv, we notice the countryside looks a lot like southern California, with palm trees and orange groves. Founded as recently as 1909, Tel Aviv is the largest and most modern city in the ancient country of Israel. Mr. Aaron calls attention to flags flying along the roads and in front of several homes. We see one apartment house where the flag flies from a third-floor balcony while laundry hangs from the second. Israel celebrates its Independence Day this week while we are here. More about this on Day Eight when we help them celebrate.

Note: On 14 May 1948, Israel proclaimed independence. Less than 24 hours later, the regular armies of Egypt, Jordan, Syria, Lebanon, and Iraq invaded the country, forcing Israel to defend the sovereignty it had regained in its ancestral homeland. In what became known as Israel's War of Independence, the Israel Defense Forces repulsed the invaders in fierce fighting, which lasted fifteen months and claimed more than six thousand Israeli lives, a large percentage of the country's Jewish population.

The country is small, only about the size of New Jersey. Jerusalem became its capital in 1950, yet most countries maintain their embassies in Tel Aviv. City

AUTHOR'S PRIVATE COLLECTION

FIGURE 1: FLAGS AND LAUNDRY

Our first view of Israel – An apartment house with an Israeli flag on the third floor, and laundry hanging from the second floor balcony.

fathers wisely built the growing city of Tel Aviv near the Old Testament biblical site of Joppa *(Jaffa)*, where Jonah had his legendary adventure with the giant fish, sometimes referred to as a whale (Matthew 12:39–41).

> **IMPORTANT INFORMATION**
>
> THE DATES ARE CONFUSING—AD, BC? Immediately we are confronted with confusing dates on Israeli antiquities and archeological sites. It becomes increasingly important to win this "dating game" before we get far in our journey. In the USA, years that follow the birth of Jesus are given the initials AD, "anno Domini" or "in the Year of the Lord," to distinguish them from the years BC, "Before Christ." Here we find dates are listed as CE and BCE.
>
> Dr. Neaves explained that some people object to time anchored to any kind of Christian or religious benchmark. Instead of using the term AD they prefer to use the phrase "Common Era," abbreviated "CE." Likewise, in place of BC they favor "BCE." "Before the Common Era." When written, BC comes after the year, and AD precedes the year. (i.e., 4 BC but AD 32.)
>
> *Tip: In Israel, AD=CE and BC=BCE

OTHER DATES IN QUESTION AND CONFUSION: Now we find the date of Christmas and the year of Jesus's birth may not be as we thought. Most scholars now assume a date of Jesus's birth between 6 and 4 BC, at least four years before previously believed. The book of Matthew tells us that Jesus Christ was born in the final years of the tyrant known as Herod the Great. Most scholars and researchers say Herod died at the end of March or early April in 4 BC. We will learn more about Herod and the importance of these dates later.

Muslims, Jews, Hindus, all believe that Jesus lived and died, as told in the Bible. To deny that fact is to deny history. People may dispute the Bible on some facts, but it remains one of the best library of history books ever written. There is confusion around dates. Scholars generally estimate Jesus began preaching and gathering followers around AD 27-29, and he continued his ministry for at least one year, perhaps as many as three.

For the first three centuries of Christianity, Christmas wasn't in December—or even on the calendar. Christians first celebrated Christmas on December 25th in the 4th Century AD, after Roman Emperor Constantine declared Christianity the official state religion of the Roman Empire. Many scholars believe the Emperor selected December 25th to counter pagan celebrations of the winter solstice. Others say the date is nine months from March 25th, the Feast of Annunciation, when the angel Gabriel visited the Virgin Mary to tell her that she would be the mother of the Christ child. In the sixteenth century, Pope Gregory the Great worked out the calendar used by us today, known as the Gregorian calendar. The average length of a Gregorian year is close to that of the solar year. According to the Jewish calendar, which attempts to count from creation itself, the current year (2020) is 5781.

WHO ARE THE ISRAELITES? The State of Israel claims more than nine million inhabitants at the end of 2020. Seventy-five percent are Jewish. The Jewish people we meet in Israel are one of three major religious groups of Jews: Orthodox, Conservative, and Reform. Mr. Aaron is Jewish Orthodox, those who maintain the most traditional beliefs and practices of the religion. They strictly observe the dietary laws (called *kosher* or *kashrut*) and the traditions of the Sabbath. Orthodox Jews are often recognized by their ways of dress and appearance, although Aaron dresses pretty much the same as we do.

Aaron tells us local Christians make up a tiny portion of the population. He explains Jews are members of a group held together for more than three thousand years by a common faith and a shared history. A person born of a Jewish mother is a Jew. Even if he or she does not practice Judaism, the religion of Jews, that person remains a Jew. Judaism is founded on the Old Testament laws and teachings, and the *Talmud*, a Jewish sacred book of manners, customs, beliefs, and instruction. *Note: Anyone not a Jew is considered a gentile. We will be reminded now and again during our visit that we are gentiles.*

NOAM CHEM, WWW.GOISRAEL.COM

FIGURE 2: MEZUZAH
You may want to place a mezuzah on your doorpost.

WHAT IS THE MOST IMPORTANT THING TO KNOW? Ritual plays an integral part in the life of every religious Jew. These ritual forms include strict dietary rules and frequent ritual baths in a pool called the *mikveh*. We will observe many of these pools at the historic sites. The *mikveh* is not merely a pool of water; it must hold stationary water and must contain a certain percentage of water derived from a natural source, such as a lake, an ocean, or rain. Jewish ritual also includes memorizing and studying the scriptures, laws, and other religious traditions. During morning prayers, many Jews wear *phylacteries,* tiny scrolls of Bible verses, on their forehead and left arm. As a sign of the covenant with Abraham, a special ceremony occurs when a Jewish male child is eight days old. Priests circumcise the boy and give him his name. Girls receive their names at a service in the synagogue. Young people become full members of the Jewish community when they reach age thirteen. That event is called *bar mitzvah* for boys, *bat mitzvah* for girls. In Day Eight, when we visit the temple in Jerusalem, we will see Jewish families celebrating this special occasion.

Original Christ-followers of Jesus's day, being Jews, observed dietary and ceremonial laws of the *Torah,* and required non-Jewish converts to do the same. Jesus's disciple, Paul, did not want those same customs such as circumcision imposed on gentile converts (Galatians 2:14).

PLACING THE MEZUZAH: A traditional Jew places a *mezuzah,* a small rectangular box, at the upper section of the right doorpost of his home and in each room. The case contains a tiny scroll inscribed in Hebrew with verses from the Bible and is a reminder of God's presence everywhere. The Hebrew word means "doorpost." According to tradition, the mezuzah is to be affixed to the doorpost at the entrance to a Jewish home. A qualified scribe called a *sofer stam*, who has undergone many years of meticulous training, will have prepared the parchment scroll you find inside the wooden, plastic, or metal casing. The scrivener uses permanent black ink to write the verses with a special quill pen, used only for that purpose. The verses comprise the Jewish prayer *Shema Yisrael,* beginning with the phrase: *"Hear, O Israel, the Lord our God, the Lord is One."* Once complete, the parchment is rolled up tightly and placed inside the case, that is often quite beautiful and artistic in design.

Dr. Neaves reminds us this is a symbol commemorating the Passover when blood was put on the doorposts, so the angel of death would pass over that home in Egypt. We will learn more about the Passover on Day Ten. We purchased a *mezuzah* in Jerusalem and brought it home to fasten on the doorpost of our first home to remind us of the scriptures, even though we are gentiles, not Jews.

WHY ARE THEY CALLED JEWS? The term "Jews" first came into use during the period of exile into Babylon. About BC 586, King Nebuchadnezzar of Babylon ravaged the little country of Judea. He destroyed Jerusalem and the temple. He marched the Hebrew captives into bondage in Babylon, a distance of about five hundred miles as the crow flies, but much farther by the path in use then. Babylon, the capital city of Babylonia in southern Mesopotamia, is located in southeastern Iraq on the Euphrates River just south of present-day Baghdad. Because these captives were from Jerusalem, Nebuchadnezzar called them Jews. Later, the term "Jews" applied to all Israelites, all Hebrews, wherever they dispersed throughout the world.

ALL ABOUT ABRAHAM – JUDAISM, CHRISTIANITY & ISLAM

Jews, Christians, and Arabs (Muslims) all share a common ancestor in Abraham. Although several religions claim belief in one God, Abraham is considered to be the spiritual father of the world's three greatest monotheistic religions; Judaism, Christianity, and Islam.

MUSLIMS ARE NOT ALWAYS ARABS: Arabs are mostly Muslim, but Muslims are not always Arabs. The main difference between the two is that Arab is a race and Muslim is a follower of the religion of Islam. Arabs are people whose place of ethnic origin is the Arabian Peninsula. Arabs speak Arabic as do twenty-three other nations. Only twenty percent of Muslims speak Arabic. There are many Christian Arabs. Christians see Abraham as a model for a man of faith and recognize him as their spiritual ancestor, just as do the Jews and Muslims. There are also Christian Muslims, but they do not understand Jesus as the son of God.

ABRAHAM, ISRAEL'S FIRST PATRIARCH: Because Abraham is so important to so many different people and religions, we will be learning more about him and his descendants on this journey. Abraham was Israel's first great patriarch (Genesis 11:27). Born at Ur in Chaldea, Abraham married his half-sister Sarah (v.29), daughter of Abraham's father, Terah, who had several wives. The ruins of Ur lie southeast of Baghdad, and southwest of the Euphrates River that once flowed past the city. Many Bible scholars believe the legendary Garden of Eden may have existed near there, just north of the Persian Gulf.

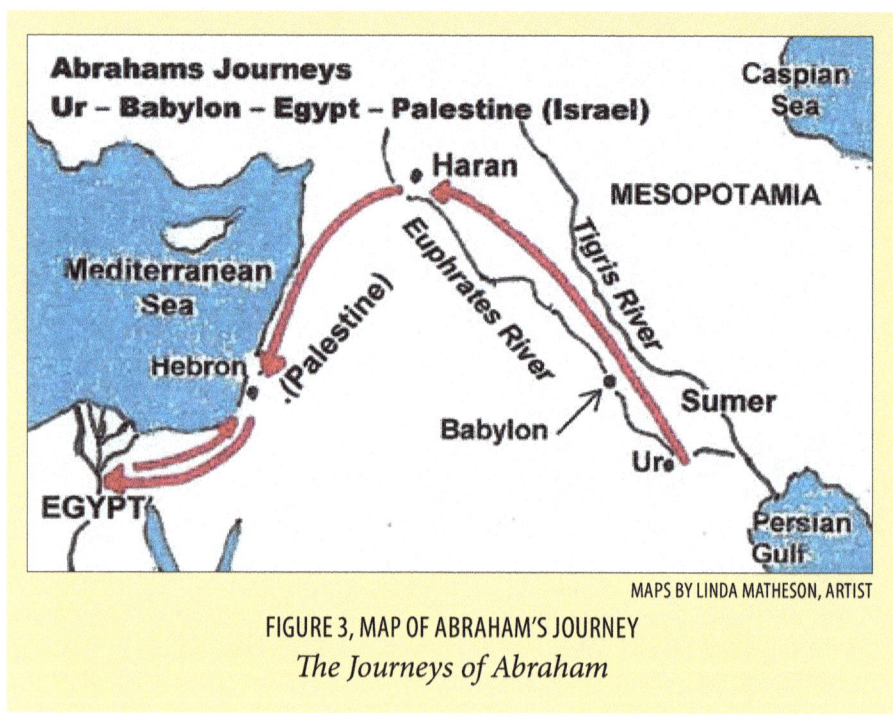

FIGURE 3, MAP OF ABRAHAM'S JOURNEY
The Journeys of Abraham

FOLLOW THE LIFE AND JOURNEYS OF ABRAHAM: God commanded Abraham to leave his home. In return, God offered Abraham land and descendants, promising he would become a blessing to all nations (Genesis 12). Abraham obeyed and migrated first from Ur to Haran, then to Canaan, near the area of modern Jerusalem, where he lived as a nomadic chieftain. Even though the countries adjoined, the distance would probably be about eight hundred miles, quite a distance on foot.

ABRAHAM'S TWO SONS, ISAAC AND ISHMAEL

- The Jews descend from Abraham's son Isaac.
- The Muslims claim descent from another son, Ishmael.

WIFE #1—SARAH AND SON ISAAC: Sarah, Abraham's wife (and also his half-sister) was gorgeous and at least ten years younger than her husband. Sarah remained attractive into her later years. She was so striking Abraham feared she would be taken away and given to another man when they were near powerful rulers. Because of a severe famine when they lived in Canaan, Abraham and his family traveled south to neighboring Egypt. When brought before Pharaoh, Abraham told Sarah to say she was his sister. Seeing Sarah's beauty, the Pharaoh brought her into his palace and gave her many gifts to gain her hand in marriage. Sarah may have acquired her Egyptian handmaid Hagar during this stay. She became part of the Pharaoh's harem for a time, but when Pharaoh learned the truth, he returned Sarah to Abraham. Abraham was happy to have his wife back, but he remained sorrowful they did not have a son.

Abraham; Sarah and Hagar; and sons Isaac and Ishmael; www.freebibleimages.org

FIGURE 4: ABRAHAM'S SONS
See the family chart of Abraham's grandchildren on the next page.

CONCUBINE #1—HAGAR AND SON ISHMAEL: Because Sarah was getting older and she knew how much her husband wanted an heir, she gave her Egyptian slave Hagar to Abraham, a custom then, to act as a surrogate mother. Hagar gave birth to Abraham's first son, Ishmael, from whom the twelve Arabian tribes claim descent. Later, in accord with a divine promise, Sarah became pregnant in her old age and gave birth to Isaac from whom the Jews declare their heritage. *Note: Certain numbers such as 7, 12, and 40, often repeat in the Bible and may be symbolic.*

ABRAHAM'S TWO SONS: Abraham's faith was put to a considerable test when God commanded Abraham to sacrifice Isaac, his beloved son by Sarah (Genesis 22:2 NIV). *Then God said, "Take your son, Isaac, whom you love, and go to the region of Moriah. Sacrifice him there as a burnt offering on one of the mountains I will tell you about."*

Isaac was Abraham's golden child, yet he felt compelled to follow the commandment. Muslims, on the other hand, feel Ishmael was the one offered up by Abraham because Ishmael was Abraham's only son for at least thirteen years before Isaac came along.

Genesis says Abraham prepared to make the sacrifice of his son. Like his departure from Ur, Abraham traveled a path unfamiliar in both geography and intent. They stopped at a rock outcrop on Mount Moriah believed to be the same "threshing floor" bought centuries later by King David, and also used for the temple by David's tenth son and heir, King Solomon. We will visit this holy place under the gilded Dome of the Rock in modern-day Jerusalem.

Whichever son it was, God spared the boy at the last moment, substituting a ram for the sacrifice. According to Genesis, Abraham became the father of the Israelite people by his faith, and he remains honored in all three religions.

Isaac's heirs would become the twelve tribes of Israel. From Moses, a Levite, to the apostle Paul, a Benjaminite, almost every person named in the Bible belonged to one of the twelve tribes of Israel based on their ancestry. Each tribe had a separate history, land, and heritage.

HAGAR AND ISHMAEL CAST ASIDE: The sin of jealousy existed in those early days because after the birth of her son Isaac, Sarah did not want any dispute over who was to be Abraham's heir. She insisted Hagar and son Ishmael must go away, so they went to live in the desert in an Egyptian community near Beersheba, between Hebron and the Dead Sea (Genesis 21:14–21 ESV). Ishmael grew up without knowing his father. When he was of age, Ishmael took an Egyptian wife and fathered twelve sons and one daughter. He became the leader of the tribe known as the Ishmaelites. Josephus says from the twelve sons of Ishmael are derived the twelve tribes of the Arabs, although there seems to be some conflict about this belief.

WIFE #2—KETURAH: According to Genesis 25:1 KJV, after Sarah's death, Abraham took another wife, named Keturah, and had at least two more children, Midian and Shuah. Midian became the leader of the tribe known as the Midianites. A few historians believe that Keturah and Hagar may have been the same person.

Abraham & Sarah are parents of Isaac.

1. **Isaac** & Rebekah are parents of the twins, **Esau and Jacob**.
2. **Esau**'s descendants became known as the Edomites, and later in Jesus's day, this tribe produced Herod. With a sincere desire to obey and please his parents, Esau married the daughter of his Uncle Ishmael (Genesis 28:9).
3. The other twin, **Jacob**, whose name changed later to Israel, had children by four different women. He married sisters Leah and Rachel and took two mistresses named Bilhah and Zilpah. He fathered twelve sons and one daughter. The daughter, Dinah, was born to Leah. The sons became leaders of the twelve tribes of Israel. (As seen on page 33.)

THE BIRTHRIGHT OF A FIRSTBORN SON: This is the story of Abraham's son Isaac and wife Rebekah, and their twins, Esau and Jacob. Esau was born first, followed by his brother Jacob holding Esau's heel. As the boys grew, Jacob became Rebekah's favorite. In Old Testament times, the firstborn son of the family received special privileges called the birthright. The birthright of the firstborn con-sisted of twice as much inheritance as any other sibling. When there were multiple wives, the firstborn was the son born before the others, apparently whether his mother was a wife or a concubine. When the boys were grown, Jacob and his mother deceived the elderly half-blind Isaac into giving the birthright blessing to Jacob instead of his firstborn twin brother Esau.

THE LOVE STORY OF JACOB AND RACHEL: Knowing he had done wrong in tricking his father and stealing his brother's birthright, Jacob took the "money" and ran away to live with some of his mother's people, specifically his uncle Laban, who lived at Haran in the desert. There Jacob met the love of his

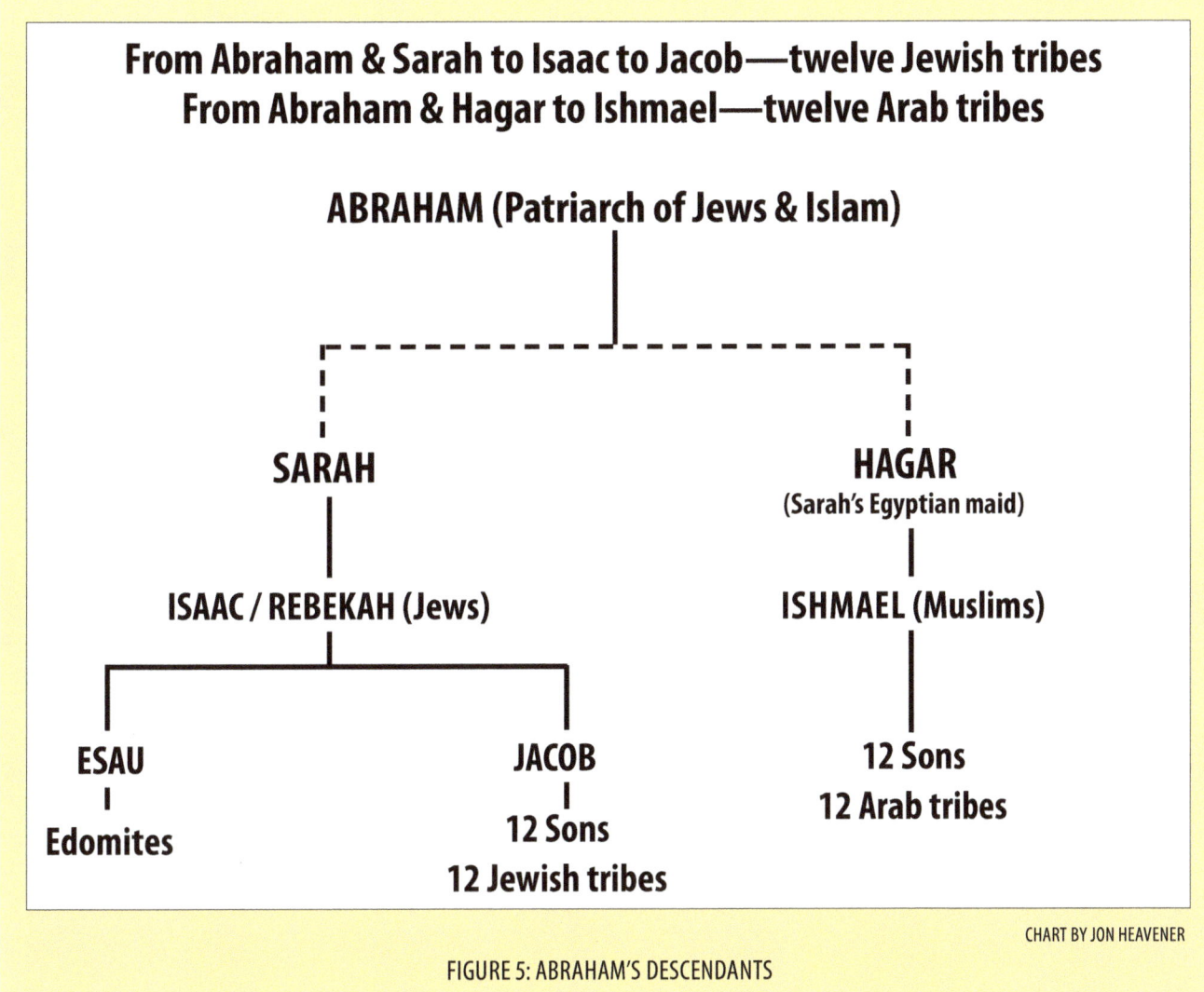

FIGURE 5: ABRAHAM'S DESCENDANTS

life. He saw his first cousin, Rachel, the younger daughter of his mother's brother, Laban. Jacob took one quick look, and it must have been love at first sight. She was a stunning girl, said to be beautiful of form and face (Genesis 29:17 NLT).

Every evening Rachel, a shepherdess, herded her father's sheep to water at the community well. An enormous flat stone covered each well to reduce evaporation in this dry country. Since the stone was too large and heavy for one man to move, the shepherds usually gathered there waiting until others arrived to help lift the cover.

Once Jacob saw Rachel, he showed off by moving the big stone by himself, and he watered her whole flock of sheep. No doubt, Rachel was impressed because Jacob finally married this woman of his dreams, but it wasn't easy to get her father's consent. Jacob had nothing to give as dowry, so he offered to serve the father seven years for his daughter's hand in marriage (Genesis 29:18 NIV). Laban agreed,

FIGURE 6: LOVE STORY

although he did mention that Rachel had an older sister named Leah. Laban said it was not customary to give a younger daughter in marriage before the first-born, but he failed to communicate more than that.

A WEDDING NIGHT SURPRISE: When Jacob completed his seven-year apprenticeship, the sly, deceitful, old trickster Laban substituted his older daughter, Leah, for Rachel on the wedding night. As a wedding gift, Laban gave Leah the servant girl Zilpah to be her maid.

Leah may have been more desirable, but it was Rachel that Jacob loved.

How could that happen? In the ancient Hebrew betrothal covenant, the groom and the bride shared a cup of wine to seal the agreement. At the actual marriage ceremony, the Hebrew bride and groom would share a second cup of wine, perhaps under a *chuppah* covering. The celebration might continue for many hours. The couple would then break the wineglass to symbolize the two people would never be the same again. During the festivities, Jacob may have had a considerable amount to drink because with a heavy veil over her face and long flowing garments, Leah made it undetected through the ceremony and the wedding night.

Come morning, Jacob discovered the deception, and he was livid.

Jacob said to Laban, *What is this you have done to me? Did I not serve you for Rachel? Why did you deceive me?* He probably also said it was a horrid trick to play on a new son-in-law. Laban knew he had done wrong to Jacob, so he promised to give him Rachel as well, if he would continue the week of wedding festivities with Leah.

As Rachel's wedding gift, Laban gave his daughter the servant Bilhah to be her maid. Jacob slept with Rachel too, and he served Laban for another seven years to keep her. Traditionally, a seven-day wedding feast would have followed for each girl.

Rachel remained the love of Jacob's life, even though her older sister Leah and the two servant girls, Bilhah and Zilpah, all bore his children.

Although Jacob made no secret he loved Rachel best, Leah became a mother to six sons and a daughter. After she stopped having babies, she presented Zilpah to Jacob to act as a surrogate mother to have more children (Genesis 30:9–13 NIV). Zilpah gave Jacob two more sons, Gad and Asher. A few years later, Leah gave birth to two more sons and a daughter.

Rachel was barren for many years and became overwhelmed with jealousy of her sister Leah, so she gave Jacob her servant Bilhah as a surrogate. As such, Bilhah gave birth to Dan and Naphtali, as detailed in Genesis 30:1–8 NIV. Finally, Rachel, the great love of Jacob's life, delivered a son, Joseph.

Their tent must have been a little overcrowded by then, with Leah's six sons, Zilpah's two sons, Bilhah's two, and Rachel's son, Joseph, the youngest, about seventeen years old. Benjamin was born later, making a total of thirteen children and five adults in their tribe. Years later, when Jacob went back to reconcile with his brother Esau, Jacob brought all his wives and children.

Over the years, Jacob, grandson of Abraham, became wealthy and a respected patriarch.

Note: Rabbinic sources—Midrash Raba, and elsewhere—indicate that Bilhah and Zilpah were Laban's daughters through his concubine, making them half-sisters to Rachel and Leah.

THE DEATH OF RACHEL: Jacob and his tribe began a move south to Bethlehem. On their way, Rachel, now heavy with a second pregnancy, went into labor. She suffered a problematic delivery. The midwife told Rachel she was sure her child would be a boy, perhaps to take her mind off her agony. With her last breath, Rachel named her son Benoni. (Genesis 35:19 NASV). Soon after the baby came, Rachel died.

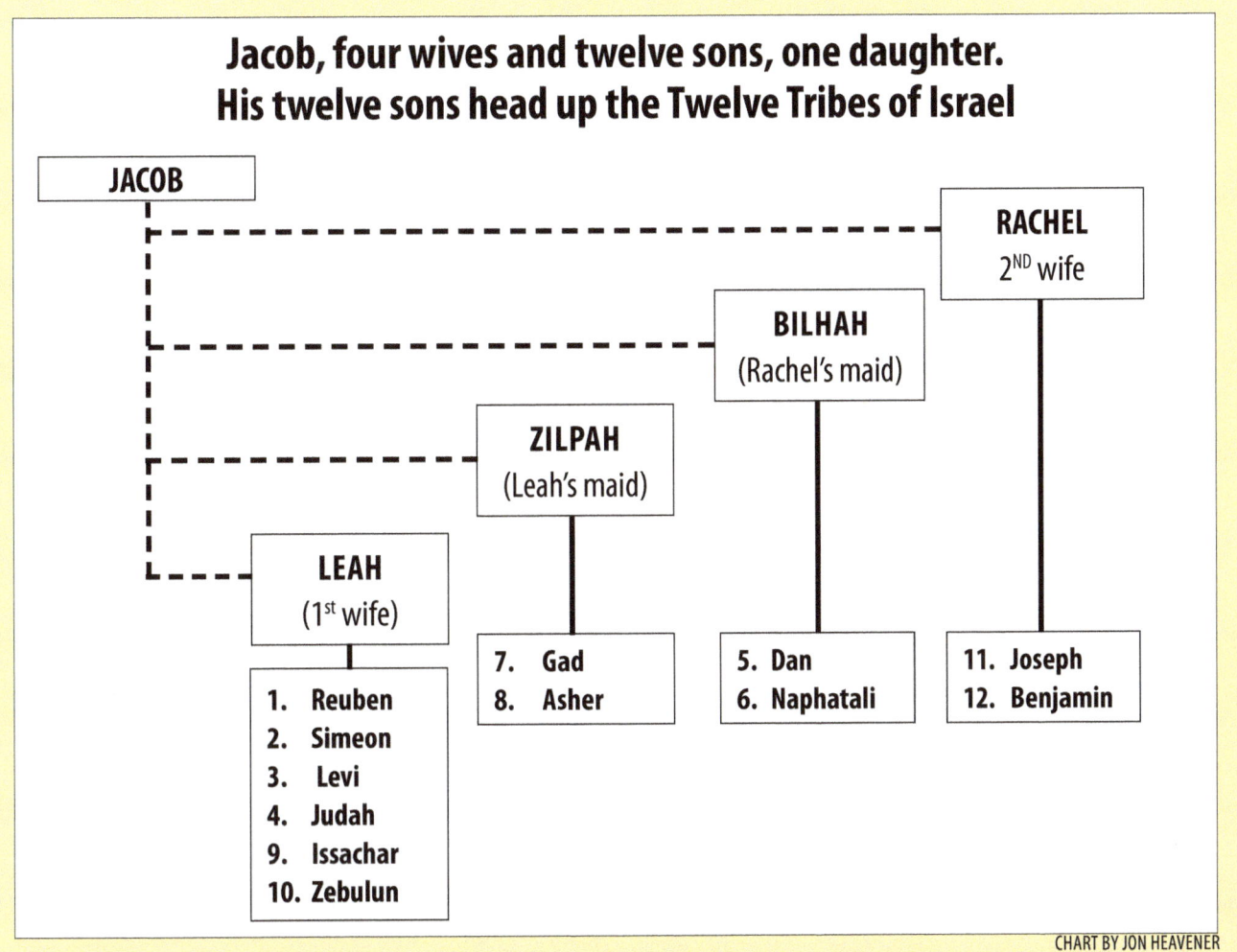

FIGURE 7: JACOB'S DESCENDANTS

Jacob, son of Isaac, grandson of Abraham became a wealthy and respected patriarch.

FIGURE 8: TWELVE TRIBES

The twelve tribes of Israel are the traditional divisions of the ancient Jewish people. Biblical tradition holds that these twelve tribes descend from sons and grandsons of the Jewish forefather, Jacob.

Jacob never recovered emotionally from the loss. Jacob called the child Benjamin, which means son of my right hand. He was now the father of twelve sons: Reuben, Simeon, Levi, Judah, Dan, Naphtali, Gad, Asher, Issachar, Zebulon, Joseph, and Benjamin. Each son became the patriarch or leader of a tribe that bore his name, hence the twelve tribes of Israel (Genesis 25 NLT).

SEEING RACHEL'S TOMB WITHOUT A BULLETPROOF BUS: In a hot country like Canaan and Israel, survivors buried the dead wherever they might be at the time. Jacob buried Rachel where she died, by the side of the road leading from Bethlehem to Jerusalem. He set up a monument to mark the spot. Early descriptions of the tomb say he placed a huge stone to mark the site, and his eleven older sons placed a stone there as well. Some argue about the correct location of her grave, but the Ottoman Turks constructed the structure visitors see now. Built about AD 1620, a cube topped by a dome marks the site. For centuries, the lonely grave lay on a deserted roadside.

We will see Rachel's tomb near Bethlehem from a distance on our way to the Church of the Nativity on Day Seven. The site is very close to the checkpoint we must drive through. The tomb is inside a fortress complete with a guard tower, soldiers, and barbed wire. A concrete barrier wall surrounds the fort as a separation from Bethlehem. Because the revered memorial is near the perilous Israel/West Bank border, only bulletproof buses are allowed direct access to Rachel's Tomb.

In 2014 this checkpoint between Jerusalem and Bethlehem saw an increase in public demonstrations, with the potential to become violent. Our not-bullet-proof-bus did not stop. Many places we will visit connect to this family, so it is necessary to learn more about them.

Tip: you may need to carry a copy of the genealogy chart with you.

A PILGRIMAGE FOR WANNABE-PREGNANT WOMEN: Although Rachel's tomb is challenging to visit, many still go there. Pregnant women and women seeking to become pregnant come to offer prayers to Rachel. Specifically, many women visit the site to wrap a red cord around the tomb. After removing the string, they cut it into smaller pieces, which they tie around their wrists. The talisman is supposed to help them become pregnant and also to make childbirth easier. We saw similar red cords for sale in Bethlehem.

Joseph, Rachel's older son, was Jacob's favorite. Jacob never tried to hide his intense love for Joseph, and this caused even more trouble for the family. Those jealous older brothers sold young Joseph into slavery in Egypt, where he became a favorite of the Pharaoh. During a famine, Jacob and all his family came to Egypt, where Joseph served in command second only to Pharaoh. They stayed in Egypt, and the Hebrew people multiplied (Genesis 41:43 NLT). That story will come on Day Ten. Along the way, we will learn the rest of the story, which features biblical lovers David and Bathsheba, Solomon and Sheba, Ahab and Jezebel, Cleopatra and Mark Anthony, Salome and her companions, and more.

THE DANIEL HOTEL, JEWISH FOOD: As our bus pulls up at the luxurious Daniel Hotel in Tel Aviv, we prepare to enjoy our first taste of Hebrew food and spend our first night in this historic

DANA FRIEDLANDER, WWW.GOISRAEL.COM

FIGURE 9: MEDITERRANEAN BEACH
The hotel beach at Tel Aviv, overlooking the Mediterranean.

country. We check in near a cascading waterfall in the lobby. The staff serves a delicious buffet dinner with several varieties of raw fish and fresh vegetables, along with a sumptuous feast of pastries and other desserts.

We had worried that Middle Eastern accommodations might be disappointing. We are pleasantly surprised and pleased with this hotel's splendor on the Mediterranean. It features three hundred rooms, six restaurants, six bars, a fully equipped health and beauty spa, shopping arcade, tennis courts, a two-hundred-fifty-seat auditorium plus a conference center to accommodate eight hundred participants. We rate this hotel as world-class excellent, and not just because we are so happy to be off the crowded airplane.

After dinner, we enjoy a relaxing dip in the hot tub, and then stroll along the deserted beach. We imagine Jonah's ride in the belly of the big fish and his landing on this very beach, (Jonah 1:17 TLB). We talk about the many generations between Jonah's time and ours; we think of the millions of other bare toes leaving footprints briefly over the centuries in this white sand. It is still hard to believe we are here; this dream came true. Our room is on the seventh-floor seaside, with a little private balcony overlooking the beautiful Mediterranean Sea, which shows us the incredible exact color of sea green.

And so ends the second day of our ten-day trip. With our balcony door wide open, we allow the sound of the waves to rock us to sleep. We rest well our first night in the promised land. It is a good omen.

FIGURE 10: HEADLESS STATUES
One tourism book identifies these headless figures in Caesarea as pagan statues of the god, Jupiter.

FIGURE 11: GATE TO THE CITY
Standing in the gates at Caesarea.

THREE

DAY OF KING HEROD

Wednesday: Caesarea, Megiddo, Herodium, Haifa, Rome, and the Kibbutz

DAY THREE: Terry, who lives in California, will not be joining our group in Israel. He wanted to tour Europe on his way here, but his passport showed he visited several countries that raised a red flag to security. The airline is meticulous, and they intend to prevent any international incidents. El Al delayed Terry's flight and rerouted him from one place to another until he became so discouraged, he decided to cancel his pilgrimage. We are all sad Terry is going to miss this incredible experience.

Tip: If you are planning to tour Israel, be careful what countries stamp your passport on the way.

IN THE GATES OF CAESAREA: We begin our tour with a short bus ride about seventy miles northwest of Jerusalem to the archaeological site of the Roman city of Caesarea (pronounced Cess-a-ree-a), also known as Caesarea-by-the-Sea and Caesarea Maritima to distinguish from inland Caesarea Philippi near Galilee. We reach the gate to the city along the coast north of Tel Aviv.

The Bible frequently speaks of "sitting in the gate" or activities taking place in the gate. The town judges, the leaders, and prophets, were there to meet and talk with the people. Controlling the gates of one's enemies meant you had conquered their city. Abraham's blessing from the Lord contained the promise *"your offspring shall possess the gate of his enemies"* (Genesis 22:17 NKJV). Built for the city's defense, this medieval gatehouse features narrow vertical channels hewn into the parallel stone arches. The long slender opening for archers guaranteed an excellent view to spot and aim while remaining protected. A massive latticed gate could drop as an extra defense. Vertical embrasures—shooting niches—narrow on the outside, become wider inside. A knight could stand and fire at a radius of nearly 180-degrees, yet still be protected by stone walls. We watch from the city gate as the desert sun bounces rays of bright reflections from the Mediterranean across the sandy stretch to the stone arches.

Caesarea adjusted over the years as it transferred control from the Romans, Byzantines, Muslims, and Crusaders. We can imagine knights in shining armor standing watch over this city.

ADMIRING HEADLESS STATUES: Walking across the road from the gatehouse to a partially restored Byzantine street shaded by tamarisk trees, we spy two majestic statues. Both are now headless, yet dressed

AUTHOR'S PRIVATE COLLECTION

FIGURE 1: GATE TO THE CITY

Caesarea-by-the-Sea featured long archery "windows" that guaranteed a good view to aim at enemies. The "gate" is actually a "gatehouse" where the elders and leaders met daily. to discuss the news, to debate, and carry out business.

in togas and seated regally, facing each other from opposite sides of the ancient street. The sculptures intrigue us. One figure is of white marble and the other red porphyry, a dense stone anciently quarried in Egypt and usually reserved for royalty. Porphyry features a unique dark, purplish-red groundmass containing small crystals of feldspar. Workers brought the broken figures from abandoned and ruined Roman temples. Marble slabs and mosaics pave this street beside the tall columns and stairs. According to a historical marker, the statues are older than the road.

We see many headless statues on this trip. No one knows which emperors the massive pieces represent, but we hear two explanations of how they came to lose their heads. They may have been victims of a religious sect offended by "graven images," or perhaps some new ruler replaced his likeness for the destroyed heads, later losing his noggin, too.

THE FIRST CONVERT: Peter, the disciple of Jesus, preached in Caesarea-by-the-Sea. A gentile of this city, named Cornelius, became Peter's first convert. The book of Acts describes Cornelius as a Roman soldier, a centurion of the Italian Regiment, an officer stationed at Caesarea. Italian volunteers became the most loyal Roman troops. A patriotic Jew would naturally dislike and avoid such a man as Cornelius, and certainly would not share a meal. Jews did not eat with gentiles because of the complex dietary laws of the Jews. However, Cornelius wanted to know more about this man, Jesus. He sent three of his servants to find Peter and bring him to his house. Peter hesitated, but after a vision he met with the family and ate with them.

PAUL IS ARRESTED: Another day, Paul came to the temple in Jerusalem, bringing four Jewish converts to be purified, according to the Torah (Acts 21:27 NRSV).

They angrily, though mistakenly, assumed Paul was bringing gentiles into a restricted area.

Temple officials knew Paul asso-
PHOTO BY MIKE CABA   FIGURE 2: THE DISCIPLE PAUL
Mural of the disciple Paul found on the wall of a grotto in Ephesus, Turkey.

That caused a riot. The Jews dragged Paul from the temple and begin beating him, trying to kill him. Claudius Lysias, commander of the Roman troops, heard the ruckus. He called some officers and soldiers to help him. They ran down to the crowd and stopped the abuse, but the Jews insisted Paul be arrested and locked up.

Paul's nephew heard the Jews making plans to kill Paul the next day. The nephew quietly went to Roman Commander Lysias, saying, "*The Jews have agreed to ask you to bring Paul down to the Sanhedrin tomorrow. More than forty of them are waiting for him. These men have sworn a solemn oath that they will neither eat nor drink until they have killed Paul. They are ready at this moment—all they want is for you to give the order.*"

> **WANT TO BE A ROMAN?**
>
> Being a Roman citizen provided a wide range of privileges and protections. You had to be born in Rome, or be wealthy enough to buy your citizenship, or become a career soldier. So, even if you weren't born a citizen, you could purchase citizenship if you had enough money. As a third avenue, you could serve in the military for at least twenty-five years and receive an honorable discharge to gain citizenship. Some of the more common rights and benefits were:
> - The right to vote and stand for office.
> - The right to make legal contracts and hold property.
> - The right of immunity from some taxes and legal obligations.
> - The right to sue (and be sued) in the courts.
> - The right to have a fair trial & defend themselves.
> - Roman Citizens could not be tortured or whipped (scourged), nor could they receive the death penalty unless guilty of treason.

THE TRIAL MOVED TO CAESAREA: Lysias decided he better get Paul out of town, so he ordered two hundred soldiers, two hundred spearmen, and seventy mounted cavalry to immediately escort just this one man, Paul, on horseback sixty miles. They were to deliver him to Governor Felix at the head-quarters of Roman rule, then in Caesarea. *Note: Four hundred seventy soldiers comprise a heavy escort for one peaceful Jewish man.* Lysias sent along a letter saying the Jews were angry. It wasn't about anything he considered unlawful, but something to do with their Jewish beliefs. So, to appease the Jews, Paul was placed in the prison at King Herod's Palace by the sea, where the governor resided.

The governor treated Paul well, and his friends were allowed to see to his needs. After two years, Nero appointed a new governor named Festus, who called Paul in for a hearing on criminal charges for provoking a riot. Paul then demanded his legal right as a Roman citizen to stand trial before the emperor.

THE TRIAL TRANSFERRED TO ROME: Just as in our courts today, lawyers knew delaying tactics. Paul was born in Tarsus, so he was a Roman citizen by birth (Acts 22:3 NRSV). Paul was also a Jew, but his nativity in the Roman city granted him citizenship, which gave him special privileges. He was arrested in Jerusalem, taken to Caesarea-by-the-Sea to be imprisoned and tried, where he filed an appeal to Rome for trial. Allowed to remain free pending his trial, Paul is eventually taken from there to plead his charges some two thousand miles away. The New Testament never tells the final disposition of Paul's case. Some people believe the charges were dropped. Another tradition holds that Emperor Nero fed Paul to the lions in Rome. There are numerous conjectures.

THE AMPHITHEATRE of CAESAREA: Standing in the open Roman amphitheater facing the beautiful green sea, we can almost imagine hearing Paul make his first defense before King Agrippa. We climb the steps and look around the enormous theatre. The acoustics are excellent in this arena, which

FIGURE 3: KING AGRIPPA II AT TRIAL OF ST PAUL

Roman Emperor Titus' lover Berenice with her twin brother King Agrippa. This stained glass window is in St. Paul's Cathedral in Melbourne, Australia.

resembles pictures of the colosseum in Rome except for the missing walls. Tourists now crowd the cut-rock stadium seats circling an enormous center arena open to the sky. The venue often hosts concerts by major Israeli and international artists. During our visit, workers were busily preparing for an opera to be held that night. As modern sounds of the flute and harp play rock and classical concerts, the ancient stones echo again with the roar of a crowd.

We sat on the not-so-comfortable stone seats and wondered what it was like here in biblical times. Our guide tells us Christians were not thrown to the lions in this arena, as they were in the arena we will visit later at the archaeological site of *Beit She'an,* or in those massive amphitheaters in Rome. However, after the Jewish revolt failed in AD 70, the crowd here did celebrate the Roman victory of Titus over rebellious Jews. Romans brought many captives to Caesarea-by-the-Sea, to perform as gladiators, and more than two thousand Jews died in gladiatorial games.

Herod's masterpiece design of the city appears on a Greek or Roman grid plan with a market, an aqueduct, government offices, baths, villas, a circus, and pagan temples. Herod worshipped at the pagan temple that commanded the port. Destroyed in AD 1291, ruins of the city lay forgotten for almost seven centuries. Archeologists began uncovering the ruins as recently as 1956, mainly employing Italian, American, and Israeli teams.

PONTIUS PILATE LEFT HIS MARK: A discovery in Caesarea is especially important to Christians. Our tour leader tells us Italian archaeologists excavating a Roman amphitheater in 1961 uncovered an ancient limestone block dedicated to Tiberius Caesar and bearing an inscription of *Pontius Pilatus*. This Pilate Stone is the first archaeological discovery mentioning him. According to the New Testament, Pontius Pilate was one of the appointed governors of Caesarea, and he authorized the execution of Jesus. *Note: The Pilate Stone mentions Pontius Pilatus, a Prefect of the Roman-controlled province of Judea from AD 26 to 36.*

ISRAEL REMAINED PART OF THE ROMAN EMPIRE: To understand what we are learning, we need to know more about the Holy Roman Empire, which included Israel. So much of Israel's history is braided together with the empire (27 BC – AD 476) which was first based in Rome, later centered in Constantinople (now known as Istanbul). The Empire controlled nations around the Mediterranean rim, including Israel. Roman leaders were not all as evil as depicted, although a few bad apples were rotten to the core. Government offices for Palestine were in Caesarea during Herod's reign, and in Jerusalem for many years. The powerful, wealthy Roman Emperors inevitably became corrupt, and many lived a depraved and immoral lifestyle. This was a troubled time. Antagonism grew between the Senate and the Emperor, causing sharp division. Either the Senate didn't like the Emperor, or the Emperor was at odds with the Senate. Constant strong conflict ruled the rulers.

LIVING CONDITIONS IN ROME: A decline in morals, especially in the wealthy upper classes and the emperors, had a devastating impact on the Roman citizens. Immoral and promiscuous sexual behavior included adultery and orgies. Constant war required massive military spending, continually threatening the government with bankruptcy. Barbarians gained skill in Roman warfare and military tactics by serving in the Roman army, later using that knowledge against the empire. The people of conquered countries and other foreign mercenaries were allowed to join the Roman army.

Life and the future seemed hopeless for the millions ruled by Rome, where an early death was almost inevitable. Life was cheap. Bloodshed led to extreme cruelty, while Christianity gave them hope. Belief in an afterlife gave courage to the desperate. In the days of the vast empire, the Emperor's number one concern was maintaining power over the state and the people. Rome and other cities had many poor and unemployed people who could not support themselves, while the middle and upper classes had a great deal of free time. The emperors found it much safer if they kept the masses fed, busy, and happy. Regular large-scale distributions of bread and foodstuffs went to the poor while even more significant sums of money went for public festivals, shows, and games. Many Romans eventually came to care about little except being fed and entertained.

The Roman Empire included present-day Israel

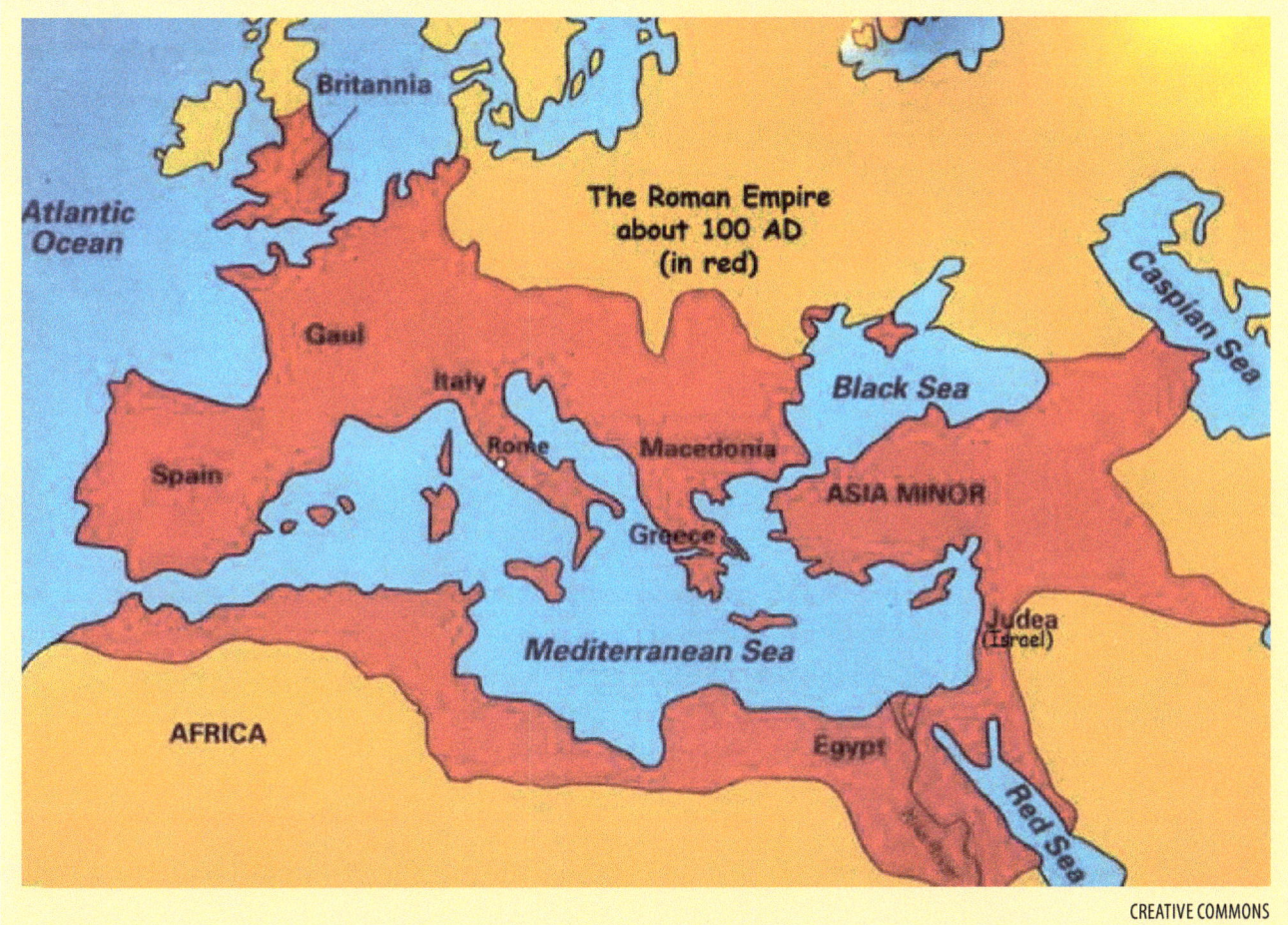

FIGURE 4: THE ROMAN EMPIRE

The Roman Empire (27 BC–AD 476) based in Rome and later centered in Constantinople, now Istanbul. Roman Emperors controlled nations around the Mediterranean, including the countries we know as Israel and Great Britain.

The life of the emperor was admired and copied, so modern man can blame the Greeks for the curse of having to shave daily. Until the third-century BC, Roman men wore beards. Then Alexander the Great of Macedonia's Greek empire introduced the "clean face" look. The Romans admired everything Greek, so shaving became fashion. Baldness was considered dishonorable. Balding men resorted to wigs and hairpieces or combed their hair forward like Julius Caesar. These men often wore a crown of laurel leaves out in public to cover their bald heads.

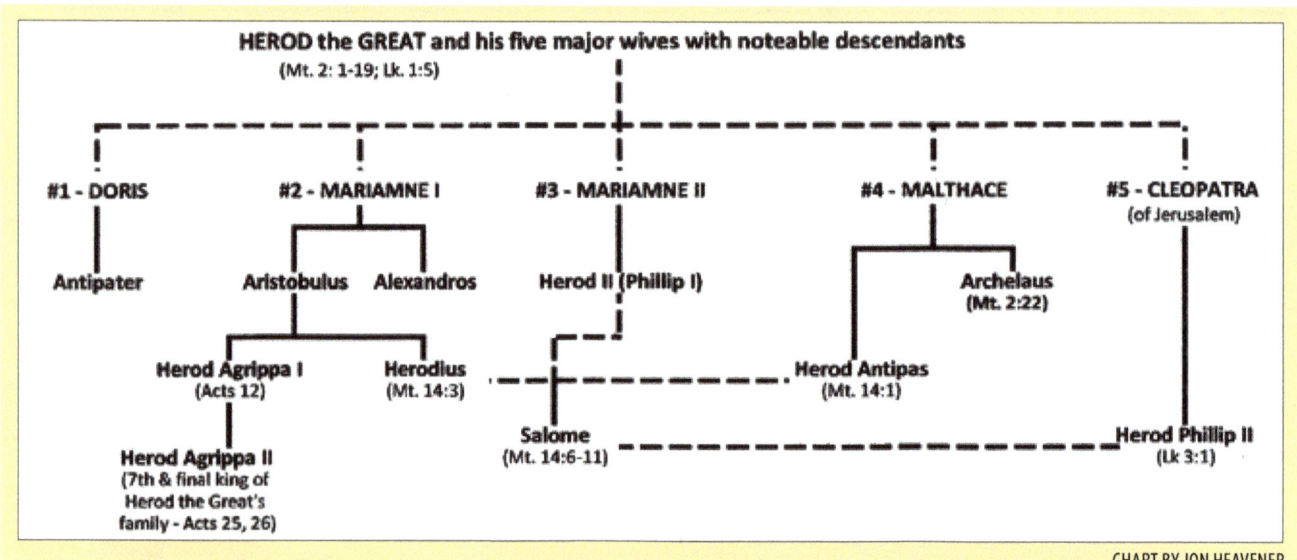

FIGURE 5: KING HEROD'S FAMILY
Herod, five of his wives, and some of his children and grandchildren in history.

KING HEROD AND CAESAREA-BY-THE-SEA: During the many years Rome controlled this country, they set up a local dynasty, the House of Herod, to rule most of Palestine. The Herodians were not of Jewish stock, but Rome required them to become nominal Jews. Herod came from the place called Edom (Idumea), where Abraham's grandson Esau first settled (Genesis 32 NRSV). After Mark Antony designated Herod the Edomite as ruler, he became known as Herod the Great. He built up the port at Caesarea about twenty years before Jesus was born and named it for Caesar.

Herod the Great named his firstborn son for his father, Antipater, a Roman military commander. Antipater Sr, who was quite an opportunist, saved the life of Julius Caesar in a campaign at Alexandria. Because of that, each of Antipater's sons received high offices in Palestine. That is how the Herods became rulers of Israel.

Herod began his career as governor of Galilee. He married Hasmonaean Princess Mariamne to secure his claim to the throne and gain some Jewish favor. However, he already had a wife, Doris, and a young son, Antipater Jr, so he banished Doris and her child. The two sons by Mariamne I, named Aristobulus and Alexander, were later sent to Rome for school. According to Jewish historian Josephus, Herod had nine other wives including two nieces—his sister's daughter and his brother's daughter—although they had no children. His older brother King Pheroras was nominally his co-regent. Still, Pheroras and their sister Salome proved an endless source of trouble with ongoing family brawls. They regularly accused his wives and sons of plotting against him.

WHY CAESAREA-BY-THE-SEA? Initially a Phoenician seaport, Caesarea took twelve years to build, and the city spread out over three hundred acres. Caesarea-by-the-Sea is where Herod constructed one palace on a peninsula jutting out into the sea, with an ornamental freshwater pool surrounded

FIGURE 6: CAESAREA-ON-THE-SEA
Looking at the Mediterranean shoreline of Caesarea, ruins of Herod's Palace may be discovered on the promontory where the disciple Paul was held prisoner.

by colonnaded walkways. Under his rule, Caesarea became a Roman city full of pagan temples. Every five years, the city hosted major sports competitions, gladiator games, and theatrical productions in its theatre. It is now a national park.

In 22 BC, Herod began building the deep-sea harbor, forum, theater, and public baths, storerooms, markets, wide roads, temples to Rome and Augustus, and imposing public buildings. The engineering work in Caesarea is amazing with piers from hydraulic concrete that hardens underwater. He protected the harbor by unique wave-breaking structures. As we walk through the ruins of the Herodian Palace and the restored Roman theater, half-forgotten Bible stories come to life and have new meaning. The Romans devoted a great deal of time to baths in this arid country, so archaeologists found many public bathhouse ruins. Women visited the water in the morning and men in the afternoon.

HEROD'S "MURDER IN THE PALACE" INTRIGUE: Due primarily to his sister Salome's persistent accusations that Mariamne was plotting against him, Herod murdered Mariamne, the only human being he ever loved, as well as his mother-in-law Alexandra. Then after intrigues of Antipater Jr, his oldest son and heir presumptive to the crown, the deranged ruler even sacrificed Alexander and Aristobulus, his sons by Mariamne. He ordered both of them strangled. Extremely paranoid, the mad-man eventually murdered not only his wife, three sons, his mother-in-law, brother-in-law, and uncle. According to Matthew 2:16 NASB, he was responsible for killing all the male children under two years old in Bethlehem. *Note: So far, researchers have been unable to confirm this mass murder.*

In addition to Herod's cruelty and lust for power, he also possessed a mania for building. His most noted constructions included Caesarea, Masada, Herodium, and the temple in Jerusalem. We will be visiting all of these sites on different days before we leave Israel. In Chapter Eight, Day of Jerusalem, we learn about his most famous endeavor, rebuilding the temple of Solomon.

ANTONY, CLEOPATRA, CAESAR, AND HEROD: How do Rome and the Queen of Egypt relate to our Journey of Discovery? History blends Israel, Egypt, and the Roman Empire throughout the early ages. Seven queens of the Ptolemaic dynasty were named Cleopatra. The most famous was Cleopatra VII, born 69 BC, a real *femme fatale* in the holy land. Her extraordinary efforts to achieve power through her forceful personality and political skill, and the romantic liaisons with prominent Romans involved in her intrigues have been the subject of much literature. She died in 30 BC, a generation before Christ was born, but she still connects to the story. Not Egyptian but Phoenician, Cleopatra became joint ruler of all Egypt with her younger brother Ptolemy XIII. Just as there were many Cleopatras in Egypt, the generations of rulers were all named Ptolemy. Cleopatra's father was Ptolemy XII.

Cleopatra was from Macedonia, a region in the north of Greece. She spoke at least eight languages, according to Plutarch, an early Roman biographer. Even though he was not one of her admirers, Plutarch said, *"It was a pleasure merely to hear the sound of her voice with which, like an instrument of many strings, she could pass from one language to another."*

Jericho once belonged to this Cleopatra, a gift from her Roman lover, Mark Antony.

WHEN CLEOPATRA MET CAESAR: Julius Caesar of Rome invaded Egypt and defeated Cleopatra's father. Caesar's son-in-law died in the battle, and Caesar was angry. He sent for the young queen and her younger brother, Ptolemy (Jr), then age twelve. Queen Cleo knew to expect death if they obeyed Caesar's order, and she had a plan.

Avoiding the guards, Cleopatra set sail at night in a little boat with Apollodorus, one of her trusted friends. They slid through the harbor undetected and landed near the palace in Alexandria. She was smuggled ashore in an oriental carpet tied around with a leather thong and carried on the back of her friend right into Caesar's palace.

Plutarch reported that when the carpet unrolled and Cleopatra fell out, Caesar fell in love with her then and there. The bewitching twenty-one year-old became the mistress of middle-aged fifty-four year-old Caesar, and she lived with him in Rome. They married in Egyptian tradition although it was not legal for a Roman citizen to marry a foreigner, and Caesar was already married to Cornelia Cinnilla.

Caesar and Cleopatra embarked on a honeymoon cruise down the Nile, providing Cleo a chance to show Egypt to her new mate, and let the Egyptian people see she was still completely in charge.

FIGURE 7: CLEOPATRA'S LOVERS
Julius Caesar, Cleopatra, and Mark Antony.

Caesar was captivated by Cleopatra's charm and kept her as his mistress until his death fourteen years later. The queen's astronomers helped Caesar create a new way of count-ing time called the Julian calendar, to replace the faulty Roman record. The new schedule had 365 days with a leap year and is the basis of today's calendar.

On several occasions, the enchantress visited Rome, residing in Caesar's villa just outside the city across the Tiber. She was there on the Ides of March 46 BC, when the Roman senators murdered Caesar. Horrified, pregnant Cleopatra immediately left Rome to return to Egypt. She gave birth to Caesar's son on the way and named him Caesarion after his father. After Caesar's assassination, his adopted heir Octavian /aka Augustus assumed the throne. Cleopatra stayed away, remaining safely in Egypt, where she ruled as joint king with her young son by Caesar.

Meanwhile, back at the Forum in Rome, General Mark Antony at age twenty joined forces with another general, Marcus Lepidus, and Octavian in a three-person dictatorship formally called the Triumvirate for Organizing the Republic. Together they defeated Caesar's murderers. Mark Antony, despite his youth, was with his third wife, Fulvia, an aristocratic Roman woman married twice before to Caesar's politically active supporters. As a result of the victory, Antony became head of Rome's eastern provinces, which included Egypt. And so, that is how he met Cleopatra.

THE FAMOUS LOVE AFFAIR: After the death of Caesar, Cleopatra set out at the head of an ostenta-tiously equipped fleet with one goal—to impress and seduce Mark Antony. Back in Rome, Fulvia loved Antony and had great ambition for him. Though she tried to keep the home fires burning, few males could deny seductive Cleopatra, now Queen of Egypt. Egyptians viewed her as Isis, the great mother goddess, and the Greeks saw her as Aphrodite, the goddess of beauty. Fulvia probably viewed her as the wicked witch. Cleo may not have been a great beauty, but she was intelligent, smart, wily, and charm-ing, and Antony fell madly in love with her

Fulvia's daughter by a previous marriage, Claudia, later married Octavian, the new Roman ruler.

she

CREATIVE COMMONS
FIGURE 8: MARK ANTONY

Cleopatra entranced Mark Antony with her charisma. No doubt, her wealth and regal connections didn't hurt either. She seems to have entirely captivated the handsome young Roman general just as had entranced Caesar. During his sojourn in Alexandria they were nearly inseparable as they enjoyed feasting, gaming, hunting, and attending plays. Rumors began reaching Rome that Antony was under Cleopatra's spell in Egypt.

Just as Caesar had married Cleopatra illegally, so did Mark Antony. Ignoring his marriage to Fulvia, he became a bigamist by wedding Cleopatra at Antioch in Egypt. Although Rome did not recognize the union, Queen Cleopatra bore Antony twin children in 40 BC, named Alexander Helios and Cleopatra Selene II.

MORE ABOUT ANTONY, CLEOPATRA, CAESAR & HEROD: Antony's passion for Cleopatra was his undoing. Several times he was summoned to Rome, and he should have gone, but like a lovesick teenager he remained in Alexandria with Cleopatra. Emperor Octavian /Augustus was furious. He told his army that Antony was a man of low morals to have abandoned his faithful wife, Fulvia, now Octavian's mother-in-law, to live with the promiscuous queen of Egypt. Hearing the rumors, Antony finally headed back to Rome to tend to busi-ness, but it was too late. Before he reached there, Fulvia died. While in Rome, although still "married" to Queen Cleopatra in Egypt, he married again. This time, to make peace with Octavian, the Roman general wed Octavian's sister, Octavia. A couple of years later, he decided he and Octavian could never work together. Although Octavia was by then pregnant with their second child, Mark Antony sailed back to Alexandria. He appealed to the mother of his twins, for fund-ing for his army. The queen of Egypt, richest woman in the world, apparently still loved this handsome Roman. She loaned him the money, allowing him to capture Jerusalem and surrounding areas in 37 BC.

The Roman general installed his friend Herod the Great as a puppet king of Judea. Lovesick Antony gave Cleopatra gifts of land in Phoenicia, Syria, Cyprus, Sicily, a coastal strip of Arabia down to the Red Sea. The greedy queen wanted more. She felt she deserved all of Judea because it once belonged to Egypt. Despite generous grants of land to his Egyptian "wife," amounting to almost all of the territory held by her dynasty at its height, Cleopatra wanted Antony to take the entire region away from his loyal friend Herod. Her paramour refused to do that.

Jericho was famous for producing balsam wood. Antony tried giving his lover smaller lots, includ-ing Herod's royal date and balsam plantations in Jericho and the oasis at Ein Gedi. (Note: we will be visiting there on Day Eight.) The royal couple planned to set up a vast kingdom to be inherited by her sons by both Caesar and Antony.

MEANWHILE, BACK IN JERUSALEM: King Herod of Judea and Queen Cleopatra of Egypt owned a monopoly over the extraction of asphalt from the Dead Sea, a great moneymaker at the time. The shipbuilding industry needed asphalt mineral. Mark Antony stayed in Egypt while his queen came to Jerusalem. Her rivalry with Herod increased to the extent some researchers claim he planned to have her assassinated. When persuaded that he would never get away with murdering her, Herod chose to claim she tried to seduce him.Octavian became enraged when he learned Antony gave Cleopatra portions of the Roman ter-ritory in Syria and Lebanon. Most Romans backed the emperor in this struggle between the two leaders. Antony divorced Octavia, then accused Octavian of forging adoption papers naming him-self (Octavian) as Julius Caesar's son.

That was the last straw for the emperor. The Roman Senate, at Octavian's direction, proclaimed Antony a traitor and declared war on Egypt. Octavian's naval forces engaged those of Mark Antony and Cleopatra on the Ionian Sea near the city of Actium. At the height of the battle, Cleopatra called her ships back, fearing capture. Antony's forces alone were not strong enough to match those of the emperor and went down in defeat. His army surrendered to Octavian in the famous Battle of Actium, where the Romans destroyed the Egyptian navy.

FIGURE 9: EGYPTIAN FEMALE.

THE DEATH OF CLEOPATRA: Mark Antony left his troops to join the queen on her ship. They fled to Egypt, pursued by the Romans. Sensing defeat when Octavian's ships entered the harbor, Antony "fell on his sword." Cleopatra surrendered to the Romans. Some authorities say she sought to establish a relationship with Octavian. Failing that alliance, she killed herself.

Here's how:
After visiting her swain's tomb, she dressed as if for dinner, and sent a sealed letter to Caesar. A slave brought her a basket of figs and an asp whose bite had the power to kill quickly. Queen Cleopatra died with the dignity she had lived—on a gold bed in her regal robes. She was about thirty-nine years old and the last active Pharaoh of Egypt. Sending everyone out of the monument but her two female servants, she closed the doors.

FIGURE 10: CAESARION
Caesarion, son of Cleopatra and Caesar, killed by Emperor Octavian.

"Opening her letter, Caesar (found) pathetic prayers and entreaties that she might be buried in the same tomb with Antony. Caesar guessed what was going on. He sent others to see, but they arrived too late. The thing had been quickly done. His messengers came at full speed and found the guards apprehensive of nothing; but on opening the doors, they saw the Queen stone-dead, lying upon a bed of gold, set out in all her royal ornaments.

"Iras, one of her women, lay dying at her feet, and Charmion just ready to fall, scarce able to hold up her head, was adjusting her mistress's diadem. When one of Caesar's men came in, he said angrily, Was this well done of your lady, Charmion?

"Extremely well, she answered, and as became the descen-dant of so many kings. As Charmion said this, she fell down dead by the bedside." (Plutarch)

Octavian ordered Caesarion killed, so the royal son of Caesar and Cleopatra died age seventeen. Antony's former wife, Octavia, was a faithful mother who raised Antony's orphaned children by Cleopatra along with her children. While King Herod and Cleopatra were rivals in their life-times, Herod survived her by decades.

Joseph and Mary, after the birth of the baby Jesus, would later flee the tyranny of Herod's son, Antipas, to become refugees in Egypt. Cleopatra was dead long before that. THE DEATH OF HEROD (40 BC–4 BC): Scholars believe Herod the Great died at the end of March or early April in 4 BC and they agree he suffered throughout his lifetime from depression and paranoia. Based on Josephus' descriptions, one medical expert diagnosed Herod's cause of death as chronic kid-ney disease. They buried him at Herodium, as he requested. *Note: We will visit Herod's palace and tomb ruins at Herodium on Day Six.*

At Herod's death, he had four remaining sons: **Archelaus, Antipas, Philip I**, and **Philip II**. Most people think Herod the Great was king during Jesus's lifetime, but he died shortly before Jesus's birth, and that office passed to two of his sons, Herod Archelaus and Herod Antipas.

- **Archelaus**: After his father's death, vicious Archelaus ruled with an iron hand the majority of Herod's kingdom. Some authors speculate that when Joseph and Mary left Egypt, instead of returning to Bethlehem (controlled by violent Archelaus), they came to Nazareth (controlled by Antipas). Like his father, Archelaus was a man of violent temper, and as bitterly as Judea and Samaria hated each other, they soon united against him. They sent an embassy to Rome to complain. As a result, Rome took away his office, his possessions, and banished him.

- **Antipas** : The second son, Herod Antipas, Tetrarch (Ruler) of Galilee, ruled during the life of Jesus and played a part in the final tragedy. Pilate arrested Jesus and sent him to Herod Antipas during Passover (Luke 23:7). Antipas is also the one who beheaded John the Baptist after his stepdaughter Salome danced for him. *Note: We learn more about this on Day Nine.*

- **Philip I:** son of Mariamne II daughter of Simon, the High Priest. This Philip never ruled; we know nothing of him except that he married his niece Herodias, the daughter of his deceased half-brother Aristobulus. Then, Philip and Herodias had a daughter named Salome, the dancer. Later, Herodias left Philip for his half-brother, Antipas.

- **Philip II:** also known as Philip the Tetrarch, he appeared utterly unlike the rest of the Herodian family. He married Salome. She was the dancer and the daughter of his brother Philip I and Herodias. He was said to be retiring, dignified, moderate, and just. Officials named the city of Caesarea Philippi for Herod Philip II.

CREATIVE COMMONS

FIGURE 11: HEROD THE GREAT

ISRAEL'S COMPULSORY MILITARY SERVICE: We see many armed soldiers, reminding us that Israel must be on constant guard against the danger of attack. Serving in the Israeli military is compulsory immediately after high school for both boys and girls. Few qualify for a deferment, and most would feel ashamed not to fulfill that military responsibility. Girls serve two years in the military, and the boys serve three. The young soldiers are encouraged to learn as much about their country's history as possible, so we see uniforms everywhere at historic sites. Touring is considered part of their education and development of national pride. As we head back to our bus from the amphitheater area, we pass a group of young Israeli soldiers sitting in the shade of the ancient Roman period aqueduct that supplied water to Caesarea. Herod began initial plans to bring water from Mount Carmel about ten miles away. After a second and third phase, the canal continued providing water for residents from an even greater distance for more than a thousand years. Ancient before Columbus discovered America, the arched base of the twelve-mile-long aqueduct is a must-do photo opportunity, especially with the uniforms adding perspective.

WHEN ISRAEL WAS UNDER ROMAN RULE: Jesus lived his entire human life under Roman rule, the first half under Octavian /Augustus (Luke 2:1), who reigned when Jesus was born in Bethlehem. Under Tiberius (Luke 3:1), Jesus lived the second half at Nazareth until moving to Capernaum on the shore of the Sea of Galilee for the final three years before his death in Jerusalem. We wonder how the soap-opera lives of those rulers influenced the lives of their subjects.

FIGURE 12: AQUEDUCT

The Herodian Period aqueduct at Caesarea-by-the-sea. The Romans used a stone soup made from volcanic ash, lime, and water with fragments of stone and brick thrown in for strength and color. This concrete made possible the many grand arches, domes, and vaults still standing, scattered around the former Roman Empire. Pipes set into the arched bridges carried running water for many miles.

FIGURE 13: SOLDIERS

Armed Israeli soldiers take a break under the perfectly symmetrical arcs of the aqueduct at Caesarea, built during Herod's time.

"It was now the fifteenth year of the reign of Tiberius, the Roman emperor. Pontius Pilate was governor over Judea; Herod Antipas was ruler over Galilee; his brother Philip was ruler over Iturea and Traconitis; Lysanias was ruler over Abilene," (Luke 3:1 NLT).

THE FIRST EMPEROR: Octavian, who later changed his name to Augustus, established his government, rebuilt the city of Rome in the year 27 BC, and became a great patron of the arts. Overall, he was a good ruler. The system of roads and a sophisticated postal system helped unify the empire. Octavian reformed the Senate, made the system of taxation more equitable, and revived the census. He allowed Jews throughout the empire to send money to support their temple in Jerusalem. He reformed the tax system by ordering a registration count of each province to find out how many people could pay taxes in support of building and maintaining roads (Luke 2:1). To ensure a correct count, he required each male to go to his ancestral home to be registered. It was this census for which Joseph and Mary would have traveled from Nazareth to Bethlehem late in Mary's pregnancy.

FIGURE 14: OCTAVIAN
Rome's first Emperor, Octavian, also known as Augustus.

His maternal grandmother, Julia, was Julius Caesar's sister, and she helped raise the boy born in 63 BC. Although he never desired to be a ruler, he delivered the eulogy at his father's funeral when he was nine and led his grandmother's services at the age of twelve. By the age of twenty, he was a senator. Julius Caesar was so impressed with this great-nephew, he adopted him and named him as heir. When Caesar died, Octavian went to claim his heritage. Mark Antony, who also expected to be named successor, got there first and refused to give Octavian the necessary papers, so the two got off to an inauspicious start.

Octavian's first wife, Scribonia, bore his only child, a daughter Julia, named for his grandmother. When he became emperor at age twenty-four, he promptly divorced Scribonia to marry Livia Drusilla, age nineteen. Livia had one son, Tiberius, and was pregnant with the second, Drusus, by her first husband. Octavian adopted both boys. As a responsible Emperor, he granted citizenship to freed slaves, and passed many other sweeping social reforms as well as laws to maintain stability in marriage (after his divorce). To raise the birth rate in Rome, he made adultery illegal, offered tax incentives to families with more than three children, and created penalties for childless marriages. So strictly did the emperor adhere to his laws that he banished his daughter, Julia, and his granddaughter, both for adultery. Although the sole master of this wealthy country, Octavian /Augustus and his wife Livia lived in a modest home and shunned the lavish lifestyle. They appeared to be happily married more than fifty years although Livia bore him no children, and her husband was frequently known to be unfaithful. During his reign, the Roman Empire at its height initiated an era of relative peace known as the Pax Romana (*The Peace of Rome*). Rome controlled all of Italy, Gaul (which included France, Belgium, part of Germany), Spain, Numidia (Algeria and part of Tunisia), Macedonia (Iraq and Iran), Greece, Palestine (Israel), Egypt, and virtually all the Mediterranean islands. The emperor died in AD 14 and his last words were, *Have I played the part well? Then applaud as I exit.*

FIGURE 15: TIBERIUS

Tiberius, Octavian's stepson and second Emperor of Rome, ruled during the adult life and at the death of Jesus.

TIBERIUS: While grooming his stepson to become his heir, Octavian forced a reluctant Tiberius to divorce his wife, Vipsania, and marry Octavian's daughter, Julia (Tiberius' stepsister). It was not a good match. The groom immediately left to fight a war in Germany.

Tiberius' unhappy marriage to Julia became unbearable, and after ten years he exiled her, supposedly for adultery, but more likely because he disliked her. After several years of intrigue at court, as candidates to succeed him maneuvered for position, he had enough. Because he had always been happiest when away from the capital and its chicanery, the Emperor simply left Rome and sailed to his getaway mansion on the isle of Capri. He never returned to the city. Tiberius was in office as Roman emperor at the crucifixion of Jesus Christ, and he reigned twenty-three years, dying in AD 37. Tiberius was succeeded by his great-nephew Caligula, legendary for a raucous lifestyle and probable insanity. Although Tiberius was seventy-seven and on his death bed, some ancient historians still conjecture that Caligula murdered him.

CALIGULA: A great-grandson of Emperor Octavian /Augustus and wife Agrippina, Caligula is still studied as one of history's biggest monsters. Executions and torture escalated, and Rome's treasury became dangerously depleted. The Praetorian Guard, an elite unit of the imperial Roman army, served as bodyguard for the emperor and they finally had their fill of him. Caligula's uncle, Claudius, was the only remaining relative of Augustus. The Praetorians assassinated Caligula and proclaimed Claudius emperor.

CLAUDIUS: The Emperor's Uncle Claudius survived the murderous reign of his nephew by playing the fool. After the Praetorian Guard assassinated Caligula in AD 41, they found Claudius hiding behind curtains in the palace, shaking with fright. Soon after being declared emperor, Claudius made a serious error. As his fourth wife, he chose a slippery and seductive beauty much younger than himself, his niece Agrippina—Caligula's sister. She had a twelve-year-old son, Nero, by a former marriage. At his bride's request, Claudius adopted Nero. Big mistake! Agrippina poisoned Claudius as soon as the adoption was final. He suffered a lingering, painful death in AD 54.

NERO: Nero became Emperor at age seventeen and married his stepsister Octavia age twelve, although he was not fond of her in the least. Unsatisfied with his marriage, he entered into an affair with Claudia Acte, a former slave. His mother, Agrippina, did not approve and demanded that her son dismiss the mistress. Nero refused. Ten years later he sent Octavia into exile on false charges of adultery and within a month Octavia was executed. He immediately married another mistress, Poppaea.

FIGURE 16: ROMAN EMPEROR NERO.

Fair-haired with weak blue eyes, a fat neck, a potbelly, and a smelly skin covered with spots, Nero usually appeared in public in a dressing gown without a belt, a scarf around his neck, and no shoes. He was a strange one; artistic, sporting, brutal, weak, sensual, erratic, extravagant, sadistic, bisexual—and later in life undoubtedly deranged.

For six days and seven nights in AD 64, the citizens of Rome watched helplessly as their city burned. The fire started at the southeastern end of the Circus Maximus in shops selling flammable goods, destroying seventy percent of the capital city. Romans blamed their emperor. Nero blamed the Christians, and ordered some Christians thrown to dogs, others were crucified and burned. His ruse did not work. The Romans still blamed Nero for the fire. During his reign, he demanded the Jewish temple treasures confiscated for the glory of the Empire.

THE GENERAL IN JERUSALEM: Meanwhile in Jerusalem, Agrippa expended large sums in beautifying the city, but he was unpopular because of the way he appointed and deposed high priests. In AD 66, the Jews revolted. Agrippa tried to persuade the citizens not to rebel against Rome, but he failed.

Nero appointed General Vespasian to put down the rebellion. He moved to the region at once with the Fifth and Tenth Legions. Vespasian's son, Titus, joined him and brought the Fifteenth Legion. Sixty thousand professional Roman soldiers quickly swept across Galilee, and by AD 69 reached Jerusalem. Supporting Rome, Agrippa fought in the campaign and was slightly wounded. The Jews, seeing Agrippa as a traitor, expelled Agrippa and Berenice from the city. *More about Berenice later.*

During this time, Nero's General Vespasian became patron of Josephus, the writer. Josephus wrote favorably about the general in *Antiquities of the Jews*. He is remembered by Josephus as a fair and humane official, in contrast to the notorious Herod Agrippa II whom Josephus goes to great lengths to demonize. The apostle Paul had pleaded his case in Caesarea before this Agrippa, last king of the Herodian line. Many people believed Agrippa and his twin sister Berenice had an incestuous relationship.

FOUR EMPERORS IN ONE YEAR: While Vespasian stayed busy besieging Jerusalem during the Jewish rebellion, the senate had enough of crazy Nero. They sentenced him to death by flogging. Nero heard about their plan and committed suicide. That plunged Rome into a year of civil war known as the Year of the Four Emperors. Galba was appointed to succeed Nero, but he did not last long enough to count. Otho quickly overthrew him. Vitellius edged out Otho, and Vespasian, the general who had conquered Jerusalem, overruled them all.

FIGURE 17: GEN. VESPASIAN
He burned the temple, and later became Emperor.

NEW EMPEROR: The Roman Senate declared Vespasian emperor in AD 69 while the First Jewish–Roman War continued. Little information survives about the government during his ten-year rule except that he moved the Roman provincial capital of Judea from Jerusalem to Caesarea.

The new ruler faced a severe deficit when he became emperor. However, the spoils of war from Judea—the riches of the temple treasury, the golden vessels from the temple, the seized personal treasures of Jewish citizens and the sale of the Jewish captives themselves—soon provided enormous wealth for the emperor as well as for the plundering army commanded by his son, Titus, who captured Jerusalem and destroyed the temple.

THE FALL OF JERUSALEM: Under General Titus' command, the Romans captured Antonia Fortress and began an assault on the gates of the temple. In AD 70 Jerusalem fell; that particular war was over although fighting would continue for another three years until the fall of Masada. According to Josephus, Titus claimed he gave an order to preserve the temple, but a soldier hurled a torch inside one of the windows, setting the entire building ablaze. Emperor Vespasian ordered all descendants of the royal line of David hunted down, causing persecution of the Jews from province to province. He may have been reacting to messianic prophecies circulating at the time. Vespasian reformed the financial system in Rome after the campaign against Judea ended successfully and initiated several ambitious construction projects. He also started building the Roman Colosseum. He became the first Roman Emperor to be directly succeeded by his natural son.

THE VICTORY ARCH: Titus is best known for completing the Colosseum begun by his father, for his generosity in relieving the suffering caused by the eruption of Mount Vesuvius in AD 79, and for finally subduing the rebellion with the capture of Jerusalem.

The victory Arch of Titus, dedicated in 85 AD commemorating Titus' victory in the Jewish War, still stands in the Roman Forum. At the inside of the arch are two panels with reliefs. In the most famous of the panels on the marble arch, Roman soldiers carry the Jerusalem Temple spoils, including the menorah, the showbread table, and trumpets. The relief does not appear to include the Ark of the Covenant. A recent *Biblical Archaeology Review* explains a digital scanning technique conducted on the famed Roman triumphal arch. The magazine reproduced the panel in beautiful colors as they believe it was initially. A hidden inscription on the Colosseum itself suggests the amphitheater was financed by plundered booty from the Jewish revolt.

THE LOVE AFFAIR: After several failed marriages, Berenice, great-granddaughter of Herod the Great, spent much of her life at the Jerusalem court of her twin brother Agrippa amidst rumors those two carried on an incestuous relationship. In Rome, after the war, she began a love affair with Titus, who was a dozen years younger. Despite concerns over his character, Titus ruled to great acclaim following the death of his father. Contemporary historians consider him a good ruler. After barely two years in office, Emperor Titus died of a fever. After his death, Berenice disappeared from the historical record. She had never been popular with the Roman people.

A JEWISH HISTORIAN'S KNOWLEDGE: Our guide describes how the people lived, including ideas and beliefs in which the biblical events took place. As a result, we feel as if we are walking on holy ground in the footsteps of David, Isaiah, Jesus, Paul, and the other apostles. Our guide is a walking encyclopedia of Jewish history, all of which he freely shares with us as we rush madly from one place to another to meet our packed schedule. His slight accent sometimes slows our comprehension. We feel caught up in a swift stream of knowledge when the words tumble too quickly around and over us. If we try to take notes, we miss out on many of the sights. If we stop taking notes to see what is around us, we forget what we just heard. We are carried ever more rapidly downstream, unable to swim, and unwilling to drown in all this information. We envy the two people in our group who carry tape recorders to review back home.

WWW.WIKIPEDIA.COM
FIGURE 18: TITUS, ROMAN EMPEROR.
Titus, Roman Emperor in AD 79, followed his father, Vespasian.

Tip: Next time bring a recorder!

VISITING HEROD'S FORTRESS AT HERODIUM: Back on the road between Jerusalem and Bethlehem, we stop to visit Herodium (also spelled Herodion), a fortified palace and the burial tomb of Herod, now a national park located a seven-minute drive from Jerusalem. The conical hill, resembling a volcano, is partially man-made. Remains of the walls and fortified towers, fragments of mosaic, and mega water cisterns indicate the original magnificence when the palace was new. Nearby we see remains of a Byzantine town with a church and other interesting buildings.

HIDING IN HERODIUM: Herod knew where he wanted to spend eternity—at his summer palace, Herodium. He commissioned this palace 42 BC. Herod's architects shaped the mountain to make it symmetrical. Earth was heaped up around the walls, creating an artificial mountain rounded off in the shape of a breast. At the foot of the artificial mound, Herod built his lower palace, a kind of royal country club, including an oversize swimming pool with an island in the middle, a bathhouse, and a roofed pool. Herod built swimming pools at all of his fifteen palaces.

Wikimedia Commons

FIGURE 19: JERUSALEM TEMPLE SPOILS

The victory Arch of Titus in the Forum at Rome has a relief panel showing soldiers carrying the Jerusalem Temple spoils in the celebration parade. The legendary Ark of the Covenant is not seen.

The bathhouse featured hot, warm, and cold bathing rooms, as well as enormous cisterns necessary in this arid country. Painted square patterns and imitation marble decorated the bathhouse walls. Colored mosaics paved floors in geometric and floral patterns, with pomegranates, grapevines and clusters of grapes.

From the top of the ruined palace, we could view great distances in every direction. Like a modern skyscraper, the structure had a commanding view of the Judean Desert, Dead Sea, Mountains of Moab to the east, Judean Hills to the west, and we watched from miles away as a shepherd boy slowly led his sheep across the valley. That reminded us of the boy David who herded his father's sheep in this barren area. Our view included the suburbs of Jerusalem and even Bethlehem.

Constructed in 23 BCE to commemorate a battle he would never forget, Herodium was meant as a summer palace that provided him with a sanctuary close to the Holy City if it became necessary to flee. A wall seven stories high surrounded what was an exquisite fortified castle. Barrel-vaulted ceilings support the lower two floors underground, while wooden ceilings separate upper floors.

ELIJAH THE TISHBITE: We drive along the coast to Mount Carmel. The book of Kings tells how Elijah offered a fiery sacrifice to prove *Yahweh*, the national god of Israel and Judea, superior to the gods of Baal. In the Hebrew Bible, this name is written *YHWH* without vowels. The prophet Elijah won the

FIGURE 20: HERODIUM
Herod's retreat palace and tomb.

contest. He was from the little town of Tishbe in Gilead, the hilly, wooded country north of the Dead Sea. Elijah, a hairy man with a leather girdle around his waist, slew four hundred and fifty priests of Baal who had come to Mount Carmel (1 Kings 18). We stop to see the monument to Elijah and tour the grounds of the Mount Carmel Monastery. We will learn more about Elijah later on the Day Five tour at *Wadi Qelt*, where we visit the cave of Elijah.

TWO KINGS, TWO KINGDOMS: During this period, Palestine held two domains, Judah (later called Judea) and Israel. Ahab reigned as king of the northern kingdom of Israel, and Asa ruled Judah.

ELIJAH + AHAB + JEZEBEL = CONFLICT: Ahab, the seventh king of Israel, took for his wife a Phoenician princess named Jezebel. Being the daughter of the King of Tyre who worshipped Baal, the new queen was from a very different lifestyle than her husband. She persecuted the Hebrew prophets so fiercely that not one prophet could raise his voice without forfeiting his life. She became a dominant influence on Ahab, and she spread idol worship all across Israel.

FIGURE 21: RESTING ON HERODIUM
A member of the group rests on top of Herodium.

The stern Jews considered Jezebel very wicked and did not approve of this marriage. Knowing this, the Queen declared war on the priests of Yahweh and insisted all citizens participate in pagan worship (1 Kings 18). The Canaanite people followed her decree and worshipped Baal, but most of the Jews refused. Elijah, a gritty, unflinching character, condemned Baal worship because it involved sexual orgies including male and female prostitutes, human sacrifice, drunkenness, worship of animal images, sexual organs, trees, and other idols.

Caught in the middle between his subjects and his wife, King Ahab managed somehow to keep things in balance for twenty years. He built a palace of ivory for his queen and a sanctuary for Baal in Samaria, while still maintaining a semblance of support for the Jewish laws in Israel, (1 Kings 16:32).

The struggle between the two religions culminated on Mount Carmel, not a mountain or a peak, but a thirteen-mile coastal mountain range. Elijah met the priests of Baal in a publicized contest to show whose God was more powerful. Although Elijah came out the victor and killed all the pagan priests, the cult soon recovered and remained active for several years. Archaeologists still occasionally discover pieces of human bone among the rocks of the altar (1 Kings 16:31–32; 18:17–40). Elijah's triumph over the pagan priests did not make Ahab's Queen Jezebel happy; she worshipped Baal, and those were her priests. She ordered Elijah killed.

THE DRAMATIC DEATH OF THE QUEEN: Elijah prophesied a violent death for both King Ahab and Queen Jezebel, and this prophecy came true. Ahab breathed his last in battle. Jezebel fell from a window to her death, and the dogs lapped her blood in the street. In his two-volume *"Guide to the Bible,"* Isaac Asimov imagines Jezebel's last act of dressing in all her finery, make-up, and jewelry. He saw this as deliberately symbolic, indicating her dignity, royal status, and determination to go out of this life as a queen, (2 Kings 9:30).

AT MEGIDDO: The text in Revelation 16:16 describes the last battle between the forces of good and the forces of evil. *"And he gathered them together into a place called in the Hebrew tongue, Armageddon."* The mountains above Megiddo, meld down to the foothills of Mount Carmel, are called the plains of Armageddon. We climbed onto the Mount Carmel monastery roof to look over the beautiful and productive valley of the Jezreel, the Plains of Armageddon. This valley served as the capital of Judea during King Ahab's rule around 865 BC.

Our guide explains this plain was a wasteland not long ago, before Jewish Zionist pioneers drained the swamps, sank wells, and planted forests. They invested energy to turn this worthless area into a fertile plain. Today the September sun beats down on us mercilessly as we peer from the rooftop. An occasional breeze provides only a moment's reprieve from the heat. Below us near the center of that vast Jezreel valley, we can see the "tel" or archeological site of ancient city-fort, Megiddo.

This place at the crossroads of the two ancient roads hosted many territorial battles. Megiddo guarded the strategic pass on the *Via Maris* coastal route connecting Egypt and Mesopotamia, the two greatest rivals in the ancient world.

In the stable ruins, we find a stone manger carved out of limestone, and learn it is the same type of cradle used for the baby Jesus at the cave grotto in Bethlehem.

AUTHOR'S PRIVATE COLLECTION
FIGURE 22: ELIJAH
The *Monument to Elijah on Mount Carmel.*

Extensive archaeological digs of numerous stables prove that Megiddo was an Old Testament chariot city. Although known popularly as King Solomon's stables, these probably belonged to King Ahab. While most paintings of the manger scene depict a wooden bed, the newborn babe in swaddling clothes probably lay in a stone manger like this one.

A STONE MANGER IS NOT SO SOFT: As we hear more about the stables reserved for horses trained to pull chariots, we can envision helmeted charioteers in armor and togas, racing at breakneck speed around pillars marking each end of the course. Our tour of the tel revealed a partially restored walled town with gates, a water shaft leading to the water source, a Canaanite temple, stables, and a small museum.

MEGIDDO: One of the walled city-states taken by Joshua, Megiddo was always a friction line of fierce battles (Joshua 12:7 TLB). Once a boundary between the Kingdoms of the South (Egypt) and the Kingdoms of the North (Mesopotamia), the city sits at the crossroads of ancient international roads.

We walked beside an altar where Baal worshippers gathered at Megiddo. An ugly stone structure sat atop the altar, carved in the image of a bull with the upper body of a man. The arms extended, and fire belched from a hollow area in the chest. According to a "Focus on the Family" 1993 newsletter, the high priest required each mother to bring her firstborn child to be sacrificed.

The priests of Baal carried the babies, one by one, up the steps to the large stone image. They lay the babies on the idol's outstretched arms and inevitably rolled them into the blazing fire. Then the priest and priestess engaged in sexual intercourse on the altar in full view of the people, while an orgy occurred among prostitutes and the men. Elijah and other Israelite prophets condemned such behavior.

DISCOVER ANCIENT SITES: Most archaeological sites around the world are hard to find because they have been hidden below the surface by the weather and by years of neglect. The sites in Israel are

FIGURE 23: STONE MANGER
In the ancient stables at Megiddo we found a manger of stone for feeding the animals.

mostly above ground, though they are covered by so many layers of soil and vegetation that they form unique looking hills. Aerial photography or, in cases such as Megiddo, archaeologists can quickly identify them with the naked eye.

Excavation involves two tasks. The archeologist must first determine the layout at each stage of the area's history, and then establish a chronology or time sequence of the things he finds. The materials of archaeological study are the things people made and the things they used, such as settlements, buildings, tools, weapons, objects of ornament, and pure art artifacts. Other items of importance include things they used but did not make, the bones of animals they ate, traces of plants either grown or collected for food, and charcoal from ancient hearths. Sometimes archaeology treasure hunters slice down through the tel or hill to catalog the strata, much like slicing a layer cake. Researchers used this method at Megiddo Tel, revealing twenty-four layers of civilization.

FROM THE TOP OF THE TEL TO THE TUNNEL BELOW: Not so professionally, we pilgrims started our investigation of Megiddo at the top of the tel. The wind sweeps fiercely across this open hilltop as we inspect the old walls and tread the timeworn rock steps.

At Megiddo, ancient engineers created a secret tunnel to the water source outside the city walls, probably completed during King Ahab's rule. The laborers had to dig a shaft, 120 feet almost straight down, and then angle another 215 feet to reach a spring outside the city. They cut through solid rock with only simple tools such as chisels and hammers.

Once outside, they camouflaged the spring so that when their city was under siege, the residents could sneak down unnoticed to get necessary water. We descend the ancient steep, carved-rock stairway of one hundred seventy-three steps down a vertical shaft like a stepladder. For the tourists' benefit, electricity lights up the stairwell. I don't believe anyone should ever attempt going through that dark tunnel at night without a light. We exited at the base of the shaft onto the old Roman road.

ROMAN ROADBUILDING: The Roman road system gave citizens of the ancient empire access to the most distant provinces. Romans built their roads right, not just ruts along a riverbank. Here's how:

QUOTE BY PERMISSION: FOCUS ON THE FAMILY, NEWSLETTER 1993. JAMES DOBSON, FOF PRESIDENT

FIGURE 24: PAGAN STATUE
Artist conception of the altar to Baal in the image of a bull at Megiddo.

- A crown at the center of the road to allow rain to run off;
- Grooved pavement in steep places to provide a foothold;
- Three levels of substructure beneath the pavement;
- Numbered signposts every Roman mile telling the distance to the next town and naming who built the road.

FIGURE 25: KING AHAB AND QUEEN JEZEBEL
King Ahab and Queen Jezebel in Naboth's Vineyard.

These paved roads and others—usually constructed of stones, rubble, and concrete—were of great strategic importance, facilitating the administration and control of conquered lands. By the end of the first century, the Romans had completed a total of about fifty thousand miles of highways through more than thirty modern nations, connecting the Roman Empire with the rest of the world.

Romans built up the highways to carry their chariots and soldiers. The main roads contained three-foot deep bedding, paved with gravel, stones, and concrete. They built roads to last and made life much easier for the many caravans of merchants in the ancient world. The Romans linked their center of administration to Galilee.

The Roman roads enabled an efficient path through the tough terrain on the ancient route of Via Maris, *"the way of the sea,"* that once connected Greece, Syria, and Persia in the North to Egypt in the South. All roads led "from" Rome because the Roman Forum marked the starting point. Road builders measured each mile from the gilded pillar Caesar Augustus placed there. They marked the roads with Via Maris milestones to and from the "Eternal City." We will see one of the Via Maris milestones on Day Four.

After all that climbing up and down, we were happy to board the bus for Haifa.

HEARING OF HAIFA, HOME OF BAHAI FAITH: Haifa, a beautiful city on the Mediterranean Sea, became one of Israel's chief seaports and home to the world center of the Bahai faith. Bahai is part of a religion founded in Persia, now Iran, in the 1800s. Baha'is believe that there have been many true prophets, not just one. Gold-topped domes of their temple and shrines sparkle like jewels in the crown of formal Persian gardens. Although the world center for the Bahai religion attracts more than a million followers from all over the world, barely a hundred members of that faith live in Haifa.

The approach to Haifa is spectacular as it nestles against a mountain while embracing the tranquil blue shoreline. Mr. Elie pulls the bus over long enough to hear a musician's flute serenade as we look out over the city to the lovely harbor below. Aaron says the young entertainer is probably one of many Russian Jews who have returned to claim their heritage. The vast territories of the Russian Empire hosted the largest population of Jews in the world after the Diaspora. Most resided in the "Pale of Settlement," which includes present-day Ukraine, Belarus, Moldova, Lithuania, and Poland. Life in Russia proved especially challenging, and the descendants are now returning. Few jobs are available for them. Some of the immigrants must "sing" for their supper. The young man's haunting music followed our bus as we moved down the highway, but as soon as the music faded, our talk turned to food.

WWW.BIBLEWALKS.COM

FIGURE 26: ROMAN ROAD
This road pictured was part of the way from the coastal city of Ashkelon to Bethlehem and Jerusalem, not the one we walked on. You should watch along the main road for sections of the old Roman road.

TAKING TIME FOR LUNCH: We piled out of our bus on a busy downtown Haifa street and purchased falafel sandwiches from a sidewalk stand. The tasty falafel is one of the treasures of Israel. It is practically their national dish, fried chick-peas topped with fresh vegetables and a variety of unknown condiments, all wrapped in delicious pita bread. The Jewish version of an American hot dog, these little vegetable rolls are readily available from roadside vendors. We hastily devoured the falafel as the natives do, standing on the street.

Falafel

2-1/2 cups dried chick-peas, soaked overnight & drained
1 tsp ground coriander seeds
1 tsp ground cumin
1/2 tsp cayenne pepper
Oil & deep fryer
1/4 cup flour

Salt to taste

Grind the chick-peas fine in a blender or food processor and mix them well with the coriander, garlic, cumin, cayenne pepper, and salt. Add flour and mix. Roll this dough into small balls about one and a fourth inches in diameter. Heat oil to 375 degrees. Drop in the balls a few at a time and deep fry about two to three minutes until golden brown. Stuff the falafel balls into a pita pocket bread, and garnish with chopped vegetables. Ready to eat!

MOVING ON TO THE GALILEE: When our tummies were full again, we headed on to the Galilee. We have reservations for our second and third nights in Israel at the Kibbutz Nof Ginosar. Our guide tells us the kibbutz is an authentic communal way of life where residents, or kibbutzim, give according to their ability and receive according to their needs.

The entire community is ruled by a general assembly of all members meeting once a week, and majority rules. Power is not vested in elected officials of the kibbutz, but all the members. The secret of success for the kibbutz, as opposed to communism, is that everyone is always free to leave at any time. Dr. Neaves reminds us the first Christ-followers shared their food and everything they had. They helped one another as Jesus taught them. They spent time together learning about Jesus and praying together. They shared bread, so perhaps that was the first kibbutz?

OUR GUIDE PLAYS A PRACTICAL JOKE: Before we reached the kibbutz, but after explaining the principle of how it worked, Aaron told us we would have to take communal showers, live in primitive dorms, and work for our dinners. Jon and I didn't mind working, and we could handle outdoor bathrooms. Still, the idea of segregated housing did not seem attractive when we had so recently said our vows to be together always, nor did we think communal showers acceptable. We heard a lot of mumbling and grumbling on the bus—even some distressing talk of deserting and heading to a nearby hotel. Aaron didn't confess the truth until we checked in and headed for our rooms.

We find our accommodations spacious, cozy, comfortable, and modern, the meals delicious. The kibbutz could compete with most modern of hotels and our stay here beside the Sea of Galilee remains a special memory a decade later. *Nof Ginosar's* one-hundred-sixty-one guest rooms are heated and air-conditioned. Each has a cable TV, a small refrigerator in the coffee corner, and a lounge area. From our window, we can see a flower-lined path to the Galilee.

We enjoy a full Israeli breakfast with individual choice or buffet dining at *Nof Ginosar's* kosher restaurant. The restaurant features big windows with beautiful sea views. Kosher foods are those that conform to the regulations of *kashrut* (Jewish dietary law). Certain foods, such as pork and shellfish, are prohibited. They never serve meat and dairy products at the same meal. Dairy products are reserved for breakfast. Food conforming to these restrictions is "*kosher.*"

"Why are they so picky about their food?" we asked. Aaron reminds the priests caution the people of Israel to be a distinct people (Leviticus 11 TLB). Just as Israel's food laws separate clean animals from unclean, so the Jewish people were to be a people separated from gentiles. There's our gentile identification again.

The concern about food laws remains so strong that in a *kosher* kitchen, meat products, and milk products are not cooked in the same vessels or even served on the same plate. Blood is not edible; all meat must be completely drained of blood and then soaked for half an hour and covered with salt an hour before cooking.

ACCESSING ISRAELI MEDICAL CARE: Being used to our American seeded olives, I bit down on what I thought was a stuffed olive—and hit the hard olive pit. I cracked a tooth. Our guide said not to worry, for we are covered by their insurance while in this land of socialist medicine. Israel's medical institutions are some of the finest in the region with convenient locations and general accessibility to foreigners.

Just like the citizens of this country, our medical care is free while we are here. Aaron says I can get my tooth repaired in Jerusalem, where dental care is excellent. I decide to wait to see my dentist at home, but that information feels comforting. No shots or vaccinations are required to visit Israel. Should you need any medications during the trip, be sure to carry them in the prescription bottle. You might also want to bring along any over-the-counter drugs and personal hygiene products as they are not always easy to find. Suggestions: moist towelettes, sunglasses, wide-brimmed sun hat, travel alarm clock, feminine products.

*Tip: Bring prescribed drugs with you in the prescription bottle or with a copy of your doctor's prescription, as well as your eyeglass prescription.

Just before sunset, Jon and I walked down and dipped our toes in the Sea of Galilee and felt a kinship with this land. The water was crystal clear and lapped against a shoreline of coarse black sand. Tonight, our second night in Israel, we are at peace.

FIGURE 27: HAIFA

An immigrant musician plays a haunting tune with the city of Haifa and the stunning Mediterranean as a backdrop.

*Tip: The Sea of Galilee is unbelievably beautiful, so don't forget to bring a digital camera, extra memory cards, and a backup battery.

FIGURE 28: THE GALILEE
Gazing at the Sea of Galilee and a boat at sunset.

FIGURE 29: MARY'S WELL
Inside the crypt under the church of Saint Gabriel we visit Mary's well, also called the Fountain of the Virgin.

FOUR

DAY OF JESUS

Thursday: Nazareth, Capernaum, Galilee, Jordan River, Golan, West Bank, Mt. of Beatitudes

DAY FOUR: At the city of Nazareth where Jesus spent his boyhood, we toured the Greek Orthodox Church of Saint Gabriel. We visited Mary's Well, located under the church. In Byzantine third century AD, a church was built over the springs and called the place of the annunciation. The church has been destroyed and rebuilt several times, and other locations in Nazareth also claim to be authentic. The church structure covers and encompasses the well and is near the reported spot where the Archangel Gabriel announced that Mary was to become a mother. The spring still supplies the town with H2O, and it is possible the mother of Jesus may have drawn water here.

The spring of the well is said to run right under the crypt or burial chamber of the church. Although we did not know we were in a burial chamber at the time, we did walk down seven steps to the lower chapel, and through a narrow aisle roofed by a barrel vault. Closed arches with colored marble, glazed ceramic, and large stone blocks decorated the vault.

As for the well, there is a surprisingly steady flow of water at the bottom through a rather small opening in solid rock. A little metal cup hangs in the well-housing. Many people, wanting to say they drank from Mary's Well, sipped from this same cup. We did not.

Twain wrote, *This Fountain of the Virgin is the one which tradition says Mary used to get water from twenty times a day when she was a girl and bear it away in a jar upon her head. The water streams through faucets in the face of a wall of ancient masonry which stands removed from the houses of the village.*

GROWING UP IN NAZARETH: We know few details of Jesus's boyhood, except that he grew up in a thriving Jewish family in the hills of Galilee province in this town of Nazareth. Jesus may have played childhood games in the same street now busy with markets. He likely studied in the town synagogue, spoke the local Aramaic language, learned to read Hebrew scriptures, and probably also studied Greek, the language of commerce. He learned a trade and worked for several years as a carpenter, a stonemason or builder, as did his earthly father, Joseph. Once a tiny town, Nazareth now boasts more than forty thousand residents, mostly Arab and Muslim. While we did visit the Church of Saint Gabriel in Nazareth, we did not go to another historic church built over some ancient ruins. Saint Joseph Catholic Church, which we did not see, claims to be on the spot where Joseph's carpenter shop and the modest family home might have stood.

FIGURE 1: NAZARETH
Nazareth's main street fills with vendor carts ready to sell to tourists.

In recent years, archaeologists unearthed remains of the first dwelling in Nazareth that dates to Jesus's era, a simple structure of two rooms and a courtyard. The team found remains of a wall and a system that appeared to collect water from the roof. Based on clay and chalk shards, the dwelling appeared to house a "simple Jewish family." The Jews used only chalk vessels to ensure the ritual purity of food and water stored in them.

Jesus had a disappointing and discouraging experience in Nazareth. He spoke twice in his hometown, but the appearances were unsuccessful. The Pharisees and scribes in the audience wanted to throw him off a cliff. Pharisees belonged to an ancient Jewish sect distinguished by strict observance of the traditional and written law, and commonly held pretensions of superior sanctity. The scribes, ancient Jewish record-keepers, taught Mosaic Law. Jesus said to them, *No prophet is acceptable in his own country,* (Luke 4:16–30 TLB). *Note: That seems to be universally true.*

Mark Twain wrote of his visit to Nazareth in 1867: *Christ did few miracles in Nazareth and stayed but a little while. The people said, 'This, the son of God? Why his father is nothing but a carpenter. We know the family. We see them every day. Are not his brothers named so and so, and his sisters so and so, and is not his mother the person they call Mary? This is absurd." Jesus did not curse his home, but he shook its dust from his feet and went away (Matthew 13:55 TLB).*

SUFFERING A BIT OF DISILLUSIONMENT: We are learning all these places so familiar to us from the Bible have been preserved by some structure, often a cathedral, covering the entire original site. As a result, nothing looks quite as expected, but without that protection, the sites would have nothing left to view after so many centuries. Our guide explains there are numerous disputes over the exact location of Gospel places in the biblical lands. When asked if we would get to visit the fabled tomb, his answer surprised us. *Which one?* He asked with a laugh. We will understand what he meant soon enough.

Back on the bus, we pass the place of Jesus's first reported miracle when he changed the water into wine at a wedding in Cana of Galilee, *Kafr Kana,* a small town about four miles from Nazareth. We did not stop to see water pots supposed to be originals from Jesus's day (John 2). Maybe next trip.

SAILING ON THE SEA OF GALILEE: The Sea of Galilee is not a sea at all, but in reality, a beautiful fresh-water lake shaped like a harp or *kinneret* and called by many names. Locally known as Lake Kinneret, the Old Testament refers to the Sea of Chinnereth, or the Sea of Gennesaret for the plain to the northwest. Sometimes the basin is even called Lake Tiberias for the modern city on the shore near where we stayed. *Note: I think they do it to keep the tourists confused.*

Herod Antipas, son of Herod the Great, established Tiberias in AD 20 and named the city in honor of the emperor. Antipas built a luxurious bathhouse, a grandiose palace, all laid out in Roman grid patterns. However, he unwittingly situated his city directly over an ancient Jewish cemetery. The Jews of Israel, who would have delighted in the free land, housing, and tax exemptions that Herod offered new residents, refused to live there until many years later after a Rabbi performed purification.

Our guide says the name Galilee comes from the Hebrew word *galil* or circle. Hebrews living in this region were surrounded, or circled, by gentiles. *There's that word again.* The once-thriving ancient cities of Magdala, Capernaum, and Bethsaida on the northern shores of the Galilee, where Jesus walked and recruited disciples from among the fishermen, are archeological ruins we will visit (Matthew 4:17–20). The Bible says Jesus, born in Bethlehem of Judea, spent some time as a baby in Egypt. He grew up in Nazareth and lived later in the Galilee area. Because of his ministry, they called him the Galilean, and other times the Nazarene, but never an Egyptian.

SAVING AN ANCIENT BOAT: At the *kibbutz,* we visit a small unique museum housing an ancient boat discovered during the drought year of 1985 at low tide of the Sea of Galilee. Two fishermen found the boat buried in the muddy bottom near the western shore when the water receded. The wood dates from Jesus's time and tells historians a lot about how early builders constructed boats. Mud covered the boat and prevented bacterial decomposition. The ancient wood was extremely fragile when exposed to the atmosphere. Historians removed the fragile shell of the boat from the lake bottom carefully. Preservationists installed fiberglass ribs and filled the craft with polyurethane foam.

Archaeologists rescued the skiff by wrapping it with fiberglass and insulating foam, which helped keep it together while floating the remains to rest in a specially built pool shelter. It was then submerged in a wax bath for twelve years for protection before it could be displayed. On our first visit to Israel, we were privileged to be the first tourist group to see the ancient boat.

Carbon 14 analysis of the wood yields a date between 40 BC to AD 80, so the craft is definitely of the right period. The boat, most likely used for fishing and transport of people and cargo, sailed or was rowed by a crew of four oarsmen and one helmsman. Possibly this boat became a casualty of war in the great battle of AD 70 between the Jews and Romans in the Galilee when thousands died, and their crafts went down in the Galilee.

FIGURE 2: THE GALILEE BOAT   ITAMAR GRINBERG, WWW.GOISRAEL.COM
The ancient Galilee Boat at Nof Ginosar Kibbutz.

THE "SEA" OF GALILEE: We climb aboard a replica of the ancient boat, probably very like the one from which Jesus calmed the waters of the Galilee during a fierce storm. The boat carries us smoothly across the lake to Capernaum. The winds are quiet today, but our guide tells us sudden storms still occur with ferocious winds whipping down through the mountain pass and churning the water into giant waves.

According to Mark chapter 6, here on the Galilee Jesus walked on water. We did not try to follow his example because the lake looks very deep, and we are not sure our faith is strong enough to keep us above the horizon. The morning seemed incredibly peaceful and the ride tranquil, in sharp contrast to reports of shelling just north of us in the Golan Heights less than fifteen miles away. Our boat paused in the middle of the azure blue lake. The morning sun dropped sprinkles of diamond sparklers on the water. That poetic moment remains a shining memory over the years.

VISITING THE SYNAGOGUE AT CAPERNAUM: The synagogue performed as the center of social life, even more than a church does today. The building offered a learning center, especially for the study of the law. Synagogues also served as tourist information centers because it was the most accessible place to find. Strangers could stop there to ask for directions. They could even sleep there if they wished. When the Romans destroyed the temple in Jerusalem, the synagogue became more vitally central to the establishment of Jewish communities all over the world. No one had a Bible like we have today, broken down into books and chapters. Leaders could not say, "Turn to Isaiah 5:33 ..." because that was not an option. The scriptures were on hand-written scrolls with Old Testament information, stored at the synagogue.

We walked through the ruins of an ancient Jewish house of worship and rested on the stone bench. This synagogue is later than the first century. Excavations reveal the foundation is from the time of Jesus, with walls of worked stone almost four feet thick. These earlier walls remain up to three-feet-high. One entire wall became the foundation of the later center. Jesus must have visited the original house of worship many times and once healed a man with a withered hand.

IN THE GARDEN: We saw one of the Roman period Via Maris milestones in the Capernaum gardens. The busy Via Maris road passed by the Galilee, and right through Capernaum as travelers moved between Megiddo in the south, and Dan in the north.

RESTING AT CAPERNAUM, *Kafir Naem*: Jesus gathered his first disciples at Capernaum, then a small Jewish fishing com-munity. Peter, Andrew, James, and John lived in the village. Matthew, the tax collector, also dwelt here. We left the kibbutz, sailed across the lake, and stepped ashore at Capernaum. *Leaving Nazareth, he went and lived in Capernaum which was by the lake* (Matthew 4:13 NIV). A remarkable new walking trail completed in 2008 traces the path from Nazareth to the Sea of Galilee. From Jesus's home in Nazareth, he could have followed this line past the hills where the zealots lived in caves. It is a forty-mile hike, but people of that time seemed to think nothing of walking such long distances. Modern-day disciples can discover the biblical landscape and sites on the same path. Jesus moved to Capernaum where he could reach a larger population. Most of his ministry, lasting about three and a half years, took place in this small northern part of the Galilee more than two thousand years ago.

AUTHOR'S PRIVATE COLLECTION
FIGURE 3: VIA MARIS
We saw a surviving Via Maris milestone from Roman rule in the Capernaum garden.

NAZARETH vs. CAPERNAUM: Nazareth remained a small town in Jesus's day, a Jewish village of only about a hundred citizens. At the same time, Capernaum's population swelled with people. According to Matthew's account, Jesus walked along the shore of the lake, where he saw Peter and Andrew casting a net into the sea. Jesus invited them to follow him and told them he would make them fishers of men. *They immediately left their nets and followed him* (Matthew 4:20). Jesus then saw the brothers James and John in the boat with their father, Zebedee, mending their nets. Jesus nicknamed them the Sons of Thunder because of their fiery style (Mark 3:17 TLB). The brothers left their father with the boat to follow Jesus (Matthew 4:21–22 TLB).

AUTHOR'S PRIVATE COLLECTION

FIGURE 4: MILLSTONES
Millstones used for grinding grain are stacked in the garden. We find it hard to imagine having one of these millstones hanging around your neck as described in the parable of Matthew 18:6.

MILLSTONES AT CAPERNAUM: Piled along the garden path, we spy several enormous millstones used to grind grain in Jesus's day. We find it hard to imagine having enormous round stones as tall as a person and twice as big around, hanging around the neck, as men-tioned in Mark 10:42. The lower section is cone-shaped, and the upper stone is hollow. A farmer places grain inside the hollow upper. They then insert wooden stakes through the upper stone and rotate it portion over the lower section. This labor-intensive operation requires at least two people. The action crushes the grain and sends newly-milled flour spilling out the bottom.

THE HOUSE OF PETER, DISCIPLE OF JESUS: Near Capernaum's synagogue. we saw ruins of a Byzantine church, believed to be the home of Jesus's disciple, Simon Peter, the one *"on whom he built his church."* Matthew mentions a house in Capernaum belonging to Peter in which Jesus frequently stayed (Matthew 8:14–16). This house was the object of early Christian attention. A fourth-century house-church was here, and in the fifth century, someone erected a large octagonal Byzantine church above the ruins. As seen in the pictures, an impressive modern Catholic church now perches above but not touching the ruins of Peter's house—crouching there like a treehouse or a flying saucer above the crumbling rock base. The church, built in the 1990s, features a glass floor in the middle so visitors can see the original meeting place for early Christians. Although slightly more substantial than most, the house was simple with coarse walls and a straw roof.

TABGHA (*Ein Sheva*) AND THE FAMOUS MOSAIC: Not far from Capernaum, we visit Tabgha, where seven springs once flowed into the Sea of Galilee attracting a variety of fish, making this a favor-ite spot for fishermen. Two churches on-site, the Church of the Multiplication and the

FIGURE 5: INSIDE THE CHURCH AND FIGURE 6: RUINS AND THE CHURCH

A Catholic church perches above ruins believed to be of Peter's house at Capernaum. The church, built in the 1990s, features a glass floor in the middle (above) to look down into the ruins.

FIGURE 6: CAPERNAUM
Resting in the ruins of the synagogue at Capernaum.

Church of St. Peter's Primacy, mark this traditional site of the feeding of the five thousand (Mark 6:35-45 TLB). We saw an ancient mosaic depicting a basket of bread loaves and two fish in the rebuilt church at Tabgha.

KURSI (Gergasa) AND THE HERD OF SWINE: Avocado trees line the eastern shore on our way to Kursi, where Jesus performed a miracle by casting out demons from a disturbed man into a herd of swine. The swine then stampeded into Galilee lake (Mark 5 TLB). Researchers know this was not a Jewish pig farm since Jewish people do not eat pork. In Jesus's day, gentiles once populated the area near Kursi in the foothills of the Golan heights.

AN OLIVE OIL PRESS: Perched on the hillside at Kursi are remains of a Byzantine church, but what we found most interesting was a nearly complete olive press, in working order. The presses have two sections something like the mill grinding stones we saw at Capernaum. Ripe olives go on the first section and a smaller stone crushes them, the fruit moves to the second section where a mechanism squeezes out the oil.

FIGURE 7: OLIVE OIL PRESS
We saw a working olive oil press at Kursi.

The pit contains most of the valuable oil. Rotating a screw in the second section lowers the weight to press crushed olives, squeezing out the oil into a groove below. Water comprises about a third of the first squeezing, so the liquid is allowed to "rest" and give the oil time to rise to the top. Virgin olive oil, the best and purest, comes from the first squeezing. Although they predominately used olive oil for cooking and salads, oil also burned in lamps for lighting.

In New Testament times, cleaning jobs required oil as well; olive oil removed dirt from the skin and provided lubrication. They prized olive oil for medicinal purposes and anointing, often with perfume added to mask the smell. These ointments were costly, like the perfumed ointment poured over Jesus's head when he was eating dinner in Bethany during his last week of life (Mark 14:3). *Note: We will see other oil presses in the Garden of Gethsemane in Jerusalem.*

CROSSING A HOLY RIVER: Today, we crossed the River Jordan—this best known and much-loved stream. The name Jordan means "The Descender" in Hebrew; the river flows **through** the Sea of Galilee on its journey to the Dead Sea. We were surprised to see the Jordan, just a small, quiet stream as it exits the Galilee, and in places only a trickle of water over stones. Throughout history, the Jordan provided cool waters from snow-clad Mount Hermon, identified as a symbol of crossing over from one way of life to another. Minimal amounts of water are available in such an arid country as Israel, and early artwork shows John the Baptist pouring water onto the head of Jesus with a shell. The scallop shell with drops of water falling is an ancient symbol of the baptism of Jesus. Perhaps that is why Methodists sprinkle instead of immersing to express their faith.

GETTING BAPTISED: The traditional place of Jesus's baptism, east of Jericho, lies in a restricted military zone. Therefore, we go to a curve on the river where it traps enough water to create a pool. The place, called the *Yardenit,* is easily accessible. We watched an unending line-up of pilgrims in white robes waiting for baptism. Dr. Neaves explains there are different traditions about baptism, considering it as either an ordinance or a sacrament. Some denominations, notably Baptist, consider baptism an ordinance; first, a person believes, are baptized and become a church member. In Methodism, baptism is a sacrament, a sign of God's grace, an outward expression of an inward decision.

We always carried bottled water to drink, so we dipped an empty bottle into the Jordan to take some of the "holy water" as a souvenir. It is hard to tell from other water, but many

FIGURE 8: BAPTISM
Traditional baptism on the River Jordan at the Yardenit site.

tourists are willing to pay a pretty penny—or in this case, a shiny *shekel*—for little plastic water vial souvenirs at the market in Jerusalem.

We hear that tankers collect four thousand gallons of water twice a year from the Jordan, which goes to a packing plant in central Israel to be bottled and sold as souvenirs. No wonder this is such an arid country, with so much water leaving the country! Israeli tap water could serve as a valid substitute since one-third of the country's household water comes from the Galilee and the Jordan River.

We bought a bottle of honey to take home instead, remembering that Israel is the land flowing with milk and honey. However, the "honey" in this land is not bee-honey, but date-honey from the fruit of the date-palm that flourishes here. It is sweet and tasty.

ST PETER'S FISH: After all that splashing in the River Jordan, we were hungry again, so Mr. Elie, drove us to the *Ein Gev Kibbutz* for lunch. We enjoyed some Saint Peter's fish, fresh from the Sea of Galilee. Many travelers come to *Ein Gev*, so there is often a long wait, but we were seated in a picturesque spot, and time passed quickly. Our table overlooked the water, and a little inlet dammed up right beside the eating area. We enjoyed throwing bits of bread in the water and watching the large Saint Peter's fish fighting over scraps. They looked like giant perch. The proprietor told us a strange thing about these fish—they dislike cold water and prefer the warm springs spilling into the lake near Tabgha. Though the Bible passage does not name the fish, we call them tilapia. Dr. Neaves says tilapia is the common name for more than forty different species of freshwater fish. The name "Saint Peter's fish" comes from the story in the Gospel of Matthew, that apostle Peter caught a fish carrying a coin in its mouth (Matthew 17: 27 TLB).

SCALING THE GOLAN HEIGHTS: We enjoyed our delicious fish dinner at Ein Gev Kibbutz resort at the base of the Golan Heights. This rocky plateau in southwestern Syria borders the Sea of Galilee. Another traveler said Syrians used to fire down at the fishermen on the Galilee. We will not have to dodge any bullets today; the Golan is now under Israeli rule. In biblical times, they referred to the heights as *Bashan*. The word Golan derives from the biblical city of "Golan in Bashan" (Deuteronomy 4:43, Joshua 21:27). According to the Bible, the children of Israel conquered the Golan from the Amorites.

WARS AND RUMORS OF WARS: The Golan is a strategically important region, extending like a finger between Lebanon, Jordan, and Syria. The Yarmouk River borders the Golan plateau in the south, the Sea of Galilee and Hula Valley in the west, Mount Hermon in the north, and the Raqqad Wadi in the east. Israel seized the Golan Heights from Syria in the closing stages of the 1967 Six-Day War, even though the United Nations declared Israel's occupation of the Golan illegal. Syrians tried unsuccessfully to retake the Golan five years later during the Middle East war.

Israel currently occupies the western two-thirds of the Golan Heights, with the eastern third controlled by Syria. Palestine theoretically includes the West Bank and the Gaza Strip. However, control over this region is a complex and evolving situation. The borders are regularly questioned and changed. Israelis have occupied many areas claimed by Palestinians for years. Most of the United Nations member countries recognize Palestine as an independent state, but Israel and some other countries including the United States, do not make this distinction.

The Israel-Syria border runs through the Golan Heights along an area known as the Purple Line, patrolled by a United Nations peacekeeping force. No one is allowed to cross the border without special permission, even at the border crossing operated by the United Nations (UN).

From the end of World War I until 1948, the area that both groups claimed was known internationally as Palestine. Following World War II this land, totaling about ten thousand square miles, was divided into three parts; the State of Israel, the West Bank of the Jordan River, and the Gaza Strip.

Note: See a map of the armistice boundary, the "Greenline," on page 89.

No wonder both sides want this area; the Golan area provides a third of Israel's water supply. The land is fertile, with volcanic soil suited for grazing cattle, cultivating vineyards, and growing orchards. Towering above is Israel's highest mountain, Mount Hermon. More than thirty different Jewish settlements crowd in on Golan residents, adding an estimated twenty thousand Jewish settlers to native Syrian residents. The inflow of Jews into this restricted area is a constant source of conflict. Residents of the Golan continue to resist Israeli occupation. As in the West Bank, Arab residents of the occupied Golan Heights say they pay taxes to the Israeli government but receive little in return. They face restricted access to their lands, confiscation of property, and tight water restrictions that impede their farming. Some news reporters say Israel expressed willingness to withdraw from a significant part of the Golan Heights if Syria guaranteed security and friendly relations. Syria refused. Relinquishing the Golan to a hostile Syria could jeopardize Israel's early-warning system against surprise attack, so there is no easy answer.

PALESTINE AND ISRAEL CONFLICT: The US Department of State periodically warns citizens about the risks of traveling to Israel, because of a complicated security environment and the potential for violence and renewed hostility. The conflict between Palestinian Arabs and Israeli Jews has been ongoing since early in the nineteenth-century. For both Jews and Palestinians trying to lead an ordinary life, the complications of living in a continuing conflict zone present an uneasy coexistence. Although the two groups worship differently, religion is not the cause of the strife. The conflict remains a struggle over land.

Ramallah, to the north of Jerusalem, is the present seat of the Palestinian government. Worldwide condemnation met the Israeli government announcement of their plan to build another one-thousand settlement homes in occupied East Jerusalem. Already at least two hundred thousand Jewish Israelis live in developments ringing East Jerusalem, which is part of the Palestinian-held West Bank.

International opinion is that a two-state solution, including a sovereign Palestinian state, appears the best, if not the only, way forward in the century-old conflict over the old country. Still, there is no visible movement toward achieving this outcome. Current information about the ongoing conflict is essential to keep in mind while visiting here.

THE DOME OF THE ROCK CONTROVERSY: Around AD 690, the Arabs built the Mosque of Omar in Jerusalem, on what most believe is the exact spot where Solomon's Temple once stood centuries ear-lier. Information about this conflict is vital to know and help us understand before we visit the Dome of the Rock on Day Eight.

In 2008, Israeli's Prime Minister stated, *Jerusalem belongs to the Jewish people and will remain under Israeli sovereignty for eternity.* However, under a longstanding arrangement, Jordanian Arabs hold custodial rights over Muslim holy sites in Jerusalem, including the compound known to Jews as the Temple Mount and to Muslims as the Noble Sanctuary. This spot is the most sacred place in Judaism and third-holiest site in Islam. Jews are permitted to visit, but prayer by non-Muslims is banned. Jews can pray silently as visitors outside the Dome of the Rock (a.k.a. Mosque of Omar) on the Mount, but not as a ceremonial service. The conflict appears to be a problem without a satisfactory solution for now.

WHO ARE THE DRUZE? Some twenty thousand Syrians in the area say they are Druze by religion. Most of the Golan residents identify as Syrian, Arab, or both. Arabs are predominant in the Muslim faith, though some are Christian, and some Arabs—including the Druse—are neither Christian nor Muslim.

The Druze, an Arabic-speaking people with a secret religion, broke off from Islam a thousand years ago. The Druze faith is secret, few of their beliefs are known to the world. However, they believe in one God, and they are quite family-oriented. The Druze prefer sons to daughters, particularly the firstborn child. They will continue to have children until a son is born.

The average family has five or six children, but Druze families might grow to include ten to twelve children. The plump and pretty Druze women wear a traditional long black or dark blue dress with a white head covering. Druze men prefer their "honeys" full-figured, believing size only produces more to love.

Men, often mustachioed, have abandoned the traditional baggy pants tight around the ankles (*shirwal*) for western-style trousers. *Shirwal* still can be purchased in Middle Eastern shops. Men working in the fields usually wear the traditional red and white-checkered *Kufiy*ah on their heads. A guide at one of our stops told us the Druze believe the Messiah is yet to come and that he will be born of a man—thus, the men wear baggy pants.

Our guide pointed out many-storied houses, explaining as children and grandchildren grow up and marry, the wife moves into the husband's family home. Usually, the family's original parents occupy the first floor, with younger couples living on the upper floors, which are added to the stucco houses as needed. Family members all spend time together on weekends.

BACK TO THE BUS: After a delicious St Peter's fish lunch at *Ein Gev*, we climb back on the bus for a ride to the Mount of Beatitudes. The Golan conflict is in deep contrast and far from our thoughts as we enjoy the serenity and peaceful beauty of our evening in the serene gardens overlooking the Sea of Galilee.

THE MOUNT OF BEATITUDES: Nazareth, Cana, Tabgha, Capernaum, our Kibbutz, and the Mount of Beatitudes, all in easy walking distance, compose the center of Jesus's ministry. Our group gathers in this natural amphitheater to sit on stones on the hillside. To our left is a remarkable octagonal building with its surrounding colonnaded portico, maintained by the Franciscan Sisters.

TAI GLICK, WWW.GOISRAEL.COM

FIGURE 9: MOUNT OF BEATITUDES
The beautiful octagonal chapel on the site known as the "Mount of Beatitudes."

The Italian ruler, Mussolini, provided financial support in 1938. Our leaders said each of the eight windows inside the chapel bears the text of a beatitude verse. The building construction exudes numerical symbolism. In front of the church, the symbols on the pavement represent justice, prudence, fortitude, charity, faith, and temperance.

In the garden beside the chapel, white-robed monks kneel at their prayers under a red-flowering African tulip tree, a stunning vision. This tranquil garden provides a good vantage point facing the Galilee while looking toward both Tiberias and Capernaum. To our right, golden wheat fields and bright wildflowers wink and sway in the breeze. Susan, standing down near the water, reads the beatitudes. There is a slight rustle of wind, and yet the acoustics are so perfect we can hear Susan's voice as if she were beside us.

Blessed are the poor in spirit, for theirs is the kingdom of heaven.
Blessed are the meek for they shall possess the earth.
Blessed are they who mourn for they shall be comforted.
Blessed are they who hunger and thirst for justice for they shall be satisfied.
Blessed are the merciful for they shall obtain mercy.
Blessed are the pure of heart for they shall see God.
Blessed are the peacemakers for they shall be called children of God.
Blessed are they who suffer persecution for justice's sake for theirs is the kingdom of heaven.

(Matthew 5:3-10).

After meditating a few moments on all we had seen and done this day, we walk silently and slowly back to *Nof Ginosar Kibbutz* through the fields of wheat and wildflowers. The *Kibbutzim* serve us a bounteous buffet dinner, which they call a dairy meal. Many different kinds of cheeses and pasta dishes decorate the table with platters of fish—both raw and cooked. Fresh vegetables from the kibbutz gardens stack on the tables along with fresh oranges from the groves near Tel Aviv, avocados from the trees of Kursi, green and black olives from all over Israel. Oranges and other citrus fruits provide Israel's chief exports.

FIGURE 10: WALKING TO GALILEE
Walking from the Mount of Beatitudes area through the fields to the kibbutz with the octagonal chapel in the background.

FIGURE 11: GREENLINE

Map showing the 1949 Green Line Division (Armistice) and the 1967 boundaries.

FIGURE 12: PRAYING AT THE WALL
Hasidic Jewish Man praying at the wall (Kotel).

FIVE

DAY OF KING SAUL

Friday: Beit She'an, Jericho, Wadi Qelt, Gideon's Spring, Saul & David, Stones of Israel

DAY FIVE: We leave the glorious Galilee to visit the archeological site of ancient *Beit She'an* and its vast ruins in the northern part of Israel. This place is known by many names: Beth Shan, Betshean, Scythopolis, and others as well. No matter what it is called, the place played an important role historically due to its geographical location at the junction of the Jordan River Valley and Jezreel Valley, some twenty miles south of the Sea of Galilee. We will walk through the ancient ruins at *Beit She'an* National Park, knowing many Old Testament stories grew from this mound.

The enormity of this dig is awe-inspiring, and we are exploring under a blazing sun. Tel *Beit She'an* contains fifteen subsequent occupation layers, meaning fifteen cities jumbled on top of each other. The most important layers are from the Egyptian occupation in Canaan. A temple once crowned the top of the tel.

FROM EGYPTIAN TO ROMAN: Egypt controlled *Beit She'an* from the time Pharaoh Thutmose III in fifteenth-century BC made it an Egyptian administrative center. Several texts mention the place, one of them a list of cities the Egyptians conquered under Pharaoh Shishak, also mentioned in the Bible. *Beit She'an* later became a Canaanite city, and then a significant Roman city, the center of government. Our guide says this place was the Washington, DC, of its time.

UNDER ISRAELI RULE: The first three kings of Israel: Saul, David, and Solomon flourished in the eleventh century BC. All these men exhibited great strengths and weaknesses when they visited this city so many hundreds of years ago. Biblical stories, such as this one about King Saul and the future King David, are essential to understand the sites we are touring.

A WAR WITH THE PHILISTINES: The Israelites and the Philistines seemed always fighting a battle somewhere. This time, King Saul and his men lost the battle. According to 1 Samuel 31, King Saul died here in a battle with the Philistines on Mount Gilboa, just south of *Beit She'an*. Saul's dramatic end accompanies a unique cast of characters including a warm-hearted witch, an outraged dead prophet, a contemptuous enemy, an ally with long-term memory, and an angry anointed successor. This story is told in 1 Samuel 28:3–25.

THE WITCH OF ENDOR, A DEAD MAN, AND THE KING: The entire Philistine army had gathered at *Beit She'an* to attack Israel's smaller and weaker troops. King Saul longed for his mentor, the prophet, to give wise advice. He moaned, *If only Samuel were here, he would tell me what to do.* However, that great prophet of Israel was dead along with all the other priests that Saul had killed in anger. The King was at his wit's end about the upcoming battle and trembling with fear. He decided to find a "woman with a spirit" to bring Samuel the prophet back from the dead. Earlier, Saul had banned all magicians and mediums from Israel, making the practice illegal. After dark, he sought out the well-known witch who lived at Endor, a neighboring Canaanite village. To get to her, Saul had to disguise himself and pass through enemy lines. He reached Endor safely, entered the witch's cave, and asked for her help.

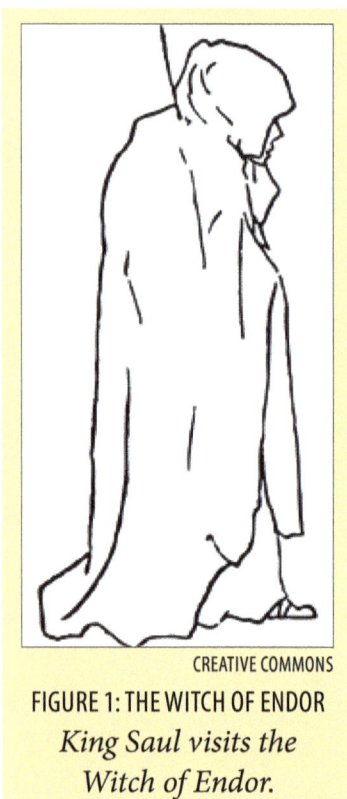

CREATIVE COMMONS
FIGURE 1: THE WITCH OF ENDOR
King Saul visits the Witch of Endor.

The Witch, though not aware of who her visitor was, reminded him that the King (i.e., Saul himself) had made witchery and mediums a capital offense. After being given a promise the king would not harm her, the witch brought Samuel the Prophet up from the dead. At least, the witch described the mantled form she saw, and Saul identified the phantom as Samuel.

At the séance, the ghostly image waved a long, crooked finger and protested, saying, *"Why are you bothering me?"*

Saul pleaded, *"The Lord has departed from me and does not answer me either by dreams or by prophets. Tell me, what should I do?"*

"Tomorrow you and your sons will be with me!" The image retorted. At these words, Saul fainted. Josephus tells this story and adds the witch felt so sorry for Saul, she tried to comfort him by killing her only calf to feed him and his sons that night. The next day the prophecy came true.

We did not go to Endor, but Mark Twain described his visit this way: *The hill is barren, rocky, and forbidding. No sprig of grass is visible and only one tree; a fig-tree, maintains a precarious footing among the rocks at the mouth of the dismal cavern once occupied by the veritable Witch of Endor.*

Saul, the first King of Israel, and all three sons, namely Jonathan, Abinadab, and Melchishua, fell in this battle with the Philistines. Josephus adds this detail: Saul and his sons threw their ardor into the fight killing many Philistines. Before the battle ended, thousands of corpses covered the battlefield. Struck by many arrows, Saul was mortally wounded. Rather than be taken alive when he saw defeat inevitable, he fell on his sword.

The victorious Philistine army found the royal bodies, decapitated the king and his sons, and hung their headless forms on the city walls. According to 1 Samuel 4, before the battle the Ark remained at the ancient sanctuary of Shiloh. The Israelites brought the revered object along anticipating a victory in the war. Instead, they suffered a terrible defeat and lost their treasure. Like capturing an enemy flag as a symbol, the Philistines carried off the revered Ark of the Covenant. This battle area now is outside Israel's border, in the Kingdom of Jordan.

Tall, dark, and handsome Saul was a popular king, so this was a great tragedy in Israel's history. The people of Gilead walked all night to come and rescue the King's body from the wall and take his remains to their city for burial. Gilead, a highland region east of the Jordan River, extended from the southern end of the Sea of Galilee to the northern end of the Dead Sea.

Even David, though he remained estranged from the King, mourned these deaths. Most of all, he missed the presence of his dear friend, Jonathan. After David became King, he went to Gilead and retrieved the bones of Jonathan and his father. He brought their remains back and buried them in one of the chambers inside Saul's father's tomb (2 Samuel 21:12 NKJV).

TRAMPING THROUGH BEIT SHE'AN RUINS: Earthquakes destroyed the city more than once, each generation rebuilding on top of previous ruins and sometimes re-using materials in creative ways. The tel (mound or hill) reveals a surprising history. As people moved down in the valley, the tel became an acropolis with stairs leading up to the temple of Zeus at the summit.

AUTHOR'S PRIVATE COLLECTION

FIGURE 2: BEIT SHE'AN RUINS
The towering tel in the background contains eighteen levels of settlement and uncountable stories of the past. Enormous marble columns and gigantic building blocks litter acres of this Israel National Park land.

Enormous marble columns and gigantic building blocks litter the acres of land dedicated to the dig. Aaron said that thirty to forty million dollars are invested each year in the excavation of this ancient city. When archeologists uncovered the house of worship, they found the skeleton of a man crushed beneath one of the columns. The historians determined he was running out of the temple when the column fell on him. Scattered on the ground near his remains, they found gold coins. So, there is a mystery. Did the man steal from the temple and bring down the wrath of God?

ITAMAR GRINBERG, WWW.GOISRAEL.COM

FIGURE 3: BLOODY AMPHITHEATRE
In this coliseum at Beit She'an the fare was brutal as gladiators fought lions or each other to the death, performing in front of thousands of spectators seated in the circular stadium.

THE BLOODY AMPHITHEATRE AT BEIT SHE'AN: The gigantic theatre built around AD 200, now with only two tiers remaining of the original three that provided seating for seven thousand spectators. White limestone imported from Mount Gilboa added the finishing touch. The limestone caps have disappeared from the middle tier, and the upper-tier seats are entirely gone. Even so, the preservation is impressive. On very hot or rainy days, they raised a canopy to cover the top. In this coliseum, the fare was brutal as gladiators fought lions or each other to the death, performing for thousands seated in the circular stadium. The score ran ten to one in favor of the Lions over the Christians. Beneath the wooden floor, slaves worked machines that pulled animal cages up to the sand-covered arena level. Fountains scented with lavender masked the stench of blood.

DIGGING UP HISTORY: Archaeologists are busily restoring uncovered mosaics everywhere in the country. As we watch, workers uncover from the sand, a stunning Byzantine mosaic of Tyche, the Roman goddess of good fortune. Her crown is a walled city, and in her hand, she holds the horn of plenty, filled with riches. *Note: Almost everywhere in Israel, history waits to be discovered; in fact, one of the residents told us it is almost impossible to find a site in Israel available to build anything new. It is now illegal for any new construction projects to begin without an excavation first taking place.* We step onto the basalt slab paving the ancient street. In the middle, flagstones cover a drain. Sidewalks line both sides of the street with evidence of shops along the western side. Stairs lead up to the temple of Zeus at the summit. Residents of this city worshipped many gods, and at the corner, we spy remains of the temple of Dionysos, the city's patron god.

FIGURE 4: PUBLIC TOILETS
The public water closets of ancient Beit She'an.

SOCIALIZING AT THE PUBLIC TOILETS: As early as 3,000 BC, according to a recent article in the *Biblical Archaeology Review*, royal palaces and homes of the elite had indoor lavatories with drains similar to sewers, to carry human waste out of the house. This public toilet contained about forty seats. Visitors sat on the slabs and straddled the opening, often sharing their stone with another person. In front of and beneath the rows, we see a ditch that washed the waste to the Jordan. Men and women used the facilities at different times; women in the morning, men in the afternoon. There were no dividers or modesty screens between the seats.

Instead of toilet paper, users carried a sponge to wash in the water channel flowing in front of the toilets. Our guide tells us this place was a popular gathering point for conversation and sharing news. However, the average citizen would not have access to this luxury. They had to make do with bushy areas outside the city.

FIGURE 5: GIDEON'S SPRING
Where Gideon chose his army of three hundred men.

FIGURE 6: SWIMMING IN THE SPRING
Sachne features a series of natural pools fed by hot springs.

MOVING ON: The enormity of excavations and discoveries becomes a bit overwhelming because of the heat. Our enlightening but exhausting walk around the grounds under the unrelenting summer sun goes at a 10k run pace. There is no time to contemplate anything at length, no time to puzzle. Just try to see as much as possible and stay close enough to the leader to hear.

We are glad to return to the bus where we can settle back under the air conditioner. Israel's tourist summer season is quite costly and very hot, so planning a trip in early spring or late fall is best.

Tip: Study hard. What visitors get out of the trip will directly relate to the amount of preparation before leaving home.

SWIMMING IN GIDEON'S SPRING: We stop on the way to Jericho for a picnic lunch at Sachne (*Gan Hashlosha)*, a charming national park with greenery and palm trees. We visit Gideon's Spring and relive the account of Judges 7, where Gideon chose his men for battle against the Midianites.

Israelis are utterly obsessed with nature. They can't get enough of their magnificent land and admire everything that grows in the soil. They might stop anywhere to enjoy a picnic in the outdoors. This beautiful park provides an entirely refreshing experience. The water is warm enough to allow swimming all year, yet amazingly cool and refreshing on a hot summer day. Sachne features a series of natural pools fed by hot springs and a stream with mini-waterfalls. Lush lawns separate the various pools. The concept is simple—go for a swim, then get out and walk around to find another spot to enjoy. A large glassy pool feeds from Gideon's Spring, where Gideon chose his army of three hundred men based on how they behaved when getting a drink of water. "*Gideon took the men down to the water. There the Lord told him, separate the ones who lap the water with their tongues like a dog, from those who kneel to drink. Three hundred of the men drank from cupped hands. All the rest got down on their knees.*" (Judges 7:5-6 NKJV).

AND WHO WAS GIDEON? A biblical judge and warrior named Gideon saved the Israelites from annual raids of the nomadic Midianites. Because he opposed the worship of Baal and also because of his dramatic victories, officials offered Gideon the kingship of Israel, but he refused. Gideon told them only God was their ruler (Judges 6-8). A few members of our group chose to enjoy the natural hot spring water. We did meet an amiable man, a professor from Jerusalem, who was there to "take the warm waters" and relax. He said he hopes someday to make a pilgrimage to America.

Tip: Wear a swimsuit under clothing, so you can peel off and jump in at will.

ON THE JERICHO ROAD: From Sachne, we head down the Jordan River Valley on the road to Jericho. Stones cover the barren desert hillsides. Our guide reminded us that on our left, we see the militarized zone of Jordan, a hotbed of Palestinian revolt and stronghold of Islamic militants. The Palestinian refugees, mostly Arab Muslims, live in refugee camps more wretched and dilapidated than any slums in America. The poverty is tragic for these displaced people. Their future is not bright unless things change. During World War I, the Ottoman Empire, rulers of this land, then called

FIGURE 7: ON THE JERICHO ROAD
Sharing the desolate road with cars, buses, and donkeys.

Palestine, allied themselves with Germany. In late 1917 British forces invaded and captured Jerusalem. After the war, the League of Nations approved a British mandate over Palestine and neighboring Transjordan. The rule intended to encourage self-governing institutions and eventual independence. Ultimately, in 1948 the State of Israel was founded, creating a homeland for the Jewish people—and displacing more than seven hundred thousand Palestinians at the same time. Even today, the conflict over borders and settlements continues to wreak havoc across the region.

Off in the distance, we see Jordan, where acres of greenhouses and signs of prosperous businesses contrast with the destitution of refugee camps. Aaron says fighting is usually north of here in the Golan Heights near the border with Lebanon and southwest in the Gaza Strip. Throughout the West Bank, Israeli settlements and nearby Palestinian villages co-exist. Conflict over resources can turn deadly. During the recent conflict between Israel and terrorist organizations, long-range rockets launched from Gaza reached many locations in Israel and the West Bank—including Tel Aviv, Jerusalem, and other cities in the north and south. Visitors staying in this area should seek information on shelters from hotel staff or building managers.

In Jesus's day, the Jordan River served as a boundary between two states, both ruled by sons of Herod the Great. Herod Antipas ruled one side of the Jordan River, and Herod Philip of Caesarea Philippi ruled the other. People who crossed the river had to pay a boundary tax, so even two thousand years ago people had reason to complain about taxation.

Finally, Mr. Elie stops the bus because we are at Jericho, once owned by Cleopatra, Queen of Egypt, before Octavian established his government in 27 BC and became the first Roman emperor.

WHERE JOSHUA FOUGHT THE BATTLE: Our guide reminds us that Old Testament cities were always built and rebuilt on a tel or mound left from the previous city. New Testament cities grew on the plains below. Jericho tel from the Old Testament lies on one side of the highway, with the New Testament city across on the other side. A well-known song about Jericho alluded to Joshua 6:20 NKJV when Joshua led the Israelites against Canaan, long before Cleopatra's day.

CLIMBING JERICHO TEL: We step out of the airconditioned bus into a fiery furnace with no trees to offer shade or protection from the sun. Slowly we climb up to the top of the Jericho tel. Ancient Jericho is a layer cake of successively destroyed cities, each new city built on the ruins of its predecessor, and it is not a picturesque ruin. While *Beit She'an* had twenty-four layers of civilization and Megiddo twenty-five, Jericho tel has many more layers than that. Archaeological dating methods place the first settlement here around 7000 BC. Those earliest inhabitants lived in mud-brick huts with lime-plastered floors. When Joshua marched around and blew his trumpet, the city walls went down. Joshua did the work so well he hardly left enough of the city to cast a shadow.

THE BATTLE OF JERICHO: Looking down from the hilltop at the different archaeological study areas, we wonder which of the excavations might verify the biblical story in Joshua. As leader of the Israelites, after the death of Moses, Joshua had to capture the fort of Jericho to achieve his goal of conquering Canaan.

AUTHOR'S PRIVATE COLLECTION
FIGURE 8: BLOWING THE SHOFAR

The city that he faced was fortified with Canaanite walls twelve to fourteen feet thick. Guards standing high atop the walls of Jericho would have observed a strange procession that first morning of the siege. In the distance, they would have heard the sound of the *shofar*, the ram's horn trumpet calling Joshua's troops to battle. The army of Israelites marched in order. First, an armed guard in ranks, with priests blowing the *shofar* and four priests carrying the Ark of the Covenant on gilded poles over their shoulders. A rearguard marched behind the priests, leading the entire Israelite army. The procession must have seemed endless. The wind whistled, the dust billowed, the horn sounded, but the soldier's voices were silent.

The *shofar*, a trumpet made from a curved ram's horn, represents the ram caught in the thicket when Abraham was about to sacrifice Isaac. The shofar is blown for a number of reasons in the Bible, most often to sound an alarm. As instructed, Joshua's army circled the city once before returning to their camp, the trumpet's sound dying in the distance as the muffled marching of the army faded.

The next morning the same strange procession occurred again and repeated each morning for six days in a row. The process made sense to those who knew the Ark they carried represented the throne of God. The seventh day the Israelites marched around the city seven times, as instructed. *Note: That magic number seven.* Then the trumpets sounded, and the walls of Jericho collapsed. Over the ages, this Bible story inspired the sound of children singing in Sunday school: *Joshua fought the battle of Jericho, and the walls came tumbling down.* NOTE: *This "Battle of Jericho" version is a good story. However, so far, there is no archeological evidence to prove this catastrophic event. Historians can neither confirm nor deny this event happened, based on what they have uncovered to this date.*

FIGURE 9: CAMELS
Camels wait for riders in modern Jericho town.

AFTER CLEOPATRA DIED EVERYTHING CHANGED: A Roman takeover followed Cleopatra's death. Octavian assumed control of the newly established Roman Empire, which included present-day Israel. He granted Herod absolute rule over Jericho, as part of the new Herodian domain.

WHEN JESUS VISITED: Jesus entered Jericho, and as he was passing through, he saw a man named Zacchaeus, the wealthy chief tax collector. Zacchaeus, a noticeably short person, or as we learned as children, Zacchaeus was a "wee little man." Zacchaeus wanted to see Jesus, but he could not see over the crowd. He ran on ahead and climbed into a sycamore tree because Jesus was going to pass that way. Zacchaeus may have been rich, but he was not popular with the Jews because he collected taxes for the Romans. They wanted to collect as much tax as possible without tying up their personnel, so they recruited locals and gave them a percentage of what was collected. The more the collectors could wring out of the people, the more they could keep. Many people filled the crowd, but Jesus zeroed right in on the little man in the tree. He had never met him before, but called him by name, *Zacchaeus, hurry down, for I mean to stay at your house today.* (Luke 19:1–4 NKJV)

A VIEW OF THE MOUNT OF TEMPTATION: From Jericho tel, our guide pointed out the Mount of Temptation, where Jesus fasted forty days and forty nights after being baptized by John in the Jordan River. One visitor said there is something about the hard rocks of the desert that bring him peace. Though the silent desert is lonely, he feels that perhaps we are not so alone after all.

Squinting our eyes to see in the distance, we can just make out walls and buildings of the Greek Orthodox Monastery of Karantel, built during the 1850s, still clinging to the barren brown cliff on the Mount of Temptation. The buildings are the same color of rock as the mountain, so they are challenging to see.

*Tip: Next time bring binoculars.

AUTHOR'S PRIVATE COLLECTION

FIGURE 10: FRESH FRUITS

Abundant crops in Jericho provide off-season fruit and vegetables, grown with the aid of natural spring water.

From early biblical times to the present, this rugged, barren beauty of the Judean Desert attracts those seeking refuge, solitude, or spiritual inspiration. For instance, the prophet Elijah, King David, John the Baptist, and Jesus all came here. Herod the Great built two fortresses in this area, Herodium and Masada, and during the sixth-century Byzantine period, someone carved magnificent monasteries into its cliffs and rock crevices. A grotto converted to a chapel is up there, where pilgrims climb to meditate. Karantel is one of only two monasteries where women are allowed. It would undoubtedly be a long hard climb, and we have far to go. No time for us to meditate, it is time to return to our modern camel. We are glad to leave this dusty old place hotter than Texas in July. We hurry on like the pilgrims we are imitating.

THE MURDER OF ARISTOBULUS: Some of Herod's murderous family activities took place at Jericho. Mark Antony gave Jericho to Cleopatra while it was still part of the Roman republic. Herod leased Jericho from her. Cleopatra and Mark Antony talked Herod into appointing Aristobulus III, Herod's brother-in-law, to the temporary office of the high priest. The people liked Aristobulus because of his handsome presence and noble descent. However, paranoid Herod feared his brother-in-law and waited for an opportunity. That opportunity came at the winter palaces near Jericho when Aristobulous mysteriously drowned in the swimming pool. The suspicious death happened during a banquet organized by Herod's Hasmonean mother-in-law. Josephus described the murder in one of his books, but there was no investigation. Herod oversaw the construction of a theatre to entertain his guests, and new aqueducts to irrigate the area below the cliffs. After construction, the city functioned not only as an agricultural center and as a crossroad, but also as a winter resort for Jerusalem aristocracy.

JERICHO, CITY OF DATE PALMS AND BANANAS: Modern Jericho, a beautiful oasis dotted with banana plantations, is the oldest city on earth. More than eight hundred feet below sea level, Jericho enjoys mild winters. Abundant crops provide off-season fruit and vegetables, grown with the aid of natural spring water. We are riding on the tour bus on our way from Jericho back to Jerusalem, a long, hot summer journey. We are thankful to be making the trip on wheels rather than donkey-back or foot power.

UPHILL ALL THE WAY: Mr. Elie drives the original Jericho road uphill east to Jerusalem for an unscheduled and unnerving adventure. Jerusalem is about three-thousand feet above sea level, and we are now eight-hundred feet below sea level. It is going to be a long climb. Even armed with that knowledge, we are unprepared for what we are about to experience. Jericho's straight-line distance to Jerusalem is fifteen miles; however, the precipitous mountain road between the two cities takes the traveler a much longer distance. In the late twentieth century, this old one-lane road, only recently paved and put into use, climbs sharply, a narrow path with sheer drop-offs twisting around the mountain, looping back and forth to reach the summit. The road and terrain from Jericho up to Jerusalem grows increasingly rugged and dangerous.

THE VALLEY OF THE SHADOW OF DEATH: Cars and buses queue up behind us like a line of army ants on their way to a picnic. Somewhere on this narrow trail, we reveal the setting for the story of the good Samaritan.

A certain man was going down from Jerusalem to Jericho, and he fell among robbers, who stripped him and beat him. They left him half dead. By chance, a certain priest was going that way. When he saw the wounded man, he passed by on the other side. In the same way, a Levite came and saw him and passed by on the other side. Along came a Samaritan. When he saw the wounded man, he felt so sorry for him. The good man bound up the victim's wounds, pouring on oil and wine. The Samaritan sat the victim on his animal, and brought him to an inn, and took care of him. When he departed the next day, he took out two denarii, gave them to the innkeeper, and said, "Take care of this man. Whatever you spend beyond that, I will repay you when I return," (Luke 10:29–37 NKJV).

The district of Samaria occupied central Palestine. Samaritans were notorious for idolatry, and Jews would not even speak to them. A devout Jew of Jesus's time would walk across the road to avoid social contact. They might even cross over the Jordan River so they would not have to walk through Samaria. When Jews spoke the word Samaritan, they would utter a curse and spit on the ground. The feeling was mutual. The two groups despised each other.

INN OF THE GOOD SAMARITAN: Ruins of a stone dwelling called the Inn of the Good Samaritan marks this road to Jerusalem. Although the structure standing there now came about long after Jesus's time, Aaron says there were always crude inns along this way, although sometimes they were little more than caves in the hillside. The "way houses" were spaced about a day's journey apart so travelers could be a little safer than on the open road.

In New Testament times, the dangerous road from Jerusalem to Jericho became known as the "Way of Blood" because of the danger.

At one point on our climb, we encountered a stalled bus, crawling around it with only inches between our tires and the edge of the precipice. Mr. Elie could not back up with the mile of vehicles behind us on that one-lane road, and it did not look like we could go forward with the stalled bus blocking the road. A couple of ladies wanted to get off and walk, but when we looked out our windows on the right side of the bus, the view from the door was straight down, actually hundreds of rugged vertical feet down. Those of us who saw that view felt ready for last rites. We heard Aaron saying, "*A little more to the right, Mr. Elie, a little more to the right!*"

Only later did we decide that remark was supposed to be a joke. Our vehicles became so tightly tangled that Mr. Elie and the other bus driver had to reach out and pull their big mirrors against their respective bus bodies to allow passage. Finally, we are beyond the stalled bus, still ascending the narrow twisting road. Finally, reaching the summit, Mr. Elie finds a spot and pulls the bus over off the road. Our guide encourages us to get off the bus to see the view, warning us to be careful of peddlers and to "mind our things," leaving any valuables on board with our trusted driver.

We think there can be nothing more to fear after that perilous journey. We were wrong.

FIGURE 11: A KICKING DONKEY
A peddler boy and his donkey at the Wadi Qelt overlook.

WHAT HAPPENED AT THE OVERLOOK: We hesitantly step off the bus, knees shaking, and follow a footpath to an observation point overlooking the deep and picturesque canyon of *Wadi Qelt*, a gorge with rocky and precipitous sides.

This area is part of the biblical wilderness of Judea. People running away from the law found shelter here, and they made a living by attacking the caravans. Anyone traveling alone was especially in danger. Outlaws preyed on people who walked or rode a donkey from Jericho to Jerusalem because travelers carried cash to pay tribute (taxes) as required.

Suddenly on this hillside, we are joined by a pack of peddlers and ragged young beggars crowding around us, offering their beasts to ride for "one American dollar." Two young boys, demanding and rude, also request dollars for any pictures we might take of them.

Several of us perch there, uncertain how to deal with the peddlers when an even more alarming thing happens. One of the donkeys becomes agitated and starts kicking. The people standing nearby move to get out of the animal's way, and in the resulting confusion, they nearly pushed our beloved minister's wife over the precipice. We will forever remember this place as our personal valley of the shadow of death. We are happy to climb back on the bus and leave the observation point.

This brief experience gave us an even greater appreciation for the danger of the journey in Jesus's day. Joseph and Mary made the long trip on foot and by donkey, not just to the monastery, but along this tortuous path through the dry and rocky mountain range to Bethlehem and later on to Egypt. They had to worry about Mary's advanced pregnancy and the ever-present danger of thieves and robbers. Later, Jesus and his disciples traveled this road also.

INVESTIGATING A GREEK MONASTERY: In the Judean Desert on the old road to Jerusalem in the eastern West Bank is the deep canyon of *Qelt* (creek). Our guide says *wadi* means the same as *arroyo* in the American Southwest. Bordered by the Judean Mountains to the West and the Dead Sea to the East, the desert's endless landscape features deep canyons and sheer cliffs. Arid hills and valleys contrast with ancient springs that create an oasis-like *Wadi Qelt*. We decide it is no wonder this arid desert has caught the attention of so many.

On the northern side of canyon is the stunning and mysterious Greek Monastery of Saint George, carved into the steep barren slope, clinging to the wall. This monastery, one of the oldest in the world, claims to protect an entrance to the cave where the ravens fed Elijah (1Kings 17:3-6), the same prophet who angered Queen Jezebel as we learned on Day Three. The strangely beautiful collection of tan rock structures topped with bright blue roofs appears as if suspended from the cliff's rocky face. Our tour guide says that five to seven monks live there year-round. They must grow a healthy garden because

FIGURE 12: THE MONASTERY OF ST GEORGE
We admire the breathtaking view of the cliff-hanging St. George's Monastery at Wadi Qelt.

they would have a very long walk to a grocery store. Our guide's organization supports the monks as missionaries who spend their days studying, meditating, and praying. Perhaps they pray for travelers like us journeying up that narrow path to look down on their monastery.

VISITING A CLIFF-HANGING MONASTERY: Arid hills and valleys contrast with ancient springs and a little distance from the monastery we see a most amazing sight. A torrent of water gushes out of a ridge on the rocky mountainside. The water brings life as it cascades down the brown cliff, growing a living ribbon of lush plant-life all the way to the bottom of the gorge. The slender green gash breaks the monotony of brown hills that stretch as far as the eye can see. Where did the water come from and where does it go? It is absorbed into the dust before it can form a river.

AUTHOR'S PRIVATE COLLECTION

FIGURE 13: THE PATH AROUND THE MOUNTAIN

Look carefully to see one of the black crosses that mark the way to the monastery. We followed the old Roman Road 500 feet up, down, and around the mountain. We had a bridge and a good path, while early-day visitors had to cross the deep ditch of the Qelt and climb up the other side.

FOLLOWING THE OLD ROMAN ROAD: Mr. Elie parks the bus, and our guide tells us his usual: "mind your things." We walk a winding avenue down and around the mountain. We cross the *Qelt* and clamber up the other side to reach the monastery, a pleasant ramble on a cooler day. The gully is dry, but an Ottoman period aqueduct runs beside the path, carrying fresh spring water down to Jericho about three miles away.

Our lane winds around the south bank of *Wadi Qelt*, following the route of the old Roman road from Jerusalem to Jericho. The walking path, wide in the beginning, quickly narrows around the first bend to accommodate a single file. There are no guardrails between the path and the sharp drop-off. Our American government safety gurus at the Occupational Safety and Health Administration (OSHA) would be appalled.

We were all quite winded by the time we reached the fourth-century monastery, rebuilt by Crusaders in the twelfth century. We stopped on the steps outside to rest and absorb all this beauty. After the Muslims conquered Jerusalem, they expelled the Crusaders, and the buildings gradually deteriorated from disuse. In 1878 a Greek monk named Kalinikos settled here and restored the monastery, finishing it in 1901.

ST. GEORGE'S MONASTERY IN THE *WADI QELT* VALLEY: Named after the most famous monk—Gorgias of Coziba—who lived in the cave of Elijah in AD 420. About two hundred years later, during the Persian invasion, the cliff-hanging monastery complex was destroyed. Persian invaders killed all fifteen of the monks living there.

The monastery chapel displays bones and skulls of the martyred monks. The remains of another priest, Saint John Jacob the Romanian, lies in state in a glass casket. He lived here alone in the monastery until his death. The body is well preserved, but the priest's worn-out work shoes almost made us cry. All visitors can see the macabre displays.

EXPLORING THE VISITOR CENTER: We asked for directions to the WC (Water Closet), and we found the room, which overhangs the cliff. Like most remote toilets in this part of the world, visitors straddle a hole in the floor. We could not decide if courtesy required facing the door or the wall. We decide to wait.

The early monks lived a hard, monastic life, dwelling in caves that cling to the cliff wall. Many believe that at the time when the earliest desert-dwelling monks sought lives of faithful seclusion, John the Baptist lived as a hermit not far from this place. The three-level monastery complex encom-

AUTHOR'S PRIVATE COLLECTION
FIGURE 14: CAMERA DISCUSSION
Father Antonios and Dr. Norman Neaves discuss cameras. We felt welcome here.

FIGURE 15: ST. JOHN'S CRYPT

The body of Saint John Jacob the Romanian lies in state in a special room of the monastery. St. John lived alone in the Wadi Qelt Monastery from 1913 to 1960.

passes the Church of the Holy Virgin and the Church of Saint George & Saint John. I do not know why there are two, but both contain a rich array of icons, paintings, and mosaics.

SPECIAL GREETING FROM FATHER ANTONIOS: Saint George's is one of only five monasteries still functioning in the Judean Desert. The monks are well known for their hospitality, and unlike most Greek Orthodox monasteries, they welcome female visitors. Father Antonios, superior of the monastery, came out to the sanctuary to greet us. He is much too young and handsome to be a monk. Long after our visit, Father Antonios replied to a letter and answered several questions. He said ten monks live there, but none in the monastery itself because that building is only for work and prayer. All services are in the Greek language. He ended with, *"Many thanks for your letter and for sending photos. I wish the holy grace of our Lord to be always with you."*

THE CAVE OF ELIJAH: Eventually the monks added a fifty-foot bell tower in 1952, a domed chapel and an open courtyard for their private use. Another steep stairway up from the main floor leads to the cave where the monks say Elijah was fed by ravens (1Kings 17:3-6). Our visit to this breathtaking, harsh, and surprising place will always be a special memory.

LEAVING THE MONASTERY: After a brief pause, we said goodbye to *Wadi Qelt*, Father Antonios, and the strangest kitty we ever saw— It was the mouse-catcher that looked more like a mouse than a pussycat.

It is time to return to our blue bus. We step down the concrete walkway from the monastery, cross the Wadi and like mountain goats, put our feet to the hard-packed dirt. It seemed like an hour-long climb back up and around the mountain in the sweltering sun. Only patience and perseverance kept us going back up, putting one foot in front of the other, ever-moving upward. Our friends remind us that such healthy physical exercise creates unforgettable memories, even if it is hotter than a firecracker lit on both ends.

About three-quarters of the way up the mountain where the road widened a bit, an Arab with a "taxi" appeared and offered to take us the rest of the way. I almost succumbed to the lure of a ride until looking more closely at the car, a beat-up 1960s model Opal hatchback, the cluttered back seat filled with junk. Two of our ladies decided they were desperate enough to take a chance. The driver turned the auto around at a "wide" spot on the path. It looked like he was doomed to go over the side. Thankfully at the last minute, he gunned the motor and managed to charge the vehicle and his paying passengers up the steep incline.

It would be difficult to find words to describe our visit to the monastery to do it justice. Though off the beaten path, the journey to this secluded bastion of desert monastic tradition is well worth the effort. It is a peaceful and unforgettable place.

And then we move on to our next adventure.

GOING UP TO JERUSALEM: Safely back in the bus, Aaron says after this trip every time we read about the Jericho Road it will never be the same for us again, and we know he speaks the truth. *People sitting next to us in church will say, what happened to these people? Did they get crazy?*

Off in the distance, we can see some of the buildings in Jerusalem. The entire city, built on the top of the hill, appears built of stone. No one can go "up" from Jerusalem, he laughs. Everywhere you must go "down" from there. Psalm 121 has a new meaning, "*I will lift up my eyes to the hills from whence comes my help.*" Our Jewish guide loves this city. Excitement and emotion build in his voice as he speaks of his promised land, his beloved Jerusalem. There are places where they have never heard of New York—but everyone has heard of Jerusalem.

A TAPED CONFESSION: The next few paragraphs are from the cassette tape of Laveta Simpson, who caught and preserved this poetry spoken by our guide in the bus on our way back to Jerusalem. This road is the highway to our guide's heart.

THE LEGEND OF THE STONES: "*As we approach the city, you might see a lot of stones. No matter where you come from, this will catch your attention, the many stones that surround Jerusalem. As a matter of fact, you will discover that the entire city is built out of stones. Everything is done out of stone. The question asked time and time again, why are there so many stones around Jerusalem?*

FIGURE 16: WELCOME TO JERUSALEM!

"There is a legend that when we are far from Jerusalem and start to read about it and study it, we start to love it. And the love we generate in our hearts for the city of Jerusalem also starts to grow hope. We have a prayer asking that one day God may grant us the privilege to come and to see Jerusalem in its glory, and as the days go by it is harder to understand the ways of life, as the love for Jerusalem grows stronger and stronger in our hearts.

"We start to understand that for his own reasons, God may not honor our prayers. Maybe we will never be able to see Jerusalem, and the love in our hearts becomes stone. As the days go by, our heart gets heavier and heavier. It is at that moment when we gain the privilege to come and see Jerusalem. It is at that moment when we make the last mile in the road, and we begin to see Jerusalem in the distance, the stone we carried in our heart for many years comes away. Those are the many stones we see around. "This afternoon as we make our approach to the city, and we see the buildings. Then the dream is not a dream anymore but is becoming a reality. A few more stones will be added to the many already around. God is giving us the privilege to come and see the city in all its glory.

JERUSALEM, A SACRED PLACE: He continues, *"I have the great privilege to be a citizen of Jerusalem. For me to live in Jerusalem is not a dream, it is a reality. To go by those places that you have dreamed of all your life, to me is a daily reality. So, as you now start to see the first buildings, we are coming to the official sign that says you are coming into Jerusalem.*

"As a citizen of this great city, I would like to welcome you to this magnificent place. It will be a time when our hearts will be ready for an unusual spiritual experience.

We will be able to listen to the stones. They want to tell us of more than four thousand years of Jerusalem history. The stones have witnessed the sad and happy occasions. So, when you leave the city you will be like us. There are many people in this world whose hearts are made of stone, but there is one place where there are many stones with the hearts of human beings. I hope you will be able at the end of this visit to Jerusalem to rejoice, for it will be a time of growing in a spiritual way."

FIGURE 17: CLIMBING UP
Jon climbed up to see the cave of Elijah.

SIX

DAY OF KING DAVID

Saturday/Shabbat: Jebus, David's Palace, Tomb of Absalom, Engedi, Masada, Dead Sea

DAY SIX: A day in which we learn about Jerusalem's Holy Voltage. Our luxurious "wayhouse" for the next days and nights of our pilgrimage is the Jerusalem Hilton, where we learned some things about "holy voltage."

We were hot, dusty, and tired on reaching the hotel, so we showered and shampooed despite the tight schedule. The expensive converter we bought for the trip refused to work with the hairdryer. Our video camera batteries were exhausted, and the recharger plugs didn't fit the room's electrical outlet. Israel's electric current is 220 volts instead of America's 110, and most Israeli sockets have three round prongs, unlike our two straight and one round. Finally, we called room service and explained our problem. Within minutes, the management delivered to our room, at no extra charge, a transformer. Viola! We have electricity again. We were ready in time for another great meal, and had our video batteries recharged. Other guests came to heat their travel irons with our converter.

*Tip: Bring a converter—but contact the hotel if the converter doesn't work.

OBSERVING SHABBAT: Jerusalem celebrates three Sabbaths every week. The Muslim holiday is Friday, the Jewish *Shabbat* is Saturday, and the Christians worship on Sunday. Of the three, Jews are the most devoted to their rules. Today is Saturday, the holy day for this Jewish city. Our guide for today, named Oodi, is not Jewish. Daniel Aaron will not be with us this day. Being Jewish, he plans to be in the synagogue with his family for *Shabbat,* the Sabbath, which begins in his words, *"when the sun touches the treetops"* on Friday evening, and doesn't end until *"you can count at least three evening stars in the sky"* on Saturday evening.

A WORD ABOUT ELEVATORS AND FIRE ESCAPES: The elevators at our Jerusalem Hilton are pre-programmed for *Shabbat*, so Jewish people do not need to push buttons. They are not supposed to perform any type of work on that day. There are no enlightening signs or posters—you just have to know.

The buttons are disabled, and the elevators are programmed to go all the way to the top without stopping, and then come back down, halting every other floor. One elevator stops only at odd-numbered levels, the other at even numbers. You must ride to the twenty-first floor, then the elevator descends slowly, halting as pre-programmed. It helps if you know this on Saturdays. We didn't.

Being unschooled in the intricacies of *Shabbat*, Jon and I boarded the elevator from our seventh floor room. We wanted to go down to the lobby and outside to catch our bus for the day's outing. To our surprise, the elevator went up instead of down, and we soon tired of the game as our carrier began its slow descent with unexpected stops. We think the lift must be broken and decide we better exit at the next opportunity.

Worried about missing the bus, we jump off about the fifteenth floor and run down the fire escape. However, Israeli fire escapes are not like American fire escapes. We exited the stairway only to find ourselves in the basement laundry room with the stairway door locked behind us. We finally locate a narrow ladder-like stairway going back up. We had no idea where it might take us, but we start climbing and are surprised to open a door and find the hotel lobby. To our delight, familiar faces greet us, and everyone has a good laugh as we share our elevator adventures.

Tip: Check your hotel elevator on Shabbat, so you don't miss your ride.

TO MASADA AND THE DEAD SEA: Oodi will guide us to the Dead Sea and Masada. There is no bustling traffic as we ride the tour bus this *Shabbat* morning through the big city of Jerusalem. All Jewish shops and stores are closed. Businesses, offices, and institutions are closed. Most public transport and places of entertainment are not operating. However, the city does not sleep.

We see people walking together as families on their way to synagogue. Men and boys wear severe black caftans and shoes, some have tall black boots almost to their knees, worn with pantlegs tucked inside. Nearly all males have some type of headgear. Some of the men wear large furry "bowler" style hats called *shtreimel* on this warm morning, and *yarmulke* skullcaps hide others. *Hasidic* boys have short hair except for one very long curl dangling over each ear. Kerchiefed women dress plainly and modestly in high-neck, long-sleeve dresses usually ending about the ankle over heavy stockings and sturdy black shoes.

We wonder aloud about the significance of the unique clothing, particularly fur hats and heavy clothing in the heat of an Israeli summer. Oodi answers that some things become custom so long that no one knows why. They just DO it.

Visitors do not have to wear hats and boots but must dress modestly with arms and legs covered most of the time. Our guide says we are permitted to wear shorts at Masada because the heat will be boiling. We thought the days extremely hot before, so with this warning, we dress in shorts and sleeveless tops but carry a wrap-around skirt in case we need to cover up later.

Tip: Pack a "modesty kit" to cover up shoulders and legs when required.

The road from Jerusalem through the Judean mountains to the Dead Sea area is not the scenic drive you might think of in America. The road slices through a mountainous desert, all barren, shadowy, and unfriendly. Along the way, we occasionally glimpse burned-out shells of military vehicles, a reminder of the country's "wars and rumors of wars," (Matthew 24:6) throughout history. This Jordan Valley separates Israel from Jordan, two countries that are not on the best of terms. Tourists can cross the border into Jordan, but Israelis cannot go there freely. The roads may be picturesque in spring when brave desert flowers try to bloom, but late summer presents only arid solitude, scorching heat, and dull-colored hills of brown sand.

THE GREAT RIFT VALLEY: Owen, a geologist in our group, explains we are over the famous Great Syrian-African Rift, or the Great Rift Valley, 3,700 miles in length and easily found on any map. River Jordan, affectionately called *The Descender*, with its mouth 1,700 feet **above** sea level on Mount Herman, in a twelve-mile span reaches sea level, drops 682 feet below sea level in another six-mile distance to the sea of Galilee, and falls to 1,200 feet **below** sea level in the sixty-five-mile stretch to the Dead Sea. Learning such detail from fellow travelers is the unexpected benefit of being part of a group.

Just forty-five minutes from Jerusalem's hills, we discover the beautiful and unique Dead Sea, actually a dead end, the lowest place on earth, and the saltiest body of water in the world—six times as salty as the ocean. Water flows in from the Jordan, and cannot escape.

AUTHOR'S PRIVATE COLLECTION

FIGURE 1: THE GREAT RIFT VALLEY
Taking the road through Judean mountains to the Dead Sea.

A sea is a part of the ocean partly surrounded by land containing salty water; a lake is an inland water body. The Dead Sea is saline for sure, yet it is also a lake. We glimpsed it from a nearby mountaintop, looking like a blue shield resting on acres and acres of golden sand.

FLOATING IN THE DEAD SEA: Several peeled off outer clothing to reveal swimsuits underneath and enjoyed the astounding experience of floating effortlessly in the water. It is incredibly easy to swim in the Dead Sea because the mineral water is so buoyant you cannot sink. Bathing in this water is a unique experience. No horizontal position can be held for long unless using your hands to stabilize. You can stand up straight in water over your head and stay dry above the chest, but you can't hold that position long. The water will soon lift your feet to the surface.

AUTHOR'S PRIVATE COLLECTION

FIGURE 2: SWIMMING IN THE DEAD SEA

Try floating effortlessly in the Dead Sea. You cannot sink. Notice one swimmer has smeared mud on his face.

HOW DID THE DEAD SEA DIE? The Dead Sea lies at the bottom of this mysterious fault in the earth's crust, this Great Rift Valley from the Jordan valley through East Africa. The same natural phenomenon that created the five-million-year-old Great Rift gash also produced the hot springs we enjoyed at Sachne. A salty liquid fills part of the Great Rift allowing the Dead Sea, no matter how low its level falls in drought, to remain one of the deepest lakes in the world. The Dead Sea contains about twelve times as much water as our US Great Salt Lake but covers a much smaller land area.

Sparkling and smooth, the pool reflects a deep blue and even turquoise blue in places. We enjoy our brief dip. However, the fluid is thick and gassy, and nothing can live in that beautiful water because it is too salty. No fish, plants, or animals inhabit the lake, and no green plants trim the water's edge. During the Middle Ages, travelers thought the air in the region was poisonous because no birds flew over the water. Now we know birds avoid this place because it contains no fish for them to eat.

Positioned between the nations of Jordan and Israel, a small peninsula extending from the eastern shore divides the Dead Sea into two unequal parts. The northern two-thirds is deepest, while the southern third is less than thirty feet deep.

WHAT ABOUT SODOM AND GOMORRAH? Several hotels and a bathing beach at the southern tip of the Dead Sea mark the infamous ancient towns. The location of the "accursed cities" is now a beehive of industry, busy with salt quarries, evaporating pans, and processing plants for minerals extracted from the salty basin. Such products as magnesium chloride, industrial salts, deicers, bath salts, table salt, and raw materials for the cosmetic industry come from there. A tourist guidebook says the cities are below the "tongue" of land that protrudes from the eastern shore, and also claims the ruins were above the water until an earthquake about 1900 BC. Lot's wife looked back at the destruction of Sodom and turned into a pillar of salt (Genesis 19:26). The Jewish legend says Lot's wife (who remains unnamed) looked back to see if her daughters were coming with them. The daughters were married to men of Sodom. Instead, she saw God raining fire and brimstone. There is a rock formation in the area that some refer to as Lot's wife; our guide claims the salt slab appears about the size of a large car and doesn't resemble a person at all. We looked and looked but never saw a grain of salt or a saline crystal of Lot's wife. She was gone—if ever she was there.

Oodi says we don't have to worry about turning into salt, and we can tan without fear because the below-sea-level location filters out the sun's dangerous ultra-violet rays.

SALTY WATER AND BLACK MUD: Many people believe in the curative and healing powers of saltwater and the black mud below surface of this pond. Several bathers dug clay from the lake floor and smeared it on their bodies. In the photo background at left, one swimmer has a face blackened with mud. Small bags of bath salts, bars of black soap, and packages of black mud souvenirs are available in the gift shop. Crystals glitter in the sun along the shore, and the water contains radioactive properties due to its high radium content. Numerous communal outdoor showers activated by pull chains dot the beach. The salty water dries quickly in the scorching air and produces an uncomfortable stinging, burning sensation, so if you swim be sure to shower as quickly as possible.

We jumped in the water long enough to take a few souvenir pictures, then quickly rinsed, pulled clothes over our damp swimwear, and ran back to the bus. We found our group patiently waiting to head for the mountaintop fortress of Masada. *Tip: When you go to Israel, don't miss floating in the salty sea. You will be glad you did.*

THE ZEALOT'S LAST STAND: Once a glamorous pleasure palace for King Herod, this mountaintop resort became a deadly fortress with a sad ending. For more than fifteen hundred years, the story of Masada was a more or less forgotten episode in Jewish history.

Now the flat plateau ranks among Jewish history's most awe-inspiring sites. The one-time Herodian fortress became a central symbol of pride and bravery in Israel. The site is now an accessible location for *bar mitzvahs* and military inductions. Shaped like a giant steamship and topped by the massive rock fortress, the mountain rises nearly fifteen hundred feet above the shore of the Dead Sea. King Herod equipped Masada for a retreat in case of revolt in Jerusalem, and he believed this mountaintop impregnable.

WWW.GOISRAEL.COM

FIGURE 3: THE CABLE CAR
We took the cable car to the top of Masada.

He built this pleasure palace, adding a twelve-foot-tall wall of white stone around the entire top of the hill and thirty-eight towers for dwellings. The completed fort featured hanging gardens, a swimming pool, an elaborate bathhouse, vast stores, a synagogue, and ritual baths. The ruins of the walls and towers remain accessible to explore.

We puzzled over how the Romans managed to deliver building materials to that height and even more how they survived the sweltering, shimmering heat of such a sinister desert mountaintop.

HOW DO WE GET THERE? Many people choose the long snake path, a tortuous climb up the mountain's eastern side. One or two of our group planned to go that way. We preferred riding the cable car to a landing near the summit. The ride overlooks the Dead Sea and Jordan across the other side. From the platform to the top, a steep open twenty-foot stairway ladder wasn't too bad except when I looked down. My advice? Do it, but don't look down. This process from the car landing to the top is no doubt much improved since our trip.

THE VIEW FROM MASADA: The remains of Herod's lavish steam room and elegant oval swimming pool drew its water from huge underground cisterns on the mountain. One source of water comes from ducts cut into the plateau's stone side, channeling rainwater into a great cave-like tank hollowed out inside the natural rock. We peeked inside this reservoir and could see it remains well-stocked. A network of large, rock-hewn cisterns on the northwestern side of the hill also guaranteed ample water supply, filled during the winter with rainwater flowing in streams from the mountain. Access to this cistern could be reached through a tunnel down from the top. Water ran through a network of dams and channels. The massive defensive casemate wall contains about seventy rooms on its inner side and twenty-seven towers, with three gates piercing the wall.

A fabulous triple-tiered palace beneath the citadel features the throne room, stone furniture, mosaics, and frescoes. Herod built this northern palace on three slightly modified natural rock terraces as a private palace for the king and his family. The two lower levels provided imposing reception halls while the family residence used the upper floor. The reception features a courtyard, storerooms, meal preparation facilities, and bathhouse. Because of size and layout, together with the opulence of decoration, this portion probably held ceremonials.

FROM A PALACE TO A FORTRESS: Herod built the fortress, but long after his death, the king's resort served as a rebel stronghold. A zealot named Eleazar ben Yair led a group of rebellious Israelites to this place, which was inaccessible on three sides. After a three-year siege, the Romans built ramparts on the fourth side

WWW.WIKIPEDIA.COM
FIGURE 4: A TRIPLE-TIERED PALACE
Model in the Israel Museum of the triple-tiered palace on Masada. (artist's conception)

FIGURE 5: RUINS OF MASADA
Herod's pleasure palace retreat.

and breached the summit. This army not only destroyed Masada but also obliterated Jerusalem and the temple. It was a brutal time, and Masada was the last fortress holdout. On this mountaintop, the brave inhabitants made their desperate last stand. Nearly a thousand Jewish men, women, and children took their lives rather than submit to capture.

At least two plastered *mikvehs* fulfilled their Jewish religious purity laws. The largest room, believed to be King Herod's throne room, featured a particularly decorative mosaic floor with floral and geometric patterns within several concentric square bands.

The movie, *Masada,* portrays very nearly those actual events of some two thousand years ago. Another film, *The Dovekeepers,* is based on the story of Masada. *Tip: Find the movies and watch them.* The mountain features a natural landscape of majestic beauty overlooking the Dead Sea. The ruined palace symbolizes the violent destruction in the first-century Jewish kingdom and memorializes the Jews' last stand in the face of the vast Roman army.

THE TENTH LEGION ATTACK: From the top, we looked down on stone remains of the Tenth Legion Roman encampments circling the fortress. Roman soldiers grouped into large numbers called legions, with each camp representing five thousand heavily armed foot soldiers and some cavalry, engineers, surveyors, stonemasons, and carpenters, and other artisans. The Tenth, bolstered with the usual auxiliaries and thousands of Jewish prisoners as unskilled laborers, settled in Jerusalem. All in all, the Roman camp numbered some ten to fifteen thousand, outnumbering the population of Masada's zealot rebels more than ten to one. Near the end, eight army camps, linked by an earthen wall, encircled Masada with an impenetrable ring. Still, the determined rebels did not surrender.

The Romans built a great stone and earthen ramp stretching upward to carry their war machines up to capture the stronghold. The ramp is still there. The movie version about this project used these same historic battlements for filming. Standing on this windswept mountaintop, we hear the whisper of the wind across the ruins, like the cries of children echoing across the centuries. Josephus wrote about the event after hearing the story from two women who survived by hiding in a cistern.

A GROUP SUICIDE PACT: After Herod's death, the Jews abandoned the mountain as a pleasure palace resort. Some seventy years later, a group of Jewish rebels with their families moved in and committed mass suicide rather than surrender to the Romans. When their leader Eleazar saw

Masada's coming demise, he convinced the men to kill their women and children and themselves rather than submit to captivity. When the Romans finally breached the wall, they found stores of food and other provisions, piles of corpses, and a deathly silence. The soldiers could not rejoice at such a hollow victory. Heart-touching remains of the zealots' last days are found, such as some tattered garments and sandals and lettered fragments of broken earthenware on which they cast their lots to see who would die first. The story only survives through the writings of Josephus. Considerable doubt still surfaces on some initial findings of the excavation, and the record may change in time.

Tip: See the exhibit at the Museum in Jerusalem before you go, if possible.

WEARING SACKCLOTH AND ASHES: Masada wears sackcloth and ashes. Perhaps the ruined for-tress stands today like the rainbow after the flood, not to glorify a mass suicide but to point to a better way of life. Oodi was right about it being extremely hot up there. Maybe September is not the best time to visit the desert, but we were indeed glad it wasn't July. Coming down the steep open stairway to reach the cable car landing was even more terrifying than climbing up. *Tip: Grit your teeth and face your fears for this once in a lifetime experience, and you don't want to miss a thing. Wear good walking shoes, light clothing, and a hat for this trip. *Tip: Pack a collapsible wide-brimmed hat and sturdy shoes.* Once off the mountain and on solid ground, we boarded our familiar bus and on the way to the next stop we discuss how this place—Jerusalem—became so special to so many people.

WHEN DAVID MET KING SAUL: Much earlier than our other stories about King Saul, this event takes place when David is still a young boy.

The prophet Samuel visited Jesse, a man of wealth, the grandson of Boaz and Ruth. Jesse lived in Bethlehem and had eight sons. The youngest child, handsome David, caught Samuel's attention. He picked this boy to be the next king of Israel and anointed him right then and there. He did not make a public announcement because it was not time for the child to take the throne, and Samuel did not want to put the future king in danger (1 Samuel 17 RSV).

DAVID THE GIANT KILLER, SCENE 1: The Philistines and the Israelites were again at war. King Saul and his Israelite army faced the Philistines from a hill near the Valley of Elah, southwest of Jerusalem.

WWW.ALLTHINGSCLIPART.COM

FIGURE 6: BOY VS. GIANT
David faces Goliath on the battlefield.

Twice a day for forty days, Goliath, the champion of the Philistines, came between the military lines and challenged the Israelites to send their best warrior to decide the outcome in one-on-one combat. They declined. They were terrified of the monstrous man.

Goliath, a giant perhaps nine feet tall, *wore a bronze helmet and had bronze armor to protect his chest and legs. The chest armor alone weighed about one hundred twenty-five pounds. He carried a bronze sword strapped on his back with an iron spearhead weighing more than fifteen pounds. A soldier always walked in front of Goliath carrying his shield* (1 Samuel 17:4–7 CEV).

Jesse's three older sons were serving in Saul's army, leaving young David home to tend the sheep. One day Jesse sent the lad to the battlefront with food. Reaching his elder brothers in the lines, he heard Saul promise to reward any man who could defeat Goliath. Young David volunteered to accept the challenge. King Saul reluctantly agreed to let the boy try, and Saul offered his armor to the young man. He refused, taking only his sling and five stones from a brook. When they met on the field of battle, the youngster hurled a stone from his sling with all his might and hit Goliath in the center of his forehead. Goliath fell on his face to the ground. The budding conqueror took hold of the Philistine's sword and drew it from the sheath. After killing the giant, David cut off his head with the sword. Here's a summary of the action.

- The Philistines flee.
- Goliath is dead.
- David is a hero.
- The Hebrews rejoice.

Note: We are sure we crossed the brook that furnished David the stone that killed Goliath, since a guide pointed out the very ground where that battle occurred.

DAVID THE MUSICIAN, SCENE 2: Another story comes from 1 Samuel 16 and 18. David is a little older, and King Saul is ill and often troubled with depression. The king hears of a young warrior famed for bravery, and his talent as a skilled harpist, singer, and songwriter. Saul sent for David. The beautiful harp music soothed the king's pain. The king was so impressed he appointed the musician as one of his armor-bearers, so now the teenager had a part-time job at the palace. The king asked Jesse to allow his son to stay in the king's court to play for him whenever he was depressed. Jesse agreed. From then on, whenever Saul became ill, David would take up his lyre and play. Living in the palace, he became close friends with Saul's son, Prince Jonathan, and other members of the family.

Saul's youngest daughter, Princess Michal (Mee-shall), fell in love with the young musician. In return for David's victory over the Philistines, King Saul made the young warrior a commander over his armies and gave him his daughter Michal in marriage. The entire kingdom seemed entranced with the handsome fellow. However, it was not long before the King became jealous after learning how much his subjects admired the young man. When the army returned from battle, the Jewish women referred to him as a greater military hero than Saul, singing, *"Saul has slain his thousands and David his tens of thousands."* King Saul considered that song an insult. He felt his people loved the new commander more than their king, and jealousy grew in his heart. Probably by now Saul had heard the story of Samuel anointing David to be the next king. In any case, from that time Saul considered his palace musician a rival to the throne and therefore an enemy. This was irrational because his son-in-law remained forever loyal. Saul tried several times to arrange David's death, but all his plots failed. David became even dearer to the people, especially to Jonathan and the other young people in the palace.

DAVID THE LOVER, SCENE 3: Michal was passionately in love with him. She had been happy as his wife. When her father's messengers came to kill David, Michal hid him. She sent Saul's messengers away, pretending he was ill and laid up in bed. Michal placed objects in the bed to make it appear he was there. She got a rope and lowered her lover down from an upper window to escape. Michal did not flee with him. She stayed in the house to buy time, to give him a better chance of getting away (1Samuel 18:20).

Judging by later events, this may have been the biggest mistake of Michal's life. The soldiers returned, entered the bedroom, and saw Michal had tricked them. David was gone. The soldiers, fearing Saul's wrath, took Michal back with them to the palace to face the King. Saul, now beside himself with frustration and anger, demanded to know how his daughter could have betrayed him.

Michal expected that after Saul's anger subsided, her spouse would come back to her, or he would send for her. She thought he would be grateful for what she had done, and he would want her with him. Instead, months passed

CREATIVE COMMONS

FIGURE 7: THE YOUNG DAVID
Michelangelo's nude statue of David in Florence, Italy.

and then possibly years, with no word from him. In time Michal eventually heard the bitter news that David had taken another wife, and then a third.

DAVID THE FUGITIVE, SCENE 4: Jonathan warned his friend that his life was in great danger and helped him flee. Although on the lam and lacking supplies, David didn't want to implicate anyone or endanger them for helping a fugitive. Where could he go? He decided to visit the high priest, who gave him food and a sword. David escaped into the wilderness, where he gathered a band of followers while evading the king's pursuit. When King Saul found out the high priest had helped his enemy, the king's paranoia overruled his intelligence. He executed not only this priest but all the priests and their families as traitors. Only one man escaped, the high priest's son, Abiathar. The priesthood was handed down from father to son, so Abiathar should have become high priest at his father's death. But now the priest's son was a wanted man also. He fled to join David, who had collected and become responsible for many followers, by now numbering about six hundred families. In the meantime, David's most stalwart supporter died, the prophet Samuel. All the Israelites gathered to lament him, but David could not even attend the funeral. He remained in constant danger while being hunted by the powerful king.

LIFE MOVES ON: In the years of her husband's absence, King Saul gave Michal to a man called Paltiel, from the city of Gallim. A woman had no choice in those days. Paltiel was a good man, and Michal became happy with him. As the years passed, her bitterness began to fade as did any lingering affection she might have held for David. During this exile, Prince Jonathan, was able to visit him once, and the two had a joyous reunion. Jonathan expressed great support for his friend, declaring, *Someday, you will be king, and I will be your right-hand man* (1 Samuel 23:17 CEV). While this was great encouragement coming from the heir-apparent to the throne, it also tells us that David could have sent for Michal.

WIKIPEDIA COMMONS

FIGURE 8: KING DAVID

King David's Statue by Nicolas Cordier in the Borghese Chapel of the Basilica di Santa Maria Maggiore, Rome.

DAVID'S SECOND WIFE: Samuel 25 tells an intriguing story about how and where he found a good wife in the wilderness. A wealthy man named Nabal owned one thousand goats and three thousand sheep. David and his men helped care for the animals in the desert. He sent messengers asking the owner to provide some food for his men since they had been helping watch over his sheep. Nabal refused rudely.

David was furious and told his men to prepare for battle, announcing they would kill that rich man and all his tribe. However, Nabal's sensible and beautiful wife, Abigail, intervened.

A servant informed Abigail about the matter, and she quickly prepared *two hundred loaves of bread, two barrels of wine, five dressed sheep, and two bushels roasted grain, one hundred raisin cakes, and two hundred fig cakes* (1 Samuel 25:18 TLB).

Abigail loaded these gifts on donkeys and sent her servants ahead to take them directly to David. When she entered into the ravine on her donkey, she dismounted and bowed low before the leader. She apologized for her husband and called him a fool. She asked David not to kill innocent people and asked him to remember her when he became king. He accepted the gifts and sent her home in peace, telling her, *Return home in peace. I have heard what you said. We will not kill your husband.*

Amazingly, Nabel died of a stroke only ten days later. When David heard of the man's death, he sent messengers to ask Abigail to marry him. She happily agreed and became his second wife. The saga does not end here. To be continued.

THE WATERFALL: For our next history lesson, our modern "camel and driver" headed for Engedi (*Ein Gedi*) where David fled from King Saul in Old Testament days, (1 Samuel 24 TLB). David and his men hid in the cave at *Engedi* upon being warned that King Saul was coming that way. Not knowing that his enemies hid further back in the cave, King Saul stepped inside the shelter to relieve himself. David was so near he could have killed Saul in the darkness, but instead he only cut off a piece of Saul's garment, later using the scrap of cloth to prove his presence to Saul. That brought about a temporary truce between them.

Jon and a few brave souls from our group climbed the long-rugged path to reach Abraham's well, and see the beautiful year-round waterfall with a pool and tropical vegetation. The cave where David hid from King Saul is beside the waterfall.

THE WEALTH OF ENGEDI COSMETICS: Not only a place of extreme beauty, the abundant springs and year-round temperate climate of this lovely oasis provided perfect conditions for agriculture in ancient times. In later years King Solomon compared his lover to *a cluster of henna blossoms from the vineyards of Engedi,* an indication of the beauty and fertility of the site (Song of Solomon 1:14 TLB).

Egypt and Rome fought for control of this area because of the income from expensive perfumes produced here. In the New

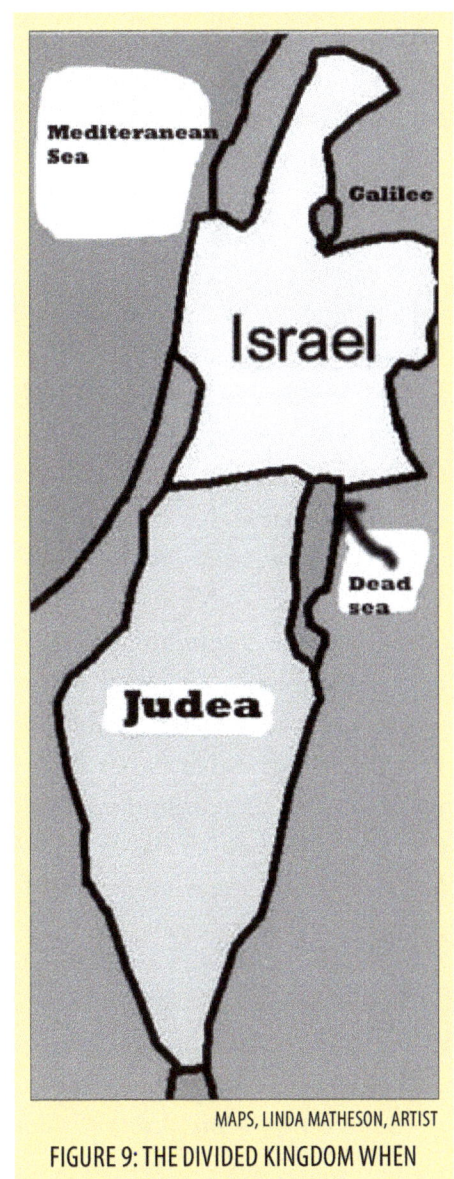

MAPS, LINDA MATHESON, ARTIST

FIGURE 9: THE DIVIDED KINGDOM WHEN DAVID BECAME KING.

Testament story of Jesus's birth, wise men from the east brought gifts of gold and resins. Frankincense, and myrrh are fragrant but bitter gums derived from plants of this region, used to make perfume and incense. At one time, those bitter gums launched commercial empires spanning the Arabian Sea. *Engedi* is still known for expensive perfumes. Several women in our group purchased Ahava cosmetics produced here.

DAVID BECOMES KING: After King Saul's death along with his three sons (Michal's father and brothers), the Jews proclaimed David king of the southern kingdom of Judea. They crowned Saul's son Ishbaal king of northern Israel/Palestine, but ambitious David wanted it all. A continuing power strug-gle ensued between the two half- brothers.

DAVID, MICHAL, AND PALTIEL: Once David was anointed King, he sent a messenger to the city of Gallim and demanded his first wife Michal be taken from her husband Paltiel and brought back to Jerusalem.

A TRAGIC LOVE STORY: Michal and Paltiel's marriage had been happy. They may have had children, although the Bible does not say. No doubt, Michal objected to the king's demand, but she was power-less. In that one battle at *Beit She'an*, when Michal lost her father and three brothers, she also lost her royal status. David's order tore Michal away from Paltiel, even though she begged to stay with him. The king wanted her back in his harem, not because he loved Michal but because her lineage as King Saul's daughter would strengthen his claim to the throne (2 Samuel 3:13-16 TLB).

Paltiel, forced to surrender the wife he loved to an uncertain future, was grief-stricken. As they took Michel away, he followed weeping. He continued his protest until one of David's envoys forced Paltiel to turn back. Michal did not go willingly. She was a pawn in the political game of that day. We know that in the beginning, Michal felt deep emotion for David because it is the only time the Bible describes a woman as loving a man. However, there is never any mention of David loving her. Just as in modern romances one is loved, the other is the lover.

Michal fell in love with the wrong young man. She lived in David's palace harem for the rest of her life as a virtual prisoner. She never conceived a child of her own, suggesting continuing animosity between David and herself, as well there might be. After all, during the years of their separation, he had married at least two other women; Abigail, the widow of Nabal, and Aninoam the Jezreelite. Both marriages brought money and supplies for himself and his followers. He would go on to marry at least five more women.

THE NEW ISRAEL: The Jews anointed David king at the city of Hebron, where Abraham pitched his tent many years before. For seven years he ruled the southern kingdom before defeating his half-brother Ishbaal and seizing the northern kingdom. He combined the two territories of Judea and Palestine into a United Israel. Although he had doubled the size of his kingdom, he still was not satisfied. Between Hebron in Judea and the northern nation of Israel lay the Jebus's mountain

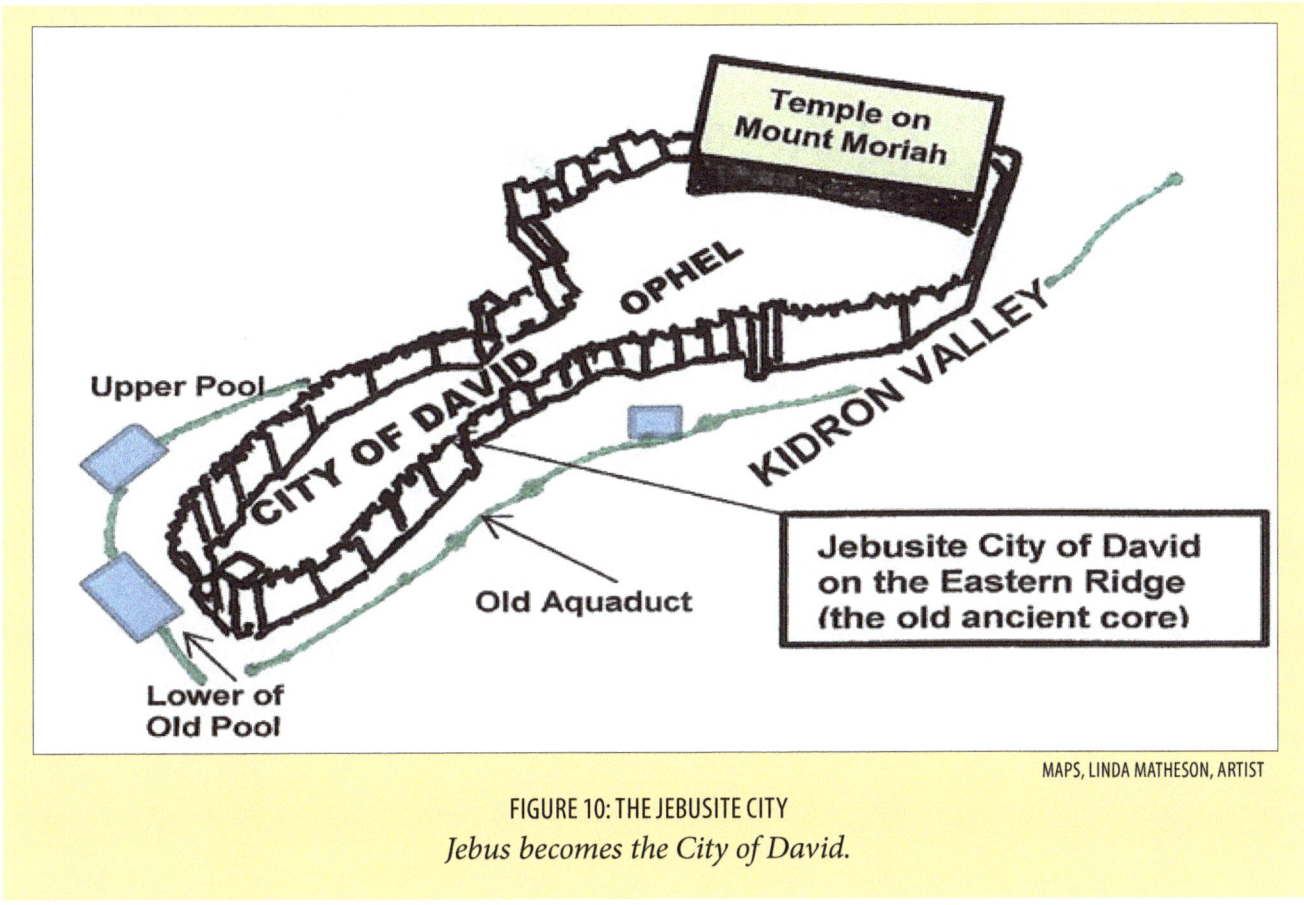

FIGURE 10: THE JEBUSITE CITY
Jebus becomes the City of David.

enclave, occupied by the warlike Canaanite clan of Jebusites. While this enemy remained, political and military control of a united country was impossible.

David wanted a different capital city. Even though Jebus was only a short distance away, the king believed he needed to move from Hebron to Jebus because of its better location, which included a good water supply. This place was also more central to the northern provinces. Only one thing stood in his way. The Jebusites did not want David and his people there. The drums of war begin cadence.

THE KING AND THE JEBUSITES: The Jebusites considered their fortress to be impregnable. They looked down from their stout walls and boasted that David's men could not defeat them or even get in (2 Samuel 5:6-8 TLB). Leading his army into the steep valley below the fortress settlement the Jewish army prepared to attack. As he and his forces gathered, the Jebusites taunted him: *You will not get in here; even the blind and the lame can ward you off.* They were wrong. David's men laid siege to the city and conquered them.

David's nephew and comrade-in-arms, Joab, went up the hidden water shaft tunnel system with his soldiers for a surprise attack on the unsuspecting city. That was the turning point, and Joab's men won the battle. This water shaft is still there to visit, now named Warren's Shaft for the archaeologist who later discovered it.

FIGURE 11: THE TABERNACLE
An actual model of the biblical tabernacle in Tinna Valley Park, Israel.

King David's sister Zeruiah is the mother of Joab and his brothers Abishai and Asahel who were much older than the king. After this victory, David named his nephew Joab as captain of his army, and he continues to be an essential part of the story of the king's reign.

David's men took the inhabitants by surprise and they surrendered the city intact, with little bloodshed. The king knew this conquest would become a proud national victory, and he moved his capital from Hebron to the former Jebusite city. His realm still appears small as empires go, covering an area about the size of the state of Maine. So Jebus was renamed City of David. Bethlehem was also known as the City of David because he was born there.

FROM JEBUS TO DAVID'S CAPITAL: To transform the Jebusite city into the Israelite capital, David recycled many Canaanite defense walls and support structures. The town was in an excellent strategic location, but its narrow hilltop location required the construction of artificial platforms to provide enough room for all his building activities. He "built up" the city from the supporting terraces to the surrounding wall while his army commander Joab restored the rest of the town (1 Chronicles 11:8 TLB). The king paid fifty shekels of silver to buy the hill to the north from Araunah the Jebusite, who may have been the king of Jebus. He used the site as a threshing floor. The purchase price included Araunah's oxen, which David sacrificed on the altar (2 Samuel 24: 24–25 NIV). This "threshing floor" is the rock protrusion on top of Mount Moriah, now known as the Temple Mount. David did not live to build the temple, but he set up a tabernacle and brought the Ark of the Covenant to his city. He also constructed a palace of cedar for himself in this new place to be known as Jerusalem. *Note: A tall landmark pillar called the Tower of David, an ancient citadel near the Jaffa Gate entrance to the Old City of Jerusalem, apparently has nothing to do with King David. This tower marks the former location of Herod's palace.*

The site of Jebus where Jerusalem began on the lower slope just outside the old city walls was quite small, only about nine or ten acres, with an estimated population of two thousand. Two major archaeological monuments lie south of the Temple Mount in the City of David, the 'large stone structure' and the 'stepped stone structure.' Building on previous suggestions, researchers use textual and archaeological evidence to identify these monuments as the remains of the king's palace; however, these locations are still tentative.

WHAT ABOUT THE ARK OF THE COVENANT? King Saul, David's predecessor, had paid no attention to the old religious symbol since its capture and subsequent return by the Philistines after the battle at Shiloh. The Ark remained in Philistine country for seven months until they decided the chest brought them so much bad luck, they wanted to get rid of it. The men of Kiriath-jearim took the chest to the hillside home of Abinadab, and the holy object remained there for twenty years (1 Samuel 7:1-2 NIV).

The revered chest held the holiest relic of the Israelites, stone tablets of the Ten Commandments received on Mount Sinai by Moses. David decided to move the item to Jerusalem, to establish his new capital as a religious center and not just a political one. But then, when an unexpected injury and death happened to one of the men bringing the box, they left the sacred item at the home of Obed-edom for three months in a house outside Jerusalem. When the owners said the Ark brought them good fortune, David decided he could safely move the object inside the walls of the palatial city, and he planned a huge celebration for the event. (2 Samuel 6:9-12 NIV)

THE KING'S DANCE: A favorite Bible story gives a vivid description of the king's jubilant entrance into the temple area. It must have been quite a parade as David and his followers made music with many kinds of instruments: harps, stringed instruments, tambourines, drums, and cymbals. The atmosphere was joyful, exciting, relevant, and engaging as the music played and the king led the people in a dance of celebration.

MICHAL THOUGHT IT WAS SHAMEFUL: Not everyone appreciated the festivity. Michal looked through a window and saw her husband leaping and whirling about, wearing only an *ephod*, part of the high priest's ceremonial dress. The ephod was worn outside the robe and kept in place by a girdle and shoulder pieces. According to Exodus 28, the ephod is a priestly garment made of two pieces of fine colorful linen, front and back, joined at the shoulders with a sash. However, the covering must have seemed too skimpy to Michal. She did not approve.

David led the procession as the priests carried the revered Ark of the Covenant. The king was dancing, whirling, and leaping to the harps and cymbal music on the way to the new tabernacle (2 Samuel

FIGURE 12: THE KING'S DANCE
King David led the joyful procession bringing the Ark of the Covenant to the tabernacle in the new City of David.

6:14-22 NIV). Michal went out to meet him, and all the pent-up anger inside her came pouring out. She was a king's daughter, now forced to watch her husband behaving like what she considered a vulgar buffoon, not at all kingly in her eyes. Michal told her husband his dancing was unsuitable to the dignity of a king. She said, *How the king of Israel has distinguished himself today, going around half-naked in full view of the slave girls of his servants as any vulgar fellow would.* This blazing quarrel is the last that we hear of Michal, except for a remark that she remained childless.

BRINGING THE ARK TO THE TABERNACLE: They brought the ark and set it in place in the City of David. They placed the tabernacle in the center of the square, and inside rested the sacred Ark of the Covenant.

AND THEN CAME BATHSHEBA: The story of David's relationship with Bathsheba is one of the most human stories in the Bible, almost like a modern soap opera. His palace overlooked the tabernacle and the city, which was on lower ground than his castle. Restless one night, the young king paced the roof of his palace from where he had a view of the homes and gardens in the city. He spied a woman taking a bath in the courtyard below and thought her figure the most beautiful in the world. David asked to learn her name, and they told him, it is Bathsheba, wife of Uriah the Hittite. The king was unable to get her out of his mind.

In the spring, when kings usually went to war, David sent Joab out with the whole Israelite army. They attacked and destroyed the Ammonites and besieged Rabbah while David remained safely in Jerusalem. Uriah, one of the generals and the arms bearer for Joab, was with the army. The King had several wives, but he could not forget beautiful Bathsheba. Even though David knew she was Uriah's wife, he sent for her. Unable to deny himself, David spent the night with her—perhaps several nights.

When Bathsheba tells David she is pregnant, the King faces a dilemma. Knowing he had done wrong, David summoned Uriah home from the army, hoping he would re-consummate his marriage and think the child his. He hoped this would hide what he had done. Uriah refused. Warriors preparing for battle commonly vowed to abstain from love-making, as a practice of discipline. After repeated unsuccessful efforts to convince Uriah to be intimate with Bathsheba, the king decided his only recourse was to have Uriah killed in battle. David confided his secret to General Joab, who ordered Uriah to the battlefront where he was more likely to be killed. And so, he was.

AUTHOR'S PRIVATE COLLECTION

FIGURE 13: DAVID AND BATHSHEBA
David and Bathsheba: David's palace rooftop in the City of David looked out over the homes and businesses.

KING DAVID'S MOST FAMOUS WIFE: After Uriah's death, the king married the pregnant widow. When she gave birth to a son who was not healthy, David considered this his punishment and became distraught over the baby's illness. He grieved and refused to eat. On the seventh day, the baby died. Then, the king got up from the floor, washed, applied lotions, changed his clothes, and went to the tabernacle to worship. After that, he went home and asked for some food (2 Samuel 12:20). *Note: The number seven seemed to be magical.*

THE BIRTH OF SOLOMON: When enough time passed, David comforted his wife and made love to her. Soon Bathsheba became pregnant again and this time she gave birth to a healthy son. Delighted, they named the baby Solomon. This baby is destined to be the golden child, gifted with unusual wisdom. After becoming King, things had gone very well for David—perhaps too well. He seemed to have the Midas touch. Everything turned to gold. He is depicted as an acclaimed warrior, musician, and poet as well as a righteous king, although not without faults. After all, we know he committed adultery with the lovely Bathsheba and caused the death of her husband.

David had at least six other wives besides Michal and Bathsheba. One of those wives was the royal Princess Maacah. King Talmai of Geshur gave his daughter Maacah in marriage to the new ruler at Hebron as a political alliance. The capital of Geshur was Bethsaida, which years later was the home of Jesus's disciples, James and John. Having a large harem was a matter of status, but also a king needed many sons because of high infant mortality. The sons should grow to lead the nation after the death of the old king. Among his many sons were four important ones who will affect the future of Israel:

- **Amnon**, son of Ahinoam, the Jezreelite
- **Absalom**, son of Princess Maacah of Geshur
- **Adonijah**, son of Haggith
- **Solomon**, son of Bathsheba

Amnon was born first. David's second son Chileab probably died young. Absalom was third and Adonijah fourth. Solomon came much later. The brothers were never close. They had different mothers and suffered much sibling rivalry. No doubt, jealousy, and intrigue always lived in the palace of the king and his harem. The Old Testament says God told David because of his history of bloodshed he would always have strife in his house.

THE SAD STORY OF ABSALOM: King David and Princess Maacah became parents of the royal babies, Prince Absalom, and Princess Tamar. As the prince grew, the country praised Absalom as the most handsome young man in all Israel. He was flawless from head to foot. Absalom was proud of his beautiful head of hair, and he would only cut it once a year. We don't know if he was wise or compassionate, but everyone said Absalom was charming. His father must have been proud to introduce this young man as his son.

THE RAPE OF PRINCESS TAMAR: Absalom's sister Tamar was equally beautiful. In this case, being beautiful was a burden. Absalom's oldest half-brother Amnon (the king's firstborn son), lusted after Tamar. He was obsessed with her. He thought about her all the time. He finally tricked her into coming into his bedroom, where he violently raped her despite her resistance. The attack ruined Tamar's life. No young man at that time would accept a deflowered girl as a wife. She would have to spend the rest of her life in the harem's backroom, childless and alone. In despair, Tamar tore her elaborate royal robes and marked her forehead with ashes. She begged Amnon to marry her. He would not. After the rape, Amnon was ashamed, but he behaved as if Tamar had seduced him.

Tamar told her brother Absalom truthfully what happened, and he vowed revenge. Absalom and his mother Maacah expected David to punish the rapist, even though Amnon was the king's heir-apparent to the throne. When the monarch heard all these matters, he became angry, but he did nothing to punish his beloved firstborn son Amnon for his misdeed. Seemingly, he adopted a "boys will be boys" attitude.

Tamar never married. At that time, a bride would be stoned to death when the husband discovered she was not a virgin, no matter the circumstances. Absalom comforted Tamar, telling her to wait. He told her she would always have a home with him; he would look after her. *So, Tamar remained desolate in her brother Absalom's house* (2 Samuel 13:20).

BROTHER HATED BROTHER: Absalom hated his brother Amnon after that. He had no intention of letting this half-brother get away with what he had done to Tamar. King David never punished Amnon, and Absalom felt honor-bound to take revenge for his sister's rape. Absalom's anger seethed for two years while he planned the killing of his evil half-brother. Finally, he carried out his plan and Amnon died. Fearing his father's wrath, the Prince ran away. He went to live with his doting maternal grandfather, King Talmai of Geshur, for three years.

The King's initial response was painful grief over Amnon's death, as anyone who has ever lost a child understands. David was willing to move on with life, but he could not bear losing two sons. Amnon was gone; Absalom was still alive, and his father loved him. No matter what his son had done, he missed him. No doubt, David also remembered a bloody past of his own. The king knew Absalom could not come back home because he was a murderer under a sentence of death. But still, the crowned head wanted his son back.

Finally, the ruler made arrangements through General Joab for Prince Absalom to return to Jerusalem under the condition he could not see his father for two more years. Absalom did not like that condition. The spoiled brat shouted, "*I might as well have stayed in Geshur.* He asked the general to intervene on his behalf so he could see his father. When Joab refused, Absalom was so angry he set fire to the commander's field.

ABSALOM'S REBELLION: Now that Amnon was dead, Absalom was next in line, but he was impatient and didn't want to wait. He was also angry that he was not allowed to have an audience with the king. This rebellious son secretly began a revolt to wrest the kingdom from his father. To impress people, Absalom bought a chariot and horses and hired fifty bodyguards to run ahead of him. He got up early every morning and went out to sit in the city gates with the judges. When people brought a case for judgment, the Prince would ask where they were from in Israel. Then he would say, *You have a really strong case here! It's too bad the king doesn't have anyone to hear it. I wish I were the judge. Then everyone could bring their cases to me for judgment, and I would give them justice!*

Absalom went to Hebron, the old capital where he had been born, and declared himself king. His charming manners, personal good looks, and insinuating ways, together with his love of pomp and royal pretensions, captivated the hearts of the people (2 Samuel 15:5). The residents of Hebron had resented the King's relocation of the capital to Jerusalem, moving the court and all the importance connected with a capital city, so they supported the youth. Reports of his son's treasonous actions came to David's ear.

Finally, the king was forced to react. He told General Joab to take his army to Hebron and stop the rebellion, but he was not to kill Absalom. In the war that ensued, Joab's army was victorious.

THE DEATH OF ABSALOM: Racing to get away from his pursuers, Absalom lost control of his chariot. He abandoned it for a mule, but the mule ran wildly through the woods, and Absalom's long beautiful hair became entangled in the branches of a tree. The mule kept going, and the handsome prince was left hanging helplessly.

King David had ordered Joab to take his son alive, but the army pursued the royal and found him dangling from a limb. Joab killed Absalom in cold blood to prevent further rebellion. While the Prince may have deserved death, the general disobeyed orders.

King David and Princess Maacah's beautiful son died like an animal, speared through the heart as he hung helplessly in a tree branch. Handsome, charming Absalom died at age twenty-nine. Upon learning of Absalom's death, his father's grief was immense. The king covered his face with his hands and wept uncontrollably, saying, *"O my son Absalom! My son, my son Absalom! If only I had died instead of you—O Absalom, my son, my son!"* (2 Samuel 18:33).

King David's mourning over his son's death is understandable. He is genuinely grieving. We can certainly sympathize. Perhaps Joab did what he thought best for the country, but the king never forgave his nephew for killing Absalom.

We saw Absalom's Tomb, also called Absalom's Pillar (*Yad Avshalom*), an ancient monumental rock-cut tomb with a conical roof in the Kidron Valley in Jerusalem. About twenty-feet tall, it is not a tomb but a monument. The lower part of the Absalom Monument is cube-shaped and carved out of solid rock, while its upper part is stone. The façade features high pillars, capitals, and decoration. Inside, the structure contained several burial rooms. No one is buried inside now, definitely not Absalom.

THE TOMB OF ABSALOM: For centuries, Jewish tradition associated the monument with King David's rebellious son. Some Jewish parents are said to visit the site with their children to warn them what happens when children misbehave. However, archaeologists say this monument came into being a thousand years after the time of Absalom. There is no record of Tamar or her mother, Maacah, after the death of Absalom. The ancient world offered no mercy to a royal who failed.

ON THE MOUNT OF OLIVES: The Kidron Valley separates the Mount of Olives from the Temple Mount and the City of David. The Mount of Olives is one of three peaks of a mountain ridge running a little more than two miles east of the Old City across the Kidron Valley. The peak to its north is Mount Scopus, while the summit to its south is the Mount of Corruption. We often hear the melancholy call of Muslims in Jerusalem across the valley summoning their members to worship. They pray five times daily; at dawn, noon, afternoon, evening, and nightfall. A crier or *muezzin* chants the call to prayer from the mosque tower (*minaret*).

THE BEAUTIFUL GARDEN OF GETHSEMANE: The now dry Kidron valley forms the eastern boundary of Jerusalem. In biblical times the bed of a small stream, Kidron, flowed south into the Dead Sea. On the other side of Kidron Valley, *Mount Olivet*, better known as the Mount of Olives, presents a ridge from north to south about two and a half miles long east of Jerusalem.

Leaving Mount Olivet, we walk down the very steep and narrow Palm Sunday Road, where you need walking shoes with good gripping soles. Although the route Jesus took began from Bethany to Jerusalem, the present road starts from the Mount of Olives and ends at the Garden of Gethsemane.

Tip: Forget your stylish Jimmy Choos. You need to wear good walking shoes with gripper soles every day.

The Hebrew word *gethsemane* means olive press. In biblical times the word «garden» designated an orchard or place where vegetables grow. So, Garden of Gethsemane would translate to an olive orchard. The oil produced at this place is well known to biblical scholars. Oil is still pressed from these gnarled, majestic olive trees, hundreds of years old. Scholars estimate the age of these trees to be anywhere between one and two thousand years, but they are not the same trees from Jesus's day. Historian Josephus reports the Romans cut down all the trees around Jerusalem for their siege equipment when they captured the city in AD 70. However, these sturdy trunks could have grown from shoots of those original trees because shoots come back from the roots to create a new tree, although you have to wait fifteen years for the tree to bear fruit.

AUTHOR'S PRIVATE COLLECTION

FIGURE 14: ABSALOM'S TOMB
Some Jewish parents are said to visit the site with their children to warn them what happens when children misbehave.

OLIVE FRUIT IS BLACK WHEN RIPE: Approximately the size of an apple tree, the olive produces beautiful clusters of white flowers in the spring. The fruit is green, turning black as they ripen. Even now, many natives harvest olives in the autumn by beating the branches with a stick, just

FIGURE 15: MOUNT OLIVET
Ancient olive trees in the Garden of Gethsemane.

as they did in Bible days (Deuteronomy 24:20). We stop at Mount Olivet and go into the Garden of Gethsemane. The famous garden, located on a slope just across the Kidron Valley from Jerusalem, boasts many ancient olive trees to this day. The garden area is full of olive trees, lilies, and other native flowers. Tall walls of stone topped with cut glass border the path where we walk, a precaution to make sneak attacks from an enemy more difficult. A warning of attack must exist today because soldiers are standing guard on top of all the buildings and streets. They are fully armed and look fierce, but we found them friendly to tourists, reminding us of our young people back home.

KING DAVID REIGNED: According to the Bible, David remained the second King of Israel for a forty-year reign. They crowned him king at the young age of thirty, and he died at age seventy (2 Samuel 5:4). Jews, Christians, and Muslims all revere David as a great prophet and king. Renowned for his composition of the Psalms, his life of faith, wisdom, and courage continues to inspire believers despite his mistakes. At his death, the city was still quite small. He had been too busy with court intrigue and hard-fought battles to think about improvements to his capital. *Note: And his children were scandalous.*

THOSE AWFUL YOUNG PRINCES: David had many wives and mistresses, therefore many sons, but those four boys—Amnon, Absalom, Adonijah, and Solomon—always vied to be the successor to the throne. As previously told, the field narrowed when Absalom killed Amnon, and General Joab killed Absalom, leaving only Adonijah and Solomon as prime contenders. The most likely successor to the crown would have been Adonijah, the elder. However, after King David became feeble and forgetful, Bathsheba created a power struggle between Adonijah and Solomon by claiming their father promised that her son Solomon would be the chosen one. The family intrigue continued even after the sovereign's death.

DOWN IN THE KIDRON VALLEY: At the bottom of the Mount of Olives close to the bed of the Kidron Valley, we noticed several awe-inspiring burial structures carved in the rock. These burial caves

AUTHOR'S PRIVATE COLLECTION

FIGURE 16: DOWN IN THE KIDRON VALLEY:
Tombs in the Kidron Valley said to be of Zachariah and Hezir.

and monuments commemorate the rich past of Jerusalem and its priests. Scholars think they date near the end of the Second Temple period (AD 70). People popularly know these tombs by names connected with the Old Testament, despite their relatively late dating. The pyramid-topped "Tomb of Zachariah" at the bottom of the Mount of Olives in the Kidron Valley is an ancient monument with no burial provision inside. Although carved out of solid rock and named after the ninth-century biblical prophet, Zachariah, the marker belongs to a much later period. We see other tombs in the hillside behind the mistakenly named Absalom's Monument. These caves of Jehosophat contain small burial niches where monks lived in the fourth-century AD.

GENERAL JOAB IS LABELED A TROUBLEMAKER: Joab and other commanders began questioning their leader's judgment in his latter days (2 Samuel 24:2-4). They may have implied the king had become a senile old fool. As David neared the end of his reign, Joab offered his allegiance to Adonijah, rather than to the promised king, Solomon (1 Kings 1:1-27). That was his last mistake. On David's deathbed, he told Solomon to have General Joab killed. He spoke of Joab's past betrayals and his disobedience in the death of Absalom. Joab needed to be gone. And so, he was.

FIGURE 17: DAVID THE MUSICIAN

The statue of King David with harp is just outside the Cenacle or Upper Room house in Jerusalem.

NOAM CHEN, WWW.GOISRAEL.COM
FIGURE 18: EAST JERUSALEM
The pedestrian mall in east Jerusalem presents a modern city.

SEVEN

DAY OF KING SOLOMON

Sunday: Jerusalem, Solomon's Palace & Temple, Babylon, Bethlehem, Shepherd's Fields, and an Arabian Wedding

DAY SEVEN: Morning meditations on the Mount of Olives overlooking the old city walls of Jerusalem, many stories of the New Testament seem telescoped into this low mound overlooking the temple where Jesus taught his disciples. From here on the Mount's slope in the Garden of Gethsemane he was taken captive and later ascended to heaven. We can see the wall around the old city, the double arches of the blocked Eastern Gate into Jerusalem, and the glistening golden dome on Temple Mount. Believers expect their Messiah to return through this now sealed double-arch golden gate.

JERUSALEM BEGAN NEAR THE CITY OF DAVID: Our guide points out a grove of cypress trees south of the temple along the lower east side of the city wall, where more than four thousand years ago Jerusalem began in the city of Jebus. In Jesus's time, both Mount Zion and the City of David remained enclosed within the city wall on the lower southern side. Wealthier members of the aristocracy and the priesthood built their homes on the higher western hill because that gave them the best view of the temple, their source of pride, and income. When Solomon became king, he decided to build his palace and temple on the large flat rock north of the City of David on top of Mount Moriah. Although he didn't know it, that area would become the future city of Jerusalem. Between the City of David and the southern side of Temple Mount was the Ophel, steps to the upper city acropolis.

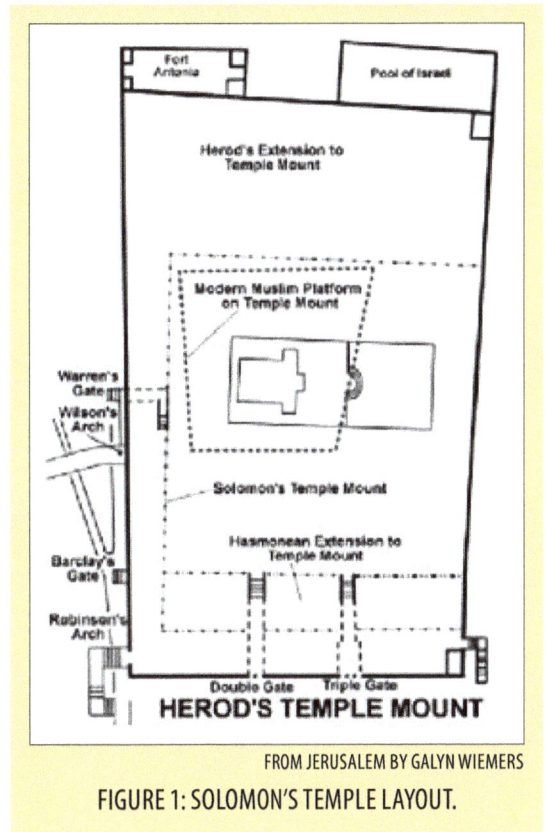

FROM JERUSALEM BY GALYN WIEMERS

FIGURE 1: SOLOMON'S TEMPLE LAYOUT.

FIGURE 2: KING SOLOMON'S WEDDING
King Solomon weds the Pharaoh's Daughter.

King David had longed to build the temple, but the Jebusite City provided too little space for the king's aggressive plan of town buildings, which included not just a place for worship but also a large royal palace and quarters. So, David gave the charge to his son Solomon.

Then David gave Solomon the plans for the temple and its surroundings, including the entry room, the storerooms, the upstairs rooms, the inner rooms, and the inner sanctuary..... David also gave Solomon all the plans he had in mind for the courtyards of the temple, the outside rooms, the treasuries, and the rooms for the gifts dedicated to the Lord... and the work of the various divisions of priests and Levites in the temple. ... he gave specifications for the items in the temple that were to be used for worship, (1 Chronicles 28:11-19 NLT).

FIGURE 3: THE OPHEL STEPS
Currently under restoration, the steps leading up to the temple in Jerusalem from the City of David.

GENERAL JOAB KILLED: King David is usually described as a kind, loving leader over his devoted followers. However, he was a fierce warrior, some would say a tyrant. King David caused his son, Adonijah, to be killed along with David's devoted commander-in-chief Joab. Then no chance of civil war over succession would remain and David could focus on building the temple while Solomon handled the country's business. The era was a much more primitive and brutal age than we know. Solomon appointed Benaiah as commander of the army to replace Joab. Then he turned his attention to planning the temple.

"David gave instructions regarding how much gold and silver he would need for the gold lampstands and lamps. He specified the amount of silver for the silver lampstands and lamps.... David also designated the amount of gold for the solid gold meat hooks used to handle the sacrificial meat and for the basins, pitchers, and dishes. He designated the amount of refined gold for the altar of incense. Finally, David gave him a plan for the gold cherubim wings that stretched out over the Ark of the Covenant. Solomon began to build the temple in Jerusalem on Mount Moriah during the fourth year of his reign. Construction started on the threshing floor of Araunah, the Jebusite, (2 Chronicles 3:1-2 paraphrased).

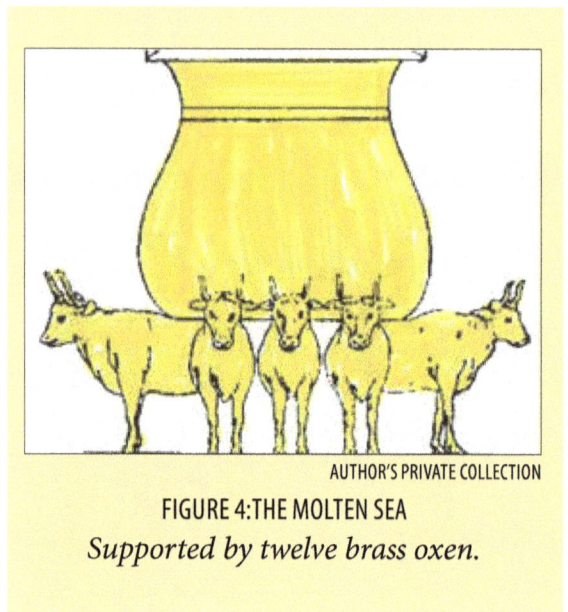

FIGURE 4: THE MOLTEN SEA
Supported by twelve brass oxen.

BUILDING SOLOMON'S TEMPLE IN JERUSALEM: If Solomon's reign was the climax of early Israelite history, the building of the temple was the climax of his reign. It was an exciting time. Rafts of timbers floated to Jaffa/Tel Aviv for construction had to pass through a dangerously narrow opening in the reef to the shore. Eighty-thousand stonecutters constructed the building with blocks dressed at the quarry. No iron tools were allowed. A wall of dressed stone trimmed with cedar beams surrounded the inner courtyard. The light came in through narrow windows placed high on the walls. Floors made of juniper appeared covered in gold, and the whole interior was first covered with cedar, and then overlaid with gold (1 Kings 6 NASB, paraphrased).

Solomon's Temple required many years to complete. The Bible describes the inside ceiling as hundred eighty feet long, ninety feet wide, and fifty feet high. The highest point was about twenty stories tall. *Note: Some authorities interpret these measurements differently.* The chapter describes ten golden candlesticks, ten tables for shewbread, and an altar for incense. *Note: Shew-bread was unleavened bread placed on a table in the sanctuary, with the seven-branched candelabra and the altar of incense.*

THE MOLTEN SEA OF BRASS: Under Solomon's direction, Hiram built a massive altar of brass for sacrifices, and a colossal brass basin called "The Molten Sea." This basin, supported by twelve brass oxen, was fifteen feet in diameter and more than seven feet in depth. The molten sea most likely contained water used in temple rituals; perhaps this is where the priests washed their hands.

Different kinds of sacrifices were offered for various reasons by the ancient Israelites and later by the Jewish priests at the temple in Jerusalem. Most often, an animal sacrifice, such as a sheep or a bull for Jewish ritual slaughter, would be cooked and eaten by the person offering it, with some parts given to the priests and other parts burned on the altar. Sacrifices might also consist of doves, grain or meal, wine, or incense.

With the destruction of the second temple by the Romans in AD 70, the Jewish practice of offering sacrifices and offerings ended.

BRINGING THE ARK: When the building was complete, King Solomon assembled the elders of Israel and all the heads of the tribes. Solomon's father David had led the procession when the Ark was carried to the tabernacle in the City of David. Now, four Levite priests carried the revered chest on poles from the tabernacle at the City of David to be installed at the new temple in Jerusalem.

When all the elders of Israel arrived, the priests picked up the Ark. They brought along the special tent and all the sacred items that had been in it. There they sacrificed so many sheep, goats, and cattle that no one could keep count! Then the priests carried the Ark of the Covenant into the inner sanctuary of the temple—the Most Holy Place. The cherubim spread their wings, forming a canopy over the Ark and its long carrying poles. Nothing was in the holy chest except the two stone tablets that Moses had placed in it at Mount Sinai. (1 Kings 8 NLT).

According to 2 Chronicles 3:11, the total wingspan of the two cherubim standing side by side was thirty feet. The Ark sat under their wings inside the inner sanctuary. Solomon gave a great feast to celebrate. There was enough food to feed a vast multitude for two weeks.

SOLOMON'S PALACE: After completion of the temple, Solomon built his palace alongside. It took seven years to build the temple, but more than ten years to build the king's house. Construction of Solomon's royal palace became much more complicated than building the temple. The royal residence presented a whole complex of buildings with many different functions. The palace building alone was said to be a hundred fifty feet long, seventy-five feet wide and forty-five feet high, constructed with blocks of high-grade stone cut and trimmed to size. Windows were placed high in sets of three, and the throne hall was covered from floor to ceiling with cedar. A wall of dressed stone trimmed with cedar beams surrounded Solomon's courtyard. The massive complex spread out near the temple.

SAUL, DAVID, and SOLOMON: Like father, like son, these three kings had many faults. Solomon became a great king, but he inherited some of his father's weaknesses and even topped David in the size of his harem. Solomon loved women. The reported claim of one thousand wives, princesses, and concubines, may be exaggerated. Still, we know many wives were political alliances, and having numerous wives was a status symbol. Yet those foreign women who worshipped idols led Solomon to forget his upbringing.

THE EGYPTIAN PRINCESS: The Egyptian Pharaoh gave his daughter in marriage to King Solomon to cement a political alliance. Although she is not given a name in the texts, out of Solomon's vast harem, this Egyptian princess is the only wife singled out. There is an actual tomb in the Kidron Valley called the "Tomb of Pharaoh's Daughter," which may or may not be authentic. According to 1 Kings 9:16-17 NLT: Pharaoh, the King of Egypt, gave the ruined city of Gezer to his daughter as a wedding gift when she married Solomon. So, Solomon rebuilt Gezer. Solomon did not take his new royal bride directly to the city of Jerusalem. He waited to bring the Princess into the city until he had completed building the palace, the temple, and the wall around Jerusalem.

SEPARATE APARTMENTS FOR THE KING'S HAREM: We learn the palace complex included harem apartments, a judgment hall for hearing cases, and many other capital city structures. The king's quarters and courtyard, and the separate house for Pharaoh's daughter no doubt used the same architect and builders. Once he completed the complex, Solomon moved all his wives into their apartments. A description of the King's home behind the palace is not described in great detail except to say his house featured a large courtyard. The majority of scholars believe Solomon to be the author of the erotic biblical book, Song of Solomon, and the woman addressed in the song the Egyptian princess. Although we still don't learn her name, this princess became the most significant person to King Solomon.

FIGURE 5: INTERIOR OF THE TEMPLE

An artist's concept of Solomon's Temple as described in the Bible, including the molten sea and the altar of brass, and a distant view of the Holy of Holies with cherubim wings over the Ark of the Covenant.

EXPLORING THE PALACE COMPLEX: According to the Bible, the buildings included:

- Judgment Hall where Solomon's magnificent ivory throne stood;
- Treasury room;
- A separate palace for the daughter of Pharaoh, Solomon's most high-born wife;
- The harem living quarters for Solomon's multitude of wives and children;
- The "House of the Forest of Lebanon," perhaps an audience hall.

Solomon brought in the best workmen. He imported an expert bronze worker from Tyre, an ancient Phoenician city now in Lebanon. He constructed the palace of expensive materials, but the emphasis in the king's residence was on elaborate stonework rather than gold plating as temple construction had been. The palace must have been magnificent. Excerpts paraphrased from 1 Kings 7:

- Forty-five pillars supported the roof of the great hall, with cedar roofing from the forests of Lebanon. Three tiers of windows added light to the wall. The royal throne room had many decorative columns. A second throne room, the Judgment Hall, held an enormous throne, decorated with ivory and overlaid with fine gold. Six steps led to the huge ornamented chair with a rounded back and armrests. The figure of a lion stood on each side of the throne. Twelve other lions marked each end of the six steps.
- All of King Solomon's drinking cups were solid gold, as were all the utensils in the palace. Silver was considered worthless in Solomon's day (1 Kings 10:21 NASB paraphrased).

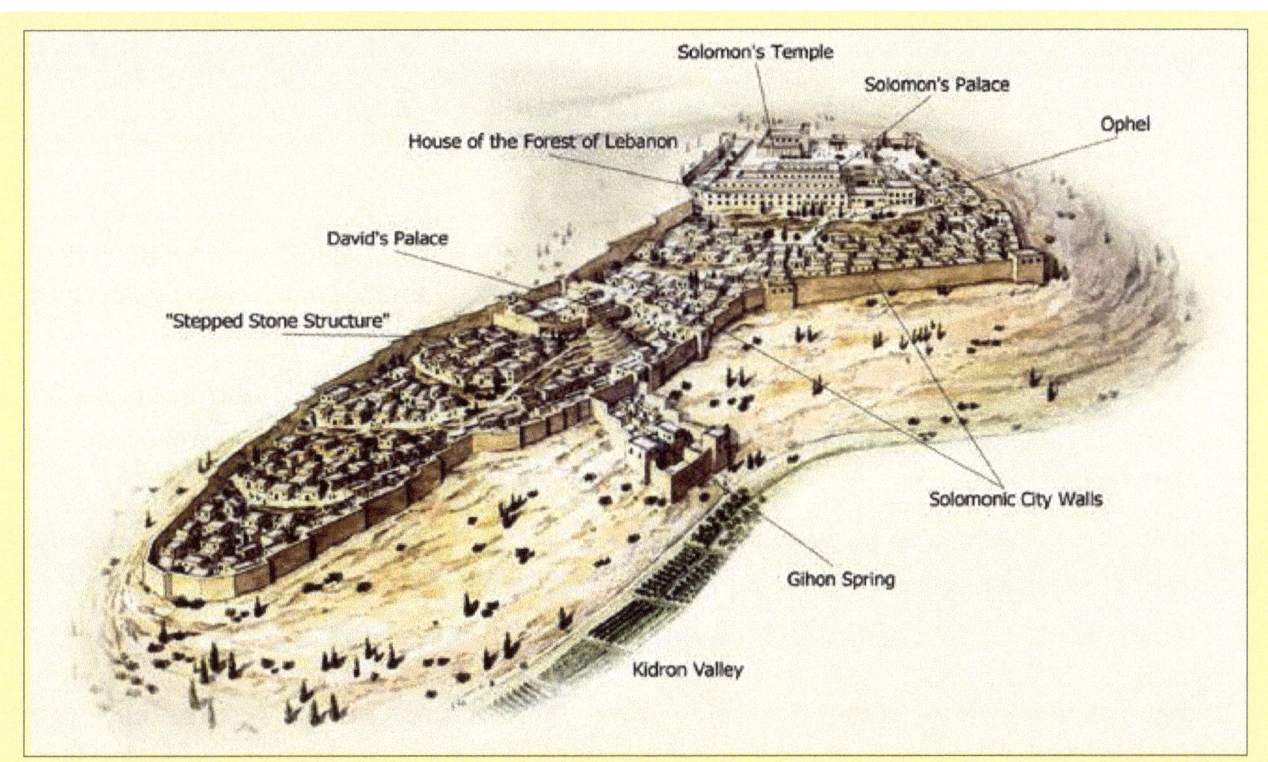

FIGURE 6: CITY OF DAVID

WATCHJERUSALEM.CO.IL

Solomon's Temple on Mount Moriah, and David's Palace on Mount Zion occupy these two small rounded mountains together, of only about 2,500-foot elevation each. This was about the year 950 BC during Solomon's reign.

FIGURE 7: SILWAN VILLAGE

The village of Silwan crouches on the rocky east side of Kidron Valley. Housing in Silwan is built over ancient tombs assumed to be the burial places of the highest-ranking officials of the ancient biblical Judean kingdom.

- King Solomon became more wealthy and wiser than any other king on earth. Kings from every nation came to consult him. Everyone who visited brought him gifts of silver and gold, clothing, weapons, spices, horses, and mules (2 Chronicles 9:22-24).
- He had fourteen hundred chariots and twelve thousand horses. Solomon imported horses from Egypt and Cilicia. He stationed some of them in the chariot cities and some near him in Jerusalem.
- The king made silver as plentiful in Jerusalem as stone. Valuable cedar timber was as common as the sycamore-fig trees that grow in Judea's foothills (1 Kings 10:26-28).
- Solomon also made a house like his residence for Pharaoh's daughter (1 Kings 7-9 NASB).

Unfortunately, we will not visit this dazzling place because nothing is left to see. The only evidence of Solomon's Palace is the written description in the Bible. No relic of the magnificent period has surfaced yet, although some archaeologists believe they can pinpoint the location. Pharaoh's daughter's palace is a legend without evidence as well.

THE PHARAOH'S DAUGHTER WAS NOT THE QUEEN: The Egyptian princess must have been Solomon's principal wife because she was the only one to be established in a separate palace. However,

FIGURE 8: TOMB OF THE PHAROAH'S DAUGHTER
Located in Silwan Village, said to be the Tomb of Pharoah's Daughter. Romans removed the pyramid cap on the tomb eons ago

she was not the queen. With so many wives, not one was named queen. The Queen Mother, Bathsheba, mother of King Solomon, claimed the title as the most important woman who lived in the harem.

The wives of King Solomon lived in a separate section of the palace, each with her separate apartment. Naturally, those wives of higher rank and greater prestige received the best quarters. No doubt intrigue lived in the harem every day, as they all lived together with the king's children they bore. There would have been both loving friendships and bitter rivalry. Perhaps life was much like the "Sister Wives" of polygamist Mormons today.

Solomon's "freedom of religion" policy with his thousand-member harem allowed the wives to build temples to their different gods. Solomon's people viewed that policy with dislike and hostility.

PHAROAH'S DAUGHTER: The once-imposing "Tomb of Pharaoh's Daughter" sits in the village of Silwan, overlooking the City of David on the opposite hill to the east across the Kidron Valley. But no one goes to visit Silwan. Our guide said the Silwan villagers have historically been an unfriendly lot.

150 To Isreal with Love

FIGURE 9: SOLOMON AND SHEBA
One of the "Doors of Paradise" in the Baptistery of San Giovanni, Florence, Italy.

Previously capped by a pyramid structure, the rock cap was cut into pieces and removed for quarry during the Roman era, leaving a flat roof. The sepulchre contains a single stone bench, indicating only one burial. In the Byzantine period (fourth-to-sixth centuries AD), monks lived inside this chamber and in the nearby Silwan caves. Their renovations raised the entrance and destroyed most of the original doorway inscription. The tomb features Egyptian style decoration, a gabled ceiling, and a cornice.

The construction does date from Solomon's temple period, so it may have indeed been the Egyptian princess' burial crypt.

ANOTHER LOVE AFFAIR The Pharaoh's daughter was not Solomon's only intriguing love affair. According to the Bible, the Koran *(Qu'ran)*, and several detailed Ethiopian texts, the Queen of Sheba visited Solomon in Jerusalem in the tenth century BC. The Queen's name may be Makeda. She had exchanged letters with the King, and when she arrived, she brought many luxurious gifts. One undocumented legend is that Solomon became bewitched by her beauty and ordered his courtiers not to disturb them for three days and three nights, after which Makeda went back to Sheba (present-day Ethiopia). *And King Solomon gave unto the queen of Sheba all her desire, whatsoever she asked, in addition to that which Solomon gave her of his royal bounty* (1 Kings 10:13 NASB).

WHO WAS THE QUEEN OF SHEBA? The Queen of Sheba, called the Queen of the South in Matthew 12:42, managed to capture much interest through the ages. Images of this queen appear in twelfth- and thirteenth-century cathedral art at Canterbury, Strasbourg, Chartres, Rochester, and Amiens. She was the subject of numerous books, fine art, a ballet, and no less than three operas. Queen Makeda came to Jerusalem ...*with a very great retinue, with camels bearing spices, and very much gold, and precious stones. Such an abundance of spices never again came, like those which she gave to Solomon* (1 Kings 10:10 NASB).

Before she returned to her country, the two ruling monarchs may have enjoyed a romantic three day and night interlude. Modern Ethiopians claim this was a queen of their nation. They believe this queen had a son by Solomon, named Menelik, from whom the entire imperial dynasty of Ethiopia is descended right down to the last in line, Emperor Haile Selassie, who died in 1975.

Tradition credits Menelik with visiting his father (King Solomon) in Jerusalem after reaching adulthood, and Solomon gave the young Menelik the Ark of the Covenant to take home with him. Even today, the

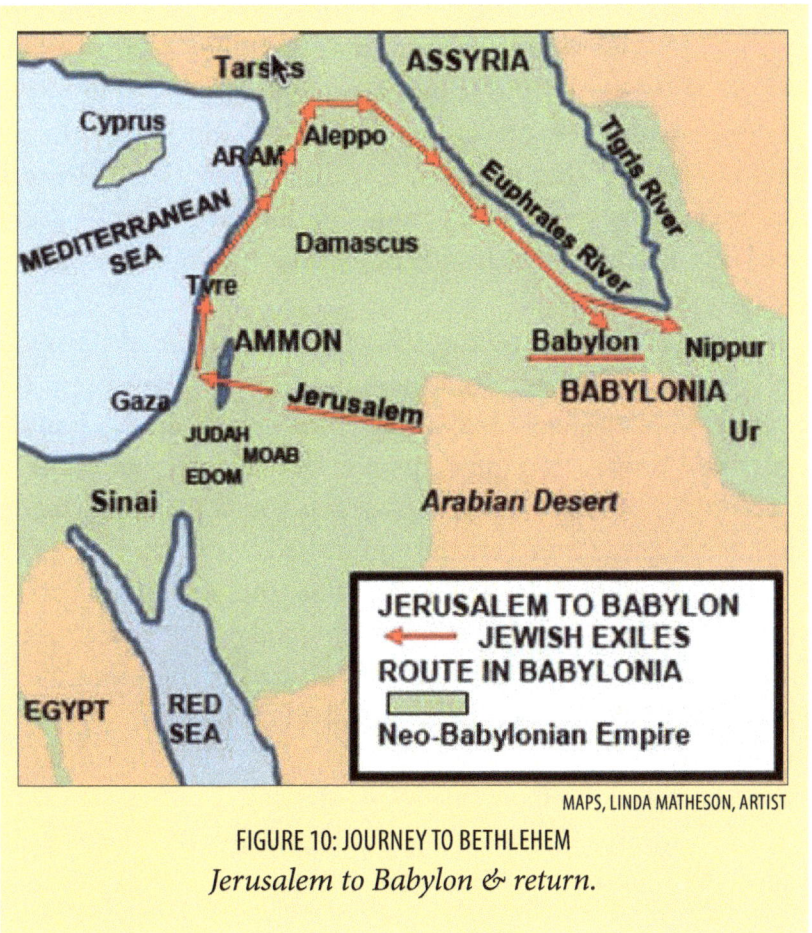

MAPS, LINDA MATHESON, ARTIST

FIGURE 10: JOURNEY TO BETHLEHEM
Jerusalem to Babylon & return.

Ethiopian Orthodox Church in Axum, Ethiopia, claims to possess the original ark that they keep under close guard. Every Ethiopian church hosts a replica of the chest with a dedication to a particular saint.

We wonder what truth is in that story as we stand on the Mount of Olives looking across the Kidron Valley. We can see the city wall of Jerusalem and the Dome of the Rock marking the spot where Solomon's magnificent palace and temple complex once stood, with the Ark inside the particular room called the Holy of Holies.

When Solomon died, they buried him in the City of David (1 Kings 11:43 NASB). Then his son Rehoboam became the next king. For Israel, it was all downhill from there. Rehoboam was not a great leader.

THE TEMPLE IS DESTROYED: Some four hundred years later the Babylonians destroyed Solomon's Temple in 586 BC when King Nebuchadnezzar conquered Jerusalem. The massive stones and beautiful temple remained a devastated heap during the Jews' seventy years of captivity in Babylon.

JEWS ENSLAVED, TAKEN TO BABYLON: When these Hebrew captives reached Babylon, now part of Iraq, they must have been dazzled by the sights in one of the greatest cities of the ancient world. The prisoners probably entered through Babylon's beautifully carved and embellished *Ishtar* gate, and looked with wonder on splendid buildings such as the seven-staged *ziggurat* or the acclaimed Tower of Babel and the famed Hanging Gardens, that provided a cool, shady place on hot days. These structures remain among the seven wonders of the ancient world. The captive Jews would have walked up that imposing avenue known as the Processional Way to Ishtar Gate. The street, nearly eighty feet wide and paved with slabs of limestone and pink marble, separated two walls more than fifty feet tall on each side. More than a hundred sculptural lions, flowers, and enameled yellow tiles trimmed the walls.

A reconstruction of the Ishtar Gate and the Processional Way to the gate is on display at the Pergamon Museum in Berlin, Germany. However, the museum reconstruction is neither complete nor original size. Initially, the Ishtar held a double gate with a door and roof made of cedar and bronze, but the Pergamon display only shows the smaller frontal part. The second gate is currently in storage. Saddam Hussein planned to use the second gate as the entrance to a museum in Iraq, but that museum remains unfinished due to war.

This ceremonial gateway guarding the main entrance to the city of Babylon featured two portals, one behind the other, each flanked by massive towers, and the whole decorated with turquoise, bronze, and pink marble. Glazed bricks decorated the front of the gate with alternating rows of dragons and bulls displayed in yellow and brown tiles, surrounded by blue lapis lazuli enamel tiles. Each stone carried an inscription underneath containing a small prayer from King Nebuchadnezzar to their chief God, Marduk.

The entrance survived the sixth-century BC Persian destruction of the city. Archaeologists found the foundations of the gate with molded, unglazed figures going down some forty-five feet.

Note: We won't see that gate built four thousand years ago, but we will see the gates of Jerusalem from almost that long ago, but they are not nearly so decorative.

The Jews remained in bondage in Babylon for some sixty or seventy years. The exact length of time seems in dispute. Then Persia invaded and conquered Babylon in turn.

The Persians allowed descendants of the Jewish captives to return to Jerusalem about 538 BC. They took the gold and silver vessels plundered from the temple by their conquerors, including the sacred Ark of the Covenant.

These returning Jews had adopted new customs and spoke a different language. The people still said their prayers in Hebrew, but the rest of the time, they spoke in Aramaic. Although Babylon's beautiful buildings no longer exist, the Jews recreated the *ziggurat* form in many of their building projects in Israel, as we will see. And we are already moving on to our next adventure.

THE ROAD TO BETHLEHEM: Onboard our bus, we are on our way to Bethlehem, a Palestinian city located in the central West Bank, about six miles south of Jerusalem. Most people think only of Jesus's birth associated with Bethlehem, but several stories featuring Old Testament characters also connect to this city.

On our way, we will see Rachel's tomb, as mentioned in Day One. Also, the prophet Samuel came to Bethlehem to visit the family of Jesse. When Samuel met Jesse's young son David at Bethlehem, he anointed him to succeed Saul as King of Israel. And we learn about Ruth and Boaz, grandparents of David, from the book of Ruth.

Naomi grew up in Bethlehem but married and moved to Moab, where she and her husband raised two sons. When her husband and both sons died, Naomi decided to return to Bethlehem. Her widowed daughter-in-law Ruth wanted to go with her. Naomi tried to discourage Ruth, suggesting she should stay at Moab where she had family, but Ruth would not hear of it.

AUTHOR'S PRIVATE COLLECTION

FIGURE 11: AN INNOCENT CHILD

She was determined to go with Naomi, saying: Don't make me leave you, for I want to go wherever you go and to live wherever you live; your people shall be my people, and your God shall be my God. (Ruth 1:16 TLB)

This verse, often used in marriage ceremonies, was a young widow talking to her mother-in-law. It was a good thing Ruth insisted on going with Naomi because Bethlehem was far away, and Naomi couldn't have traveled all that way by herself. At Bethlehem, Ruth met and married Boaz. They became grandparents of a shepherd boy at Bethlehem, who became the great ruler, King David.

TRAMPING THROUGH SHEPHERD'S FIELDS: We stop along the road to visit the shepherd's fields where shepherds watched over their flocks at the time of Jesus's birth. From here, there is a good view up to the slopes of Bethlehem. There is also an excellent view to the east of the distinctive conical shape of Herodium, the breast-shaped hill in the desert that King Herod developed as his bunker.

As a young boy, David would have practiced with his slingshot right below that hill as he was herd-ing his father's sheep.

We pause to examine an ancient hand-dug well, still in use near a Bedouin shepherd's tent home. The Bedouins draw water for daily needs and live much as their ancestors did in the Old Testament days of Abraham. This life does not appear a happy one, and women catch the worst of it. The family must often move from place to place, always seeking new pasture for their flocks. Men rule the house-hold and can have as many as four wives. Even today, women have no rights at all. Their days are filled with work and childbearing, although each wife may have a separate area of living quarters and occa-sionally her tent. The first wife claims seniority, but the favorite wife—usually the youngest—gets the best location.

The Bedouin tent we visited featured one room of canvas, supported by long sticks, with only the barest of necessities. It did not at all resemble a colorful romantic "Sheik of Arabia" tent style. This one offered only a pile of thin mattresses and blankets stacked in one corner on the hard-packed dirt floor. A young woman sat on the only chair, a straight-back hardwood. She was heavily pregnant, probably the favorite youngest wife. Two youngsters, with olive skin and snapping black eyes and hair, shyly peeked around a curtain from the back of the tent. The scene reminds me of photos of desolate frontier life in America.

STEPPING INSIDE A BEDOUIN TENT: We did not explore inside the tent, but there is a description in *National Geographic,* saying they roll out mats or carpets and sleep in their clothing at night. In evi-dence, we see a leather bucket to draw water from the well, and a pitcher to carry the liquid. They cook over a fire with stones around the hearth hole, have mats and platters for serving dishes and cups for drinking. If they have a camel, then their saddle provides seating inside the tent. In hot weather, the cooking fire is outside. Another reference says the men occupy an entrance room, which also serves as a reception area. A cloth curtain separates a living space for women and children, and sometimes a third area for servants or livestock is found.

MEETING A SHEPHERD GIRL: One little girl, about four years old and without shoes, followed us silently, first with her enormous dark eyes and then with her bare feet, as we walked out into the stony brown pasture. Little tufts of grass only occasionally broke through the stone carpet. We wonder how animals find enough forage to survive.

Our guide leads us to a hillside and motions for us to sit. Visitors choose a large flat rock, brush it off and crunch down as Aaron tells the history of shepherding. From this vantage point, we can see in the distance the little town of Bethlehem, now a good-sized city. Homes clinging on a rough and rocky hill in the distance, appear as a cluster of whitewashed square blocks occasionally accented by the green exclamation point of an olive tree.

The child sat quietly, all by herself, on a rock. She waited patiently while our guide spoke to us in a language the Bedouin girl obviously could not understand.

AUTHOR'S PRIVATE COLLECTION

FIGURE 12: THE SHEPHERD CHILD AND HER MOTHER.

After the talk, we took photos of the little girl and handed her money. She solemnly put the coins in her pocket and never smiled at all. We walked back to the tent where the child and her family lived. I asked if we could take pictures outside the tent. A woman, also barefoot, squatted on the ground wearing a shapeless long dark skirt and a loose top. She never spoke but nodded agreement. A white cloth covered her head as she pulled the free end of the fabric across her face for a veil. Her wrinkled, leathery skin raised a question about her age. I posed the child beside her mother. As we walked back to the bus, I turned to wave and saw the mother take the silver coins from the child's pocket. Only then did we hear the child's voice, a small whimper of protest.

Our guide says Bedouins are not impoverished. They have money but choose this lifestyle because they believe it is Allah's will, and they prefer to remain free. Tent life, with its simplicity and so much time spent out-of-doors, carries a real charm for some. Most would not live otherwise if they could.

FIGURE 13: BETHLEHEM MANGER SQUARE AND CHURCH OF NATIVITY COURTYARD

Their motto is "*Allahu Akbar*," Arabic for "God is Great." Sometimes the children go to school, more often they do not.

The families stay in one area for a time, then move on. The goats-hair cloth used in making these tents is porous when dry but becomes waterproof after the first rains shrink it. The material of a Bedouin tent is the same as the sackcloth of Bible days. I wonder if it keeps them warm in the winter when temps may go down below 30° Fahrenheit. Our guide says some Bedouins have modern camels, a car or truck, to make life easier.

The little shepherd girl's face reminds me of my children and grandchildren far away in America. I say a prayer for their safety as we head for Bethlehem, the legendary birthplace of David, who became King, as well as the baby Jesus that Christians call their promised Messiah. I am even more thankful for our country and our comfortable home. I wish these people well.

BATTLE FOR BETHLEHEM: A friend who recently returned from Israel was disappointed Bethlehem was off-limits to them because of danger. The situation was volatile when we were there. Our guide told us not to worry because Bethlehem's primary economic income is tourism. We hope he is right. The peak season hits at Christmas when Christians make a pilgrimage to the Church of the Nativity, returning as they have for more than two thousand years. Many artisans sell "holy hardware" to tourists. Jews and Arabs mix freely during business hours and treat each other with courtesy, but they do not socialize, nor do they trust the other. There are years of bad blood between them, since the days of Isaac and Ishmael (Genesis 25:5–6).

The town of Bethlehem has a checkered history, changing hands many times over the ages, being ruled at different times by Romans, Byzantines, Arabs, Crusaders, Mamelukes, and Turks. Yet Christians continue to cling to Bethlehem throughout the ages despite many centuries of frequently hostile non-Christian rule, which often made pilgrimages difficult and even hazardous.

THE WALL: If Bethlehem appeared as a cluster of whitewashed boxes from a distance, up close the city resembled a war zone. A massive twenty-five-foot-high concrete wall topped with barbed wire divides the West Bank area from the Israel section. A raised scar snaking through the "holy city" of Bethlehem, the barricade features periodic watchtowers hiding armed guards. It cuts across fields and olive groves separating citizens from schools, hospitals, and workplaces. Israel started building the wall in 2002. Citizens must stand in long lines in all kinds of weather to show credentials at checkpoints. One tourist said he stayed at a Bethlehem hotel but found the wall separated him from Rachel's Tomb where he wished to visit. Some gift shop owners lost their business when the barrier separated them from the tourists.

Soldiers and police officers outnumber both tourists and pilgrims as we enter the city and arrive at the legendary birthplace of Jesus. Graffiti decorates many structures, and abandoned buildings become apparent. Tourists crowd the sidewalks. Shutters hide occupied shops, and the few residents we saw seemed to wear a permanent distressed expression.

FIGURE 14: CHOOSING SOUVENIRS
A treasured hand-carved olivewood souvenir from Bethlehem.

JON HEAVENER

A WORD ABOUT SHOPPING: Make your plan for souvenir purchases before you leave home. You will find many worthy items to choose from and lit-tle time to debate about what you want to take home. The tourist trade is Bethlehem's life blood. Back on the bus, Mr. Elie drove through Bethlehem's city to an olivewood shop named "The Three Arches," owned by a friend of our tour guide. Mr. Aaron joked about Israelis who might offer to take us to their cousin's shop, where we would be encouraged to purchase shoddy mer-chandise at an inflated price. He says he has many "uncles" instead of "cousins." These products appear to be of excellent quality, not overpriced. We brought home a delicate hand-carved olivewood Madonna and child, signed by the artist. The artifact will serve as a precious reminder of our trip to the holy land, perhaps somewhat like the religious relics collected by Middle Eastern Christians in the early days. *Tip: Choose your souvenirs with care. Keep them small to fit inside your suitcase.*

CAN THE CHURCH OF THE NATIVITY BE SAVED? The structure of the Church of the Nativity is an odd combination of two churches with a crypt beneath—the Grotto of the Nativity—where tradition holds Jesus of Nazareth was born to fulfill prophecy. Various denominations share control over different parts of the church. Although the building is on the "endangered" list, there is no great hope to save it. One authority said it would take a miracle to get the three custodians to work together: the Greek Orthodox Church, the Armenian Orthodox Church, and the Franciscan order. Discord has reigned for centuries. The Israeli government and the Palestinian Authority would also need to cooperate, which is not likely to happen. The "status quo" including customs, rights, and duties of the various church authorities holding custody of the holy places was legally fixed under the Ottoman Empire in the sixteenth-century, remaining in force to this day, as it does at the Church of the Sepulchre in Jerusalem, (see Day Nine).

Bethlehem is important to **Jews, Christians, and Muslims.**

Judaism: Bethlehem (Bet Lechem) relates to several Jewish ancestors: the burial place of the matri-arch, Rachel, and David's birthplace. King David's ancestors Ruth and Boaz married in Bethlehem. Additionally, Samuel anointed David as King of Israel in Bethlehem at the home of Ruth and Boaz.

FIGURE 15: THE DOOR OF HUMILITY
Entering the Church of the Nativity through the door of humility. Look closely in front of the man in the dark suit to see the tiny black door only four feet tall and two feet wide. Visitors must stoop or bow to enter.

Christianity: Bethlehem is named in Matthew and Luke's gospels as the birthplace of Jesus and is one of the holiest sites around the world. The town is inhabited by an ancient Christian community, although many have fled the city in recent times out of fear.

Islam: Bethlehem has meaning for Muslims as well since they also honor Jesus. However, Muslims believe that Jesus was only one of many prophets.

THE CAVE UNDER THE CHURCH: Manger Square, the Mosque of Omar, the Palestinian Peace Center, and The Church of the Nativity form the center of the city to create a magnet for pilgrims. Palestinian police patrol the area. The church structure is over a grotto or small cave. The entrance to the famous church features a large open, but not at all impressive courtyard. Originally built under the direction of Constantine's mother Helena in the fourth century, Roman Emperor Justinian rebuilt the current structure around AD 530. We wondered how to identify and preserve a site like this for more than two thousand years. The Romans are responsible, though that was not their original intent.

The second Jewish revolt against Rome led by Judah Maccabee failed again some sixty years later. As part of the punishment to Jews and Christians, Roman emperor Hadrian surrounded the cave of the nativity by a shrine in a sacred grove of trees dedicated to Adonis, pagan God of beauty and love. Hadrian, a staunch adherent of paganism, caused Christ-followers to suffer even more grievously than did the Jews. Hadrian's pagan shrine stood above the cave for two centuries. His attempt to eradicate evidence of Christianity must have preserved it.

INSIDE THE CHURCH OF THE NATIVITY: We enter Bethlehem's Church of the Nativity through a tiny door, an opening so small we must bow to go through. This "door of humility" is only four feet high. Legend claims the door was reduced to this size in the seventeenth century so Muslims could not ride into the church on their horses. However, it might also be an attempt to cut down on looting.

The interior of the structure confronts on such a grand scale to be somewhat overwhelming, with a large central nave and four aisles divided by rows of robust red limestone Corinthian columns, eleven to a row. We learn these are the original columns while the roof is a little younger, only about seven hundred years old.

We circle the enormous sanctuary and continue through the church, behind the choir loft, and down a curving stairway under the pulpit to reach the revered place. We descend stairs jammed with tourists, seemingly hundreds of pilgrims crowding on the small stairway at once, seeking that tiny room.

THE BIRTH GROTTO IN BETHLEHEM: Three altars at the bottom of the stairs dominate the room: Nativity, the Manger, and the Magi. This cave, selected in the fourth century to mark the site of Jesus's birth, is controlled by the Greek Orthodox Church. The Nativity grotto appears cave-like, yet gaudy clutter assaults our eyes with black and white marble, gold and silver lamps, red and gold brocades, var-ious candles, and bright silk hangings. Paintings cover the walls, and everywhere we see those unique Greek-style hanging lamps.

A giant silver star on a marble slab on the base of the cave marks the spot where Mary reportedly gave birth to the Christ child. Inside the crèche, fourteen silver lamps, each one a little different design, light space. Many people fell to their knees, bowed, puckered up, and planted a kiss on the marble slab's star with no concern for the germs that might live there. The design features fourteen points, representing fourteen generations between Abraham and David and then from David to Jesus.

THE MANGER GROTTO: We find the manger area, situated in a little chapel to the left of the birth cave, where the floor is a step lower. This cavern is also draped in silks and lit by candles. According to tradition, Queen Helena removed the simple stone manger and replaced it with a silver one.

A second small altar in the Grotto of the Manger is dedicated to the Magi, the three wise men described in Matthew's Gospel as coming from the east, probably Persia, to worship the newborn Jesus. Catholics often celebrate Mass (communion) in this small room, which is only about 9x40 feet. I don't even remember seeing that altar to the Magi. Perhaps so many people viewing the area blocked my view.

AUTHOR'S PRIVATE COLLECTION

FIGURE 16: THE BIRTH GROTTO
A look at the Nativity grotto with its fourteen-point star and a variety of oil lamps. Hundreds of people visit the grotto in Bethlehem every day. Many kneel and kiss the star.

FIGURE 17: THE CHURCH OF THE NATIVITY

Inside the Church of the Nativity, trapdoors in the floor allow glimpses of the ancient mosaic floor dating from Constantine's time in the fourth century.

This place of Jesus's birth is not at all as we imagined, and in fact, some modern scholars are doubtful Jesus was born here, believing instead the delivery was at Bethlehem-of-Galilee in northern Israel. Like religious relics of Queen Helena's day, perhaps this grotto only represents the original. If this place is the correct "city," then it was probably somewhere near here that Mary gave birth to her firstborn. In this century, in addition to worrying about robbers on the road through the desert, Mary would have to negotiate a concrete wall, armed guards, and enormous crowds of tourists.

The verse we learned as children reverberates in our heads: *And it came to pass that when they were there, her days were accomplished that she should be delivered. And she brought forth her newborn son and wrapped him up in swaddling clothes and laid him in a manger* (Luke 2:7 KJV).

After Jesus was born, the family stayed in Bethlehem for a time. The Magi or wise men saw a star in the East and came to Bethlehem to see the baby who was prophesied to be the Christ (Matthew 2:1-23).

THE CHURCH OF THE NATIVITY: The Bethlehem church stands like a citadel, with defense a significant consideration. The building is still standing despite frequent battles raging all around this area. This church is the only one to survive the Persian invasion of AD 613. Some say the church endured because the Persians saw a mural of the three wise men from their country on the wall inside. Trapdoors in the floor allow glimpses of the ancient mosaic floor of Constantine's time, and we could find faint traces of mosaics on the walls. Huge oil lamps hang from supports between columns and around the sanctuary area. Gaudy colored glass balls of red and green and silver hang beneath the oil lamps. Our guide said the colored balls on our Christmas trees today come from this Greek Orthodox tradition. He said the crusaders came to this land in the thirteenth century, and they liked the beauty of the glass balls hanging from the oil lamps, so they took some back to Europe to decorate for their Father Christmas holiday. Eventually the balls became a part of our Christmas tradition.

AN ARABIAN WEDDING: When we came up from the manger cave, a formal Arabian wedding party was forming, and we paused to see the bridal couple. The bride was a vision in an exquisite American style satin and lace gown. Many members of the wedding party and guests dressed in the robes and turbans of native Bedouins. Several flower girls with halos of white blossoms carried baskets of petals, and one little boy in a miniature monk's robe may have been the ring bearer. Colorful flower garlands and candles brightened the dark sanctuary. The name *Bedouin* in Arabic means "desert dweller." As we watched this beautiful wedding in action, I couldn't help remembering the somber little shepherd girl we just visited. We wonder what this Bedouin bride's life might be.

164   *To Isreal with Love*

AUTHOR'S PRIVATE COLLECTION
FIGURE 18: WEDDING CEREMONY
We were wedding crashers at an Arabian ceremony in the ancient Church of Nativity in Bethlehem.

And they lived happily ever after …?

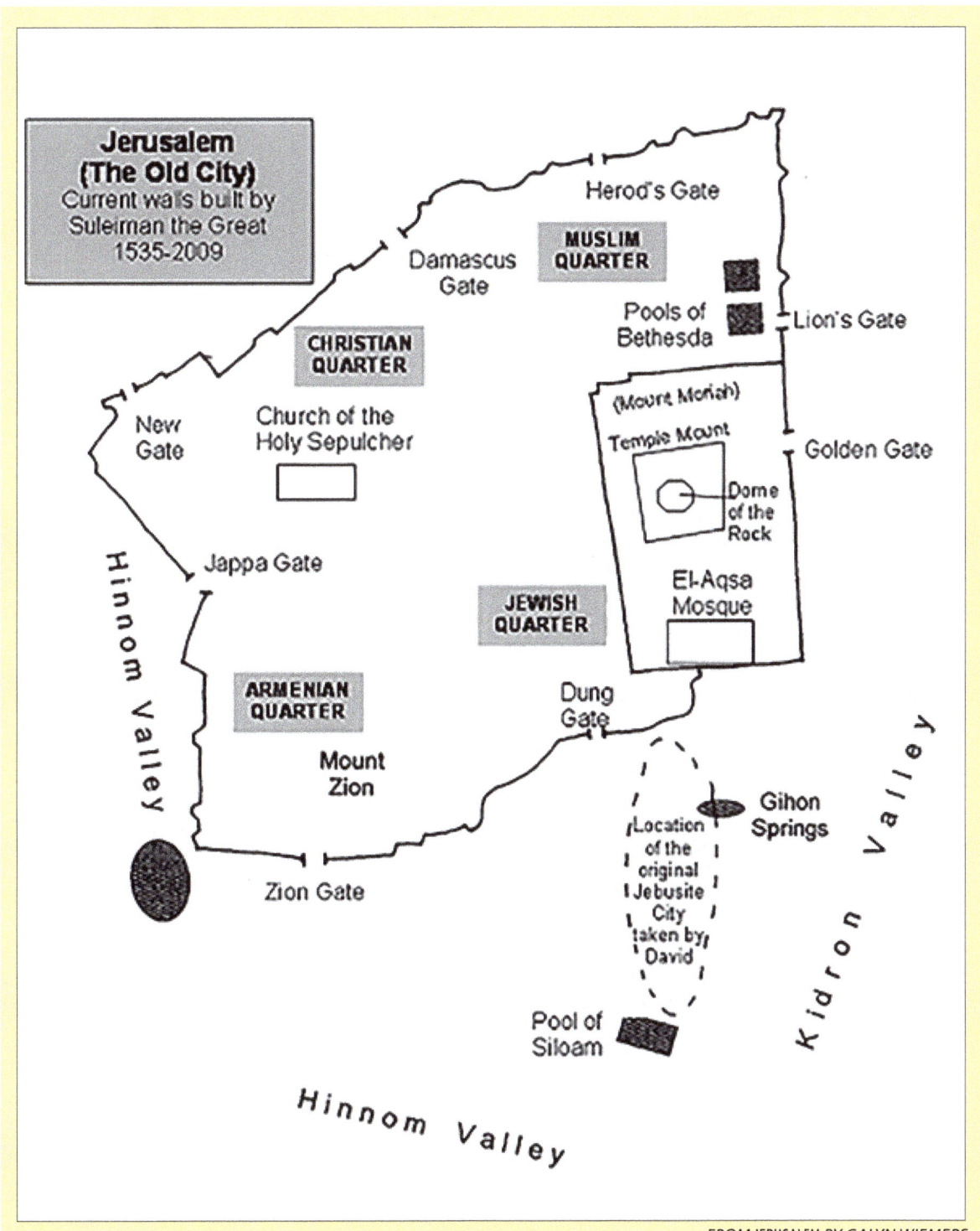

FROM JERUSALEM BY GALYN WIEMERS

FIGURE 19: JERUSALEM IN AD 635

EIGHT

DAY OF JERUSALEM

Monday: The Gates of Jerusalem, The Western Wall, Zedediah's Cave, Hezekiah's Tunnel, Dome of the Rock, the Model City, and Independence Day

DAY EIGHT: Today is a holiday, Israel's Memorial Day, a day to honor the military dead. Fully armed soldiers are everywhere. Soldiers peer from rooftops and from behind trees. They walk among the tombstones, jostle with the crowds in the streets, and guard the city gates. Thirty-four towers and eleven gates circle the old city, although not all are open. We Americans are not familiar with city walls, but in ancient times defensive walls enclosed settlements, protecting a city from attack. Generally, people refer to such structures as city walls or town walls. However, other walls extend far beyond the borders of a city to mark territorial boundaries, like the Great Wall of China.

WWW.GOISRAEL.COM

FIGURE 1: MACHICOLATION
Ancient city gates often feature a machicolation, a protected opening at the top of the wall where residents could drop boiling oil or rocks on the invading enemy below.

THE WALLED OLD CITY: We see Jerusalem today as a large city spread out over a vast area, but for most of its history, Jerusalem remained a small town. The walled "Old City" portion near the Temple Mount consists of four very unevenly-sized quarters: Christian, Armenian, Muslim, and Jewish.

We will walk in all four sections to understand why the invisible walls of fear, anger, and hatred often divide the people living there. These quarters form a rectangular grid, but they are not equal in size. The division between the quarters is as old as the city itself. Names of these four neighborhoods represent the ethnic affiliation of the people who live there.

FOUR QUARTERS: Tiny shops line most of the narrow streets, where merchants sell foodstuffs and handicrafts. The average shop size compares to a residential washroom in the United States. Homes cluster around courtyards surrounded by high walls. Dividing lines include the street running from Damascus Gate to Zion Gate, dividing the city into east and west. The road leading from Jaffa Gate to Lion's gate bisects the city north and south.

AUTHOR'S PRIVATE COLLECTION
FIGURE 2: SHOPPING
Stalls of colorful fabrics and smells of exotic spices line the rebuilt Cardo walkway.

- **Christian**: The most visited quarter of the Old City hosts a seemingly endless grouping of churches and holy sites whose roofs, domes, and facades bump together. Narrow shotgun-style storefronts line a noisy street crowded with pilgrims and merchants advertising their wares.

- **Armenian**: The first nation to declare itself a Christian nation even before the days of Constantine, Armenians have lived in Jerusalem since 95 BC. This smallest Jerusalem old city neighborhood boasts only a couple of souvenir shops and eateries but holds the heart of the oldest Christ-following communities in the world. Today the Armenian quarter covers only about one-sixth of the Old City.

- **Muslim**: Herod the Great first developed this most populated of the four quarters. Later the Byzantine Empire occupied it and afterward the Crusaders. We will visit many churches and shrines, including the *Via Dolorosa*, a path symbolic of the one taken by Jesus on his way to Calvary.

- **Jewish**: This quarter, a thriving residential community, houses more than a thousand families. Rebuilt out of the rubble left from Jordanian occupation from 1948 to 1967, the Jews first excavated archaeological remains and then built their city over and around these ancient discoveries. The Roman *Cardo* (AD 135), with its Byzantine bazaar (AD 325), features trendy businesses selling a wide variety of items. This quarter also contains the western or wailing wall, a holy place for the Jews. We will visit the remains of a house burnt by the Romans more than two thousand years ago.

WE SEE A NEW CITY: In addition to the four quarters of the walled Old City, the larger area of Jerusalem itself breaks down into three sections: Old City, New City or West Jerusalem, and East Jerusalem. Mark Twain was amazed by the smallness of the old city when he visited in 1867. *A fast walker could go outside the walls of Jerusalem and walk entirely around the city in an hour. I do not know how else to make one understand how small it is.* Most of Jerusalem's religious landmarks are in this area. *Note: Of course, Mark Twain's visit was more than 150 years ago. Jerusalem is not that small now, but the old walled city remains that size. I believe you are still allowed to walk the ramparts on the top of the wall.*

SURPRISE AT HOLY TOILETS: We had a new educational experience on our first visit downtown. We learned to watch out for "holy toilets." We carried tissues because the public rooms stocked something similar to waxed paper. However, our experience in the city became even more unique. Several of us needed to go, and we located the facilities. A woman sitting in the doorway held out her hand. We gave her a *shekel* (about 25 cents US), and she motioned us through the door. A long trough along the wall led to three stalls, each with a plastic curtain for privacy. If I thought about it at all, I probably presumed the long trough was for washing hands. I went in one of the stalls, took care of my business, and came out to discover a couple of men facing the trough. Thank goodness, they kept their backs turned, and this country girl didn't hang around to make conversation. **Tip: Other countries do not have the same hang-ups we do about bodily functions.*

KIND STRANGERS: Downtown in the new city (East Jerusalem), we found the people friendly and curious about where we are from and why we came. As an example, Jon's glasses needed repair. He lost one of the little screws holding the earpiece. We located a shop in the pedestrian mall with eyeglasses in the show window. Using a mixture of English and sign language, Jon explained his dilemma. The language of Israel is mostly Hebrew, though some speak Arabic. Many Israelis also speak English, but Hebrew is how most Israelis conduct commerce and even order a falafel. The young male clerk disappeared into the back of the store, reappearing with an older man who spoke our dialect very well. The shopkeeper quickly repaired Jon's glasses while we answered his questions about America. He refused to take any pay and wished us a pleasant journey.

A yogurt kiosk provided us a delicious snack. Fruit and nuts tempted us with a variety of flavoring choices. The operator placed a frozen vanilla yogurt patty in a large blender with three or four fruit and nut toppings, then whipped the ingredients into a nourishing snack. I chose blueberries and strawberries with pecans in a honey sauce. Jon selected walnuts, pineapple, and cherries. After tasting the heavenly results, we decided someone should open a franchise like this in the United States. We leave the kiosk and walk through Damascus Gate back into the Old City. We remember the importance of gatehouses.

THE GATES OF JERUSALEM: The Old City has a total of eleven gates, with seven main ones named Lion's, Jaffa, Dung, New Gate, Herod's, Zion, and Damascus. Each gate also has one or more alternate names, just to keep us confused.

Damascus Gate (pictured above) The main entrance and busiest gate to the Old City can be found on the northwest side flanked by two towers trimmed with stone gingerbread. On the lintel to this second-century gate, we see the city's name under Emperor Hadrian's Roman rule, *Aelia Capitolina*.

FIGURE 3: DAMASCUS GATE
Damascus Gate, the main gate into the old city.

Damascus Gate is the largest and most attractive of all Jerusalem gates. Ottoman ruler Suleiman-The-Magnificent constructed Damascus Gate in AD 1541 on top of two older gates, one built by Herod the Great and another by the Roman Emperor Hadrian. This gate leads directly into the Muslim Quarter of East Jerusalem. An increased police presence is apparent here, particularly on Fridays. The police often impose restrictions on visitors to the Temple Mount, so the area might be closed without warning. One day on our way, the police stopped us before we reached the western wall. A shooting happened there earlier that day. They warned us to visit only in daylight hours.

Other Gates

Lion's Gate, also called Stephen's Gate or Sheep Gate, in the East Wall should not be confused with Zion Gate on the south wall, even though it looks similar. Lion's gate features four faint figures of panthers, often mistaken for lions, two on the left and two on the right. The lion is the emblem of Jerusalem. All roads from Mount of Olives, Bethany, and Jericho meet here. Both pedestrians and vehicles use the gate, although maneuvering is tricky. Cars can exit but not enter here. Christians may call it the Gate of St. Stephen, because the Via Dolorosa is just inside the gate, and every Friday afternoon, hundreds join a procession through the Old City, stopping at fourteen Stations of the Cross. These stations identify with the suffering of Jesus on his way to crucifixion. Muslim escorts lead the parade in Ottoman uniforms of red fez, gold-embroidered waistcoat, and baggy blue trousers. These escorts bang silver-topped staves on the ground to signify their authority. The route is not easy to identify, so if this is something you want to do, better follow the baggy blue trousers. This path is not documented and is symbolic.

Herod's Gate, In ancient times this gate led to the sheep market. A floral design above the opening may be why it is sometimes called flower gate, but also because local merchants sell fruit and flowers there. This gate adjoins the Muslim Quarter. Law enforcement and tax collectors might meet there, people come to beg or pray for mercy. Depending on their purpose, the same gate might be called by different names.

Dung Gate, near the southeast corner of the old city, is the main passage for vehicles. This gate's unusual name derives from refuse dumped here in antiquity, where prevailing winds would carry odors away from the city. Dung Gate opens into the Jewish Quarter. Pedestrians and vehicles both use this gate to reach the Western Wall.

Jaffa Gate, positioned at a right angle to the wall, stands near the Tower of David. The street leading east from Jaffa Gate is best for souvenir shopping. Like the rest of the Old City walls, the stones of this gate are large, hewn, sand-colored blocks.

New Gate is the newest gate in the walls. Built to provide direct access between the Christian Quarter and new neighborhoods going up outside the walls in 1889, New Gate provides the quickest route from the Old City to West Jerusalem. New Gate is not nearly as grand as the other Jerusalem gates in stature or history.

Zion Gate, also known as David's Gate. Zion gate leads to the Jewish and Armenian Quarters. Lepers used to gather there. Stones in the wall around the gate remain pockmarked by weapon fire and bullet holes from the 1948 war. Both pedestrians and vehicles go through here, although maneuvering is challenging. Cars can exit but not enter via this gate.

FIGURE 4: GOLDEN GATE
The sealed Eastern/Golden gate formerly provided a direct entrance to the temple area.

THE GOLDEN/EASTERN GATE OF THE OLD CITY: The Golden (or Eastern) Gate is a double-arch sealed gate, facing Mount Scopus and the Garden of Gethsemane. The now–sealed entrance led to two vaulted halls. Christians expect Jesus to return to Jerusalem and enter the city through this gate. All the sealed gates have a historical connection to the ancient Jewish temple. Most of the open gates have historical significance to Islam.

Many people believe Jesus rode into Jerusalem on a donkey through the now-sealed Eastern Gate on that first Palm Sunday. Our guide told us it would have been most unusual for Jesus, a Jew, to enter through this gate leading directly into the gentile area of the temple. Aaron said they used this Eastern Gate for ritual purposes, not for public access. He suggested Jesus probably came in through the Lion's Gate a little further on the wall. Although the Golden Gate remained open in Jesus's day, the Turks walled the big doors up and sealed them with great stones in the 1500s. Toward the end of World War I, British troops led by General Sir Edmund Allenby invaded Palestine, capturing Jerusalem in December 1917. Britain's occupation in the twentieth-century ended four hundred years of Turkish rule and Ottoman sovereignty. The British left the Eastern Gate sealed—as it remains.

SIX SEALED GATES REMAIN VISIBLE BUT INACCESSIBLE: The **Huldah Gates** show two sets of bricked-up gates in the southern wall of the Temple Mount. The left set is a double-arch gate, and the right (eastern side) is a triple-arch. During the second temple period, these Huldah gates led to the Temple Mount. While the temple stood, the public walked through the double gate. Only priests used the triple gate. These Huldah gates served as the main public gates to the temple. The gates led to tunnels, now closed, leading under and up into the temple mount. Entrance through the double gate led to a staircase in an underground tunnel, then about forty-five feet up the stairs to the surface of the Temple Mount complex. This enormous staircase enabled thousands of pilgrims to walk directly there.

The staircase up to the triple gate consists of fifteen pairs of alternating broad and narrow steps to force the climbing priests to keep their eyes downcast as they followed the steps.

The priests went up the stairs singing the Psalms of Ascent, beginning with Psalms 130, one on each level. (from *Stepping Up: A Journey Through the Psalms of Ascent* by Beth Moore.) The Mishna, second century AD books of Jewish practices, references the Huldah gates: *Five gates were in the temple mount: the two Huldah Gates on the south, that served for coming in and for going out....*

AUTHOR'S PRIVATE COLLECTION

FIGURE 5: HULDAH GATES
Two sets of bricked-up gates in the southern wall of the Temple Mount.

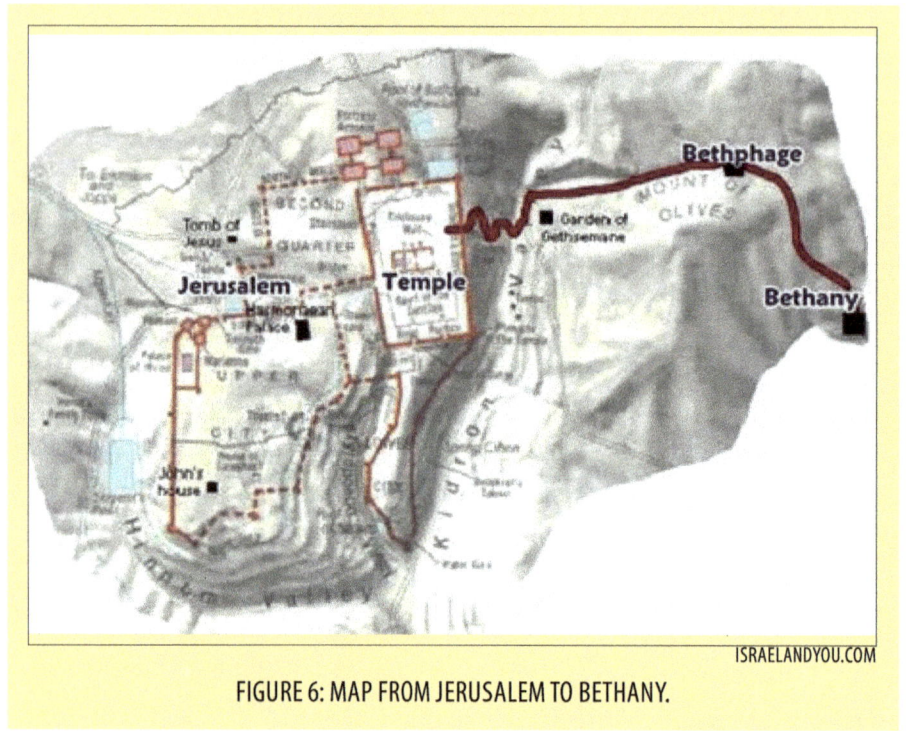

FIGURE 6: MAP FROM JERUSALEM TO BETHANY.

JESUS SPENT THE NIGHT IN BETHANY: Jesus and the disciples spent the night after Palm Sunday in Bethany on the other side of the Mount of Olives at the home of Mary and Martha, sisters of Lazarus. Having set out from Jericho that morning, Jesus must have arrived in Bethany, about two miles from Jerusalem, in the late afternoon to enjoy dinner with his friends. It was during this meal that Mary anointed the feet of Jesus and wiped them with her hair. *"Six days before the Passover Jesus came to Bethany where Lazarus was, whom Jesus had raised from the dead. So, they gave a dinner for him there* (John 12:1 ESV). All four Gospels tell the account of Jesus's entry into Jerusalem, but none gives the name of the specific gate Jesus entered. He returned to Bethany each evening.

WHY DID JESUS RIDE A DONKEY? Palm Sunday, the Sunday before Easter, is the only recorded instance in the Gospels where Jesus rides rather than walking. The two-mile ride was symbolic, riding a donkey because he came in peace. The Israelites were happy to welcome Jesus into Jerusalem on Palm Sunday because they saw Jesus as the one who would restore the monarchy of King David. That was how they understood the idea of the Messiah, but that was not Jesus's plan. Many people view Judas that same way, not so much as a betrayer of Jesus but as one who was impatient and wanted to call Jesus's hand. Judas, a zealot, may have thought if he tipped off the soldiers, it would get the reform movement underway and that Jesus would put down the oppression and re-establish the Kingdom of David. That is not what happened (John 18:36).

By waving palms, the people were fanning the flames of Jewish nationalism. Other books say people threw their cloaks and leafy branches in his path. Only John mentions "palm branches," which the people would have to bring from Jericho since palm trees are not native to Jerusalem. *Note: You do see palm trees throughout the city today.*

After entering Jerusalem, Jesus went into the temple, drove out the merchants, and knocked over the money-changers' tables and the stalls of those selling doves. 'The scriptures say my temple is a place of prayer,' he declared, 'but you have turned it into a den of thieves' (Matthew 21:12-14 TLB).

FIGURE 7: STONES OF MEMORY
"Stones of Memory" pile up on graves in the ancient cemetery on Mount of Olives.

FILLED WITH STONES OF MEMORY: Leaving Jerusalem through the Dung Gate, we walked down the mount and took the so-called Palm Sunday path beside high walls topped with shards of glass. We can see the Jewish Cemetery on the Mount of Olives through an open gate on the path. The oldest cemetery in the world still in use, it is undoubtedly the most famous cemetery in Jerusalem. These tombstones are all horizontal rather than vertical. The flat cement tops are piled high with small stones. People place a stone for remembrance instead of flowers. This way the poor and the rich are equal. Tradition declares someday the Messiah will appear here first, so it is an honor to be buried in this sacred Jewish cemetery. Christians believe the dead will be resurrected and will follow the Messiah into Jerusalem through the now-blocked Eastern gate.

MOVING TO TEMPLE MOUNT: Past the cemetery, we enter the temple mount area which covers about thirty-five acres and is the most sacred place in the world to the Hebrew people. David's palace and temple sat to the left on Mount Zion (in Jebus, City of David), and Solomon built his temple to the right, on nearby Mount Moriah. Thousands of years ago, when Abraham went to seek the land shown to him by God, this is where he came—to the hill of Moriah, meaning "fear" in Hebrew. So, the hilltop where the Solomon built his temple eventually came to be called Holy Mountain. *Zion* later referred to the combined area of Zion and Moriah, or Jerusalem itself.

WHY IS IT CALLED DOME OF THE ROCK? The enormous flat rock on top of Mount Moriah, where Abraham prepared to offer up his son as a sacrifice, is believed the same threshing floor King David bought from the farmer, Araunah the Jebusite. Solomon later made this a "home" for the particular receptacle called the Ark of the Covenant. Jews believe the rock served as the floor of the designated room, Holy of Holies, in Solomon's Temple, built about a thousand years before Jesus was born.

Now, this particular spot is held and controlled by the Muslims and is sacred to them because of their religious traditions concerning Abraham. The Abrahamic faiths are any or all of the religions (Judaism, Christianity, and Islam) that revere Abraham, the biblical patriarch. Monotheistic faiths grew out of the Abrahamic heritage, worshipping one God. *Note: The rock of Abraham and Isaac's sacrifice, the threshing floor of Araunah, and the Rock under the Dome are all the same rock.*

A SANCTUARY FOR PRIESTS: In Jesus's day, the Jewish temple sanctuary was for priests only. Gardens and an inner courtyard surrounded the temple, and only Jewish men could enter that area. A larger outer courtyard surrounded the inner courtyard. Gentiles and women could enter this area, along with money-changers and sellers of sacrificial lambs and other businesses. The "western wall" of this outer courtyard is all that remains of Herod's Temple. Jesus came to this courtyard at age twelve. *After three days, they found Him in the temple, sitting amid the teachers, listening to them, and asking them questions* (Luke 2:46 NASB). When he was older, he threw out the corrupt money-changers in this outer court on Palm Sunday (Matthew 21:12 TLB).

JERUSALEM'S THREE TEMPLES:
1. **Solomon's Temple,** built by Phoenician artisans, was dedicated about 950 BC and remained in continual use for some four centuries until destroyed by Nebuchadnezzar and the Babylonians in 586 BC. *Note: Mark Twain says they saw the columns from Solomon's temple in Saint Peter's Cathedral in Rome.*

2. **Zerubbabel's Temple,** built three-quarters of a century after the destruction of Solomon's temple. The rebuilt structure was not nearly so grand as the first. Zerubbabel's temple housed treasure, including more than five thousand gold and silver vessels taken by the Babylonians in the first siege and later returned by King Cyrus of Persia. Over the next several centuries, Zerubbabel's temple also fell into disrepair.

3. **Herod's Temple,** the one Jesus knew, was rebuilt by Herod the Great in a project he began around 20 BC. The previous temple had been allowed to fall into disrepair. Herod claimed he was just improving the work of Zerubbabel. Herod's construction incorporated and restored what was left.

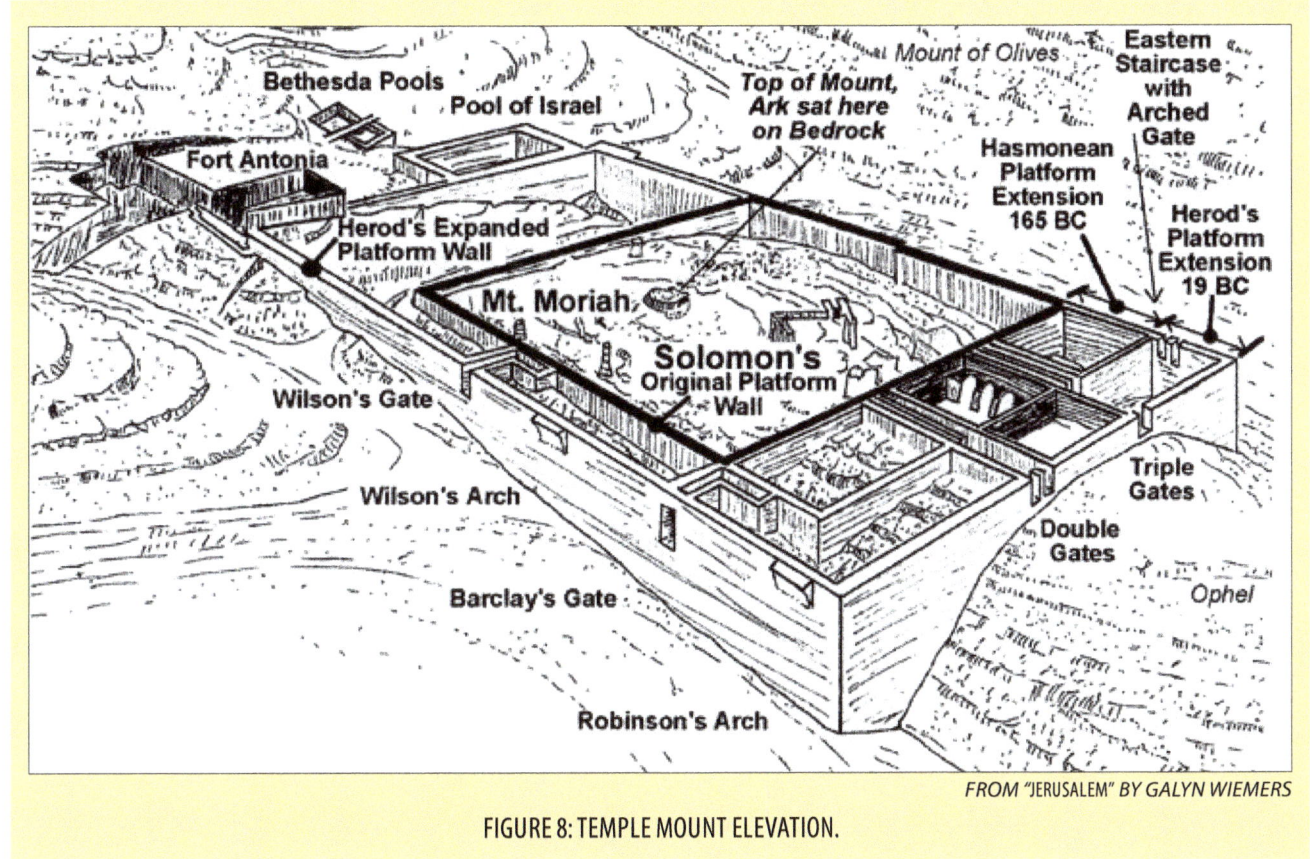

FIGURE 8: TEMPLE MOUNT ELEVATION.

LOCATING ROBINSON'S ARCH: Near the southern end of the Western Wall, we see remains of a monumental staircase supported by an unusually wide stone arch that once stood at the southwestern corner of Temple Mount as part of Herod's Temple construction. Called Robinson's Arch for the discovering archaeologist, this stone arch supported an overpass connecting the street at the foot of the Mount with the porch at the southern end. The portico housed law courts, moneychangers, and shops. The Romans destroyed the massive arch during the sacking of Jerusalem in AD 70.

Our guide showed us a picture of himself at this site in 1960 when this wall appears almost underground. Aaron is standing at ground level with his hand on the mantel that is part of Robinson's Arch, but that spot now extends at least twenty feet above excavations.

For many centuries, visitors had to present a certificate they had bathed in a *mikveh* baptismal before entering the temple. South of the monumental staircase researchers uncovered many ritual baths, used for Jewish purification. These *mikvehs* may have baptized some of the three thousand new Jewish believers on the Day of Pentecost, described in the New Testament book of Acts, chapter two.

ZERUBBABEL'S SECOND TEMPLE WAS BIGGER: After returning from Babylonia, the Jews completed a new structure, which became known as Zerubbabel's temple on the site of Solomon's. Traditional rabbinic sources state Zerubbabel's temple stood for hundreds of years. Who was he? Zerubbabel, an ancestor of Christ, was considered a Prince of Israel while they were in exile in Babylon.

178 *To Isreal with Love*

FIGURE 9: TEMPLE RECONSTRUCTION
Herod's temple reconstruction in the model city at Jerusalem's museum.

Then King Cyrus of Persia conquered Babylonia. He allowed the Israelites to return to their "promised land," a nine-hundred-mile hike. Josephus says the Jews carried back with them all the sacred vessels. Cyrus appointed Zerubbabel governor of the province. After being selected, his first project was erecting an altar, and rebuilding the temple. The foundation alone took two years. Four years later, in 515 BC, the second temple was completed and dedicated with great fanfare (Ezra 6:16 RSV).

Zerubbabel's temple with its gilded walls was bigger than Solomon's but far less magnificent. It was ready for consecration in the spring, twenty years after the return from captivity. Zerubbabel's Second Temple stood for more than four hundred years—but without the Ark, because they could not find it.

HEROD'S TEMPLE (Often called the second temple): About 20 BC, Rome appointed Herod as king of Judea. He started restoring and enlarging the remains of Zerubbabel's temple. Although Herod did not finish during his lifetime, this third structure became known as Herod's or the second temple. Jewish historian and writer Josephus described this structure as, *To approaching strangers, the temple appeared from a distance like a snow-clad mountain, for all that was not overlaid with gold was purest white.* Jesus visited Herod's temple many times while the building remained under construction. Many years after Jesus's death, builders completed the complex (about AD 64), and then Romans obliterated the building during the Jewish Revolt of AD 70.

Herod generally respected traditional Jewish observances in his public life. For instance, the Jews did not approve of human images on coins, so he minted coins without human images to be used in Jewish areas. He acknowledged the sanctity of the structure by employing only priests in the reconstruction. However, when Herod erected at the entrance a golden eagle, the symbol of Rome, his Jewish subjects were livid. Herod's errors in leadership eventually became one of the causes driving the Great Revolt of AD 70. To this day, traditional Jews pray three times a day for the temple's complete restoration.

THE DIASPORA SCATTERED THE JEWS: Our guide fills in the empty spaces of our knowledge of Jewish history, reminding us the year AD 70 changed everything.

When Jerusalem fell to Rome, the Diaspora, or scattering of the Jewish people, began. The Romans did not force the Jews out of all Judea in a single expulsion. At first, the Romans expelled them only from Jerusalem. Jews left the country slowly over centuries as conditions in Judea became too harsh. Palestine passed from one conqueror to another, and the Jews settled in other countries throughout the world. Although the term refers to the physical dispersal of Jews throughout the world, it also carries other connotations, because the Jews perceive a special relationship between the land of Israel and

FIGURE 10: WEEPING AND WAILING AT THE WALL.
A low fence divides the men from the women visiting the Kotel western wall.

themselves. Our guide feels this diaspora is the basis of the ongoing conflict in Israel. However, the Jewish people have been returning by the millions.

JERUSALEM AND THE TEMPLE DESTROYED: Roman conquerors destroyed Herod's temple in AD 70. It lay in complete ruin for many years, until Roman Emperor Hadrian built a pagan temple to Jupiter on the site. Later, Arabs conquered the area, removed the Roman structure, and constructed their mosque, the Dome of the Rock, over the threshing floor. Christianity became permanently separated from Judaism during the first century after Christ. The traditional view is Judaism existed before Christianity and that Christianity separated from Judaism sometime after the destruction of Herod's temple.

WEEPING AND WAILING AT THE WALL: The much-publicized *Kotel* (wailing wall) that supported Herod's temple's outer courtyard is the only piece of the fabled Jewish building still standing. The dazzling structure ornamented with gold, with high double walls and outer courts—long gone. When the Jews returned to this place, they would stand here and say their prayers, fervently crying out their loss to *Yahweh*, hence the name "wailing wall."

Separate areas designate where men and women may pray, as did the temple. Women go right, and men go left, separated by a low fence which has been criticized and may go away in time. This "wall of tears," still a very sacred and holy spot to the Jews, was not a part of the original building itself but an outer wall that circled the gentile wall around the inner sanctum, which enclosed the temple itself. One of four retaining walls supporting the immense platform on which the second temple rested, it became a place of prayer and yearning for Jews around the world. This remaining wall alone measures 105 feet high from foundation to peak and is 1,600 feet long, the length of more than five football fields.

WWW.GOISRAEL.COM
FIGURE 11: PRAYERS FOR PEACE.
We left our prayers for world peace and prosperity at the wall.

PRAYING FOR PEACE THROUGH CRACKS IN THE WALL: Not only tourists but also high-profile dignitaries visiting Israel from abroad come to the wall for inspiration. Millions of prayers written on tiny pieces of paper stuff cracks between the rocks, all around the wall. An unusual internet option is available for people unable to attend in person. "Window on the Wall," promises those unable to come in person may send a prayer to Jerusalem. A student will print and place the note in the wall. All prayers are collected from the wall twice a year for burial on the nearby Mount of Olives.

THE JOY OF A BAR MITZVAH CEREMONY: We felt privileged to see a special coming-of-age celebration the day we were near the wall. A priest circumcises every Jewish boy at eight days old, as a symbol of the covenant God made with Abraham. At the age of thirteen, his family presents him at bar mitzvah, to become a full member of the community. Often the boys come with all their family for this special occasion. We saw a young boy riding on his father's shoulders on their way into the worship area. A large group of people followed, all clapping and singing. Many others threw candy at the boy. Our guide says the candy is symbolic of wishing them to have a sweet life. The women make a clucking noise. The girl's ceremony is called *bat mitzvah*. Once a person is celebrated this way, they are old enough to understand and accept the Jewish commandments.

THE "MAN CAVE" AT THE END OF THE WALL: Only males are allowed to enter a large cave at the end of the western wall. Adult males take the boy, place a unique cap on his head, and place a specially decorated gown on him. They present him with a scroll printed with Jewish law and invite him to read to the group as a symbol of his coming of age. The ceremony is full of joy for all.

INSIDE THE DOME OF THE ROCK: We are ready for the most exciting revelation of all. We are on Temple Mount about to enter Dome of the Rock, now a Moslem Mosque. Our guide will not go with us. As an Orthodox Jew, he is forbidden by his faith to enter. Many Orthodox rabbis regard entry to the compound as a violation of Jewish law, because the precise location of the Holy of Holies, the sanctuary that could be entered only by the High Priest, is unknown.

The Muslin rule of who is allowed to go inside changes off and on. We were very fortunate to go when we did. Our guide tells us we can go in, but our bags, shoes, and cameras must remain outside the Mosque where he will guard them. *"Take off your shoes, you are standing on holy ground,"* he said. Mr. Aaron and other Orthodox Jews do not enter. Some rabbis believe modern archaeological evidence makes it possible to identify accessible areas of the Mount without violating Jewish law, but even those opinions forbid Jews from entering what Muslims call the Noble Sanctuary.

THE BEAUTY IS AWE-SOME! Beautiful ceramic tiles decorated with arabesques, inlaid with quota-tions from the *Koran* edge the outside walls. These tiles, laid during the reign of Suleiman the Magnificent (1520-1566), took seven years. Sixteen arches reclaimed from different churches in Jerusalem support the dome. In 1955 the government of Jordan replaced many tiles dislodged by heavy rain. Beautiful inlay and marble of incredible detail greet us, gold and silver, and tiny pieces of stained glass sparkle in the sunlight. Colorful rugs cover the floors. At the center is the gigantic rock, the threshing floor, that sacred rock of Abraham's intended sacrifice on Mount Moriah. This place where we stand with the Foundation Stone and its surroundings, is the holiest site in Judaism and Christianity. We are surprised to notice a few of the columns still marked with the sign of the cross. We stand amazed by the scene around us once inside the doors. The gilded dome rests on columns of porphyry and other tinted stones salvaged from the ruins of Roman Jerusalem. This place is sacred to Jews because they believe the rock was a part

FIGURE 12: DOME OF THE ROCK AND THE WESTERN WALL

AUTHOR'S PRIVATE COLLECTION

FIGURE 13: THE JOY OF A BAR MITZVAH CEREMONY
We watched a joyful bar mitzvah ceremony at the wall.

FIGURE 14: DOME OF THE ROCK

This magnificent octagonal structure of turquoise and gold, is covered with what appears to be marble, overlaid with various color tiles, and topped by that sparkling gilded cupola. This mosque is the holiest place the Muhammadan knows, outside of Mecca.

of the "Holy of Holies" altar in their temple, because they claim it as the historic stone "threshing floor" which King David bought from Araunah the Jebusite and because it was the base of their temple. We pause a moment to absorb the stunning beauty of the building. The exterior of this magnificent octagonal structure appears to be marble overlaid with various turquoise and gold colors, topped with a gilded cupola, a stunning sight. Scaffolding had kept the dome partially hidden during our first visit. King Hussein of Jordan financed overlaying the bronze-aluminum dome with eighteen-karat gold, a donation of eight-point-two million dollars with a total cost of more than thirty million dollars.

THE ROCK IS UNDER CONTROL OF MUSLIMS: This Mount Moriah bedrock protrusion is holy to them because of the connection with Abraham and his son, and because they believe this place is where Muhammed rode through the sky on his horse to pray at the rock and leaped skyward into heaven. Muslims refer to the Dome of the Rock as the "Mosque of Omar" because Muslims under the Caliph Omar in the year AD 636 built the magnificent dome over the rock. This incredibly beautiful structure is almost fourteen hundred years old. Each new group that conquered Jerusalem laid claim to the monument.

Recently a treasure of gold coins and a large medallion showing the symbol of the menorah was discovered at the base of the Temple Mount in the southern wall area. These items appear as from the time of the Persian occupation around AD 600. Persian control of the city did not last long. Archeologists speculate that Jewish officials may have stored the treasure to help the Jewish community survive or rebuild.

PINTEREST.COM

FIGURE 15: DOME CROSS-SECTION
A diagram of Dome of the Rock, from the gold-coated aluminum covering the wooden dome. Marble and mosaics decorate the exterior wall. You can see the location of the sacred stone with the mysterious "Well of Souls" cave below.

FINDING THE WELL OF SOULS: The threshing floor itself is about forty feet by fifty feet. A cave beneath the rock provided a drainage system for cleaning up Jewish sacrifices because so many butchered animals resulted in a tremendous amount of blood. We walked around the boulder, down steps bringing us inside and under the sacred stone to a natural cave, called the Well of Souls.

The Temple Mount itself is rife with a network of some forty-five cisterns, chambers, tunnels, and caves. This particular cave attracts many legends associated with Old Testament figures and incidents. In the movie *Raiders of the Lost Ark,* the intrepid Indiana Jones finds the Ark of the Covenant in the Well of Souls. However, in the Hollywood version, the site was moved from Jerusalem to the ancient Egyptian city of Tanis. The movie is an exciting fiction story—a nonfiction version would be even more so.

WHAT'S UNDER THE DOME? Some people believe the Ark of the Covenant is hidden somewhere under this sacred rock. One member of our group is well informed about the Ark and gave a talk one evening saying those in power will not allow searching because they fear finding the revered object might start a disastrous war.

Soon after the beginning of the twentieth century, a curious group of Englishmen managed to get under the great rock into the cave where they found a hidden cache of precious objects, as both Jewish folklore and Islamic legend suggest. However, Muslim officials discovered the Englishmen, and they had to flee for their lives. In the chamber, we did see a hole through which Muhammed reportedly ascended into Heaven. It did not look big enough for a body to go through, but perhaps only his spirit was released. At one point, a guard directs us to reach into a protected spot to feel a "footprint" left in the rock by Muhammed. I can't say I buy into the footprint theory.

THE MYSTERY OF THE ARK OF THE COVENANT: Described in Exodus 25:10–22 as a chest made of acacia wood overlaid with gold, the object held stone tablets of the agreement between God and Israel—or as we know them, the Ten Commandments. At the time of King Solomon, the Old Testament says the vessel contained only the two tablets. Other verses in Hebrews report the chest held Aaron's rod, a jar of manna, and the first Torah scroll written by Moses.

A solid gold mercy seat served as the lid or cover of the Ark. No one knows what the cherubim looked like, but artists usually depict them as angelic winged creatures. Above the mercy seat or lid between two hovering cherubim, they believed God could communicate with His people (Exodus 25:22 NLT). The sacred chest always traveled with the Israelites in the desert. Some students speculate this arrangement of wings over the box might operate as a primitive radio conductor.

In early Old Testament days, the object stayed in a tabernacle in the desert. When King David set up a new church during his reign, he danced as he led the procession bringing the special coffer to the tabernacle. The form of the tabernacle became the pattern for the temple later built by Solomon. During construction, Solomon ordered a particular inner room, called the Holy of Holies, to receive and house it (1 Kings 6:19 NLT).

The Book of Deuteronomy describes it as a simple wooden container with no mention of ornaments or gold. Similarly, the *Koran* refers to it as a wooden box with holy relics inside.

When priests carried the talisman into the bed of the Jordan, they said the river separated, opening a pathway for the group to cross (Joshua 3:15-16 NLT). The riverbed grew dry as soon as the feet of the priests touched its waters and the bed remained dry until they left the river. So, the Jewish people have always revered this object.

When the priests dedicated Solomon's Temple, and later Herod's, the special chest containing the original tablets of the Ten Commandments was placed in a particular place (1 Kings 8:6-9 NLT). That spot is where we are standing now, but I can look all around and see for myself, the Ark is not here. Where is it? That mystery has been eluding researchers for centuries.

REMINDERS OF THE ARK'S HISTORY AND TRAVELS: Seven priests sounding seven trumpets of rams' horns (the *shofar*) carried the revered Ark in a seven-day procession around the wall of Jericho and took the city with a shout. During the days of Samson and Delilah, about 1050 BC, the Philistines routed the Israelite army and carried off the sacred chest as spoils of war (1 Samuel 4:10-11 RSV). The Jewish relic must have brought them bad luck because the Philistines soon returned the talisman.

As said earlier, Solomon placed the chest in his temple. However, in 597 BC, Babylonians destroyed both Jerusalem and the temple.

FIGURE 16: ARTIST'S CONCEPT OF ARK OF THE COVENANT

The Old Testament mentions the Ark for the last time when King Josiah instructed the Levites to return it to the temple (2 Chronicles 35:3 RSV). When Rome conquered Jerusalem in AD 70, they took all the treasures from the temple, and they carried these items in their victory procession to Rome, where they displayed them in the imperial palace as we learned earlier. The sculpture on the Victory Arch of Titus in Rome does not show a chest with the other objects carried in that parade. No one knows for sure where those other holy objects shown in the sculpture are today.

Most of the Jewish inhabitants had been killed or sold as slaves. To keep the remaining residents from rebuilding, Emperor Titus stationed a garrison of eight hundred Roman soldiers on the ground.

According to 2Maccabees 2:4-10, the prophet Jeremiah, "being warned of God," took the tabernacle, the altar of incense, and the Ark, and buried them in a cave on Mount Nebo. Most interested parties believe the sacred vessel is hidden somewhere under the temple. *Note: Just for the record, we did not see it anywhere in, around, or under the rock floor, if it is indeed there.*

RON WYATT, ADVENTURER, AND SEEKER: An adventurer and explorer named Ron Wyatt who died in 1999, spent his entire life researching and trying to find the talisman. He claimed to have found the Ark in an underground cave in Jerusalem. Wyatt said he ran DNA on the blood he found there, which showed no paternal chromosomes except for one Y chromosome. Could he have seen the blood of Jesus verifying he had only one earthly parent?

After a lifetime of study, Ron Wyatt's conclusions:

- Someone hid the chest in a cave between the time Josiah took the object to Solomon's Temple, and thirty-five years later, when the Romans destroyed the temple.

- The revered vessel was placed somewhere between the confines of the city wall of Jerusalem and the Babylonian siege wall. The entire city and temple were destroyed in 586 BC by the Babylonians, so the box could only escape destruction or captivity in one of two ways:

    a) by not being anywhere inside the city, or

    b) by being carried to Babylon.

- Based on information describing which religious items went and what returned, the Ark did not go to Babylon, so the chest remained here.

- Most likely someone hid the objects when the Babylonian siege wall still surrounded Jerusalem; and

- Wyatt quotes from the apocryphal book of 2Maccabees: *Jeremiah found a cave-dwelling; he carried the tent, the ark, and the incense altar into it, then blocked the entrance.*

THE SECRET HOLLOWS OF JERUSALEM: Jerusalem area is honeycombed with caves. Ron Wyatt believed the Ark to be hidden outside the ancient city wall but within the siege wall. So, he is specifying a cave just outside the city wall of Jerusalem. For instance, "Zedekiah's Cave," also known as Solomon's Quarry, is located beneath the Muslim section of the city, extending seven-hundred-fifty feet into Mount Moriah. During several visits to the chamber, Wyatt tried to explore the contents thoroughly. He determined this cave was three hundred twenty feet wide at the maximum point and average height about fifty feet. Zedekiah's cave was a stone quarry, but Wyatt could not determine at what point the quarry was in use.

The first item he listed finding is the Ark. He said the tablets of stone (the Ten Commandments) were still inside under the mercy seat lid. Wyatt said he saw a small open cubicle containing the book of Law, presumably the one written by Moses. Wyatt lists other found items, but he did not eyeball the book of Genesis. He saw only Exodus, Leviticus, Numbers, and Deuteronomy. The thing Wyatt said amazed him most was that these sacred scrolls, written on animal skins, were in perfect condition.

After paying all expenses over his years of work and research, Wyatt talked to authorities about his discoveries. He said the officials did not encourage or discourage him. He said they felt such a discovery announcement would "most likely set off a bloody clash between the Arabs, Muslims, and those who would want to immediately destroy the mosque on the temple mount to rebuild the temple." They felt it best not to release any of the information.

Wyatt permanently sealed the entry after his last visit to the chamber. He said because of the honeycomb of tunnels, no one would be able to find the correct passage without him. The blocked entry looked like a natural stone wall. He said he learned many lessons over the years, sometimes the hard way. One lesson he learned was to be very careful with whom he shared his information.

Do I believe Wyatt's story, that these sacred relics hide in a cave under the Temple Mount? Do you? Scientists, historians, biblical scholars, and leaders in his own Seventh-day Adventist Church dismissed Ron Wyatt's claims, but his work continues to have a large following. The cave Ron Wyatt explored is directly under "Golgotha" hill. He believed the Garden Tomb was the true crypt that held the body of Christ. Ron Wyatt died a few years ago, but his family maintains a website where you can read about his discoveries: http://ronwyatt.com

WHAT THE GARDEN TOMB ASSOCIATION SAYS: If you request information from the Garden Tomb Association of Jerusalem, they send a prepared letter. "*The Council of the Garden Tomb Association (London) refutes the claim of Mr. Wyatt to have discovered the ark of the covenant or any other biblical artifacts within the boundaries of the area known as the Garden Tomb in Jerusalem. Though Mr. Wyatt was allowed to dig within this privately-owned garden on several occasions (the last time being the summer of 1991), staff members of the Association observed his progress and entered his excavated shaft. As far as we are aware, nothing was ever discovered to support his claims, nor have we seen any evidence of biblical artifacts or temple treasures. Zedekiah's Cave and Solomon's Quarry are not part of the Garden Tomb property.*"

AUTHOR'S PRIVATE COLLECTION

FIGURE 17: THE SACRED ROCK
The foundation stone on Mount Moriah under the golden dome. Some authorities believe the square indentation at lower right became the usual resting place for the Ark.

In the previously mentioned adventure film, *Raiders of the Lost Ark*, Indiana Jones confronts a group of Nazis searching for the holy item, which Adolf Hitler believes will make his army invincible. In the movie, Indiana Jones finds the Ark. He takes it to officials in Washington, DC, where Army Intelligence agents inform the adventurer, they have placed the chest in a safe place for study. They store the object in a giant government warehouse among countless similar crates.

"*Putting it anonymously on a shelf and forgetting it,*" is what happened to Ron Wyatt's discovery. Ronald Eldon Wyatt, born in 1933, died of cancer on August 4, 1999, in Baptist Hospital, Memphis,

Tennessee. His lifetime of research and work to locate the hiding place for the Ark of the Covenant remains inconclusive, an intriguing mystery. His detractors are many, but on his death bed, Wyatt made a sworn confession every word was true.

ZEDEKIAH'S CAVE a.k.a. SOLOMON'S QUARRIES: Amazingly, we visited this five-acre cave, the limestone quarry near Damascus Gate, where Ron Wyatt claimed to have found the holy chest. At the time, we had not heard of Ron Wyatt and had no hint that someone believed the Ark was hiding there. This ancient quarry near the Temple Mount under the old city of Jerusalem is, as Wyatt said, an enormous labyrinth of caves. This place may be where Solomon's slaves quarried the enormous rock slabs to build the first temple, and hundreds of years later, Herod brought out blocks for the temple's renovation, including the western wall.

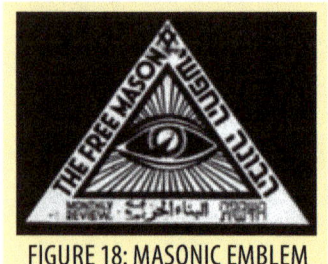

FIGURE 18: MASONIC EMBLEM

MASONIC LODGE SECRETS: This cave has special meaning for Freemasons in general and Mark Master Masons and the Royal Arch group, in particular. They believe King Solomon to be the founder of the order and its first grandmaster. The cave has continued to be used for the ceremony of Mark Master Mason's degree since the British Mandate, except while under control of Jordan's Arab Legions between 1948 and 1968. The Supreme Grand Royal Arch Chapter of the State of Israel conducted a ceremony in the cave in the spring of 1969 and continues every year since. Large stones are quarried from the cave and sent to various countries to serve as cornerstones for new Masonic lodges.

HOW BIG IS SOLOMON'S QUARRY? This vast cavern under the Old City's Muslim Quarter spans five city blocks. Used for a time as a quarry, traditional beliefs have also attributed it to being an escape route, a burial ground and now, perhaps also a hiding place for the biblical Ark. Over the years, the quarry has been known by many different names. We saw the chiseled grooves in the stone walls, several partially quarried blocks, and mounds of stone chips and slabs removed during the quarrying process. The cave stretches from under Jeremiah's Grotto and the Garden Tomb to the walls of the Old City. In our opinion, the cave is so big an entire city could almost be housed inside. One reference said the cave led to an underground route all the way to the plains of Jericho. After having been there, we believe that it is possible.

KNIGHTS TEMPLAR AND THEIR STABLES: (Refer to Day One, Queen Melisende and the Crusaders.) The Templars were initially established as militia to defend pilgrims on their route to the holy land. The Roman Catholic Church officially endorsed them in AD 1129 and permitted them to make Solomon's Temple their headquarters. In their distinctive white mantles with a red cross, Knights Templar were among the most skilled fighting units of the crusades. They were wealthy as well as powerful and existed for almost two centuries during the Middle Ages. The Templars established themselves in Jerusalem because the site represented the earthly power of King Solomon, and the remnants of the temple contained big secrets. The Crusaders used a single gate on the south wall to access the

FIGURE 19: KING SOLOMON'S MINES
Down, down, down – the entrance to Solomon's Quarry.

caverns below the Temple Mount, also called Solomon's Stables, where they kept their horses. The Templars housed in the temple for the next seventy years.

THE TURKS TAKE OVER: German Emperor Frederick I, known as "Red Beard," led the third crusade, with three religious-military orders—the Knights of St. John {Hospitallers}, the Knights Templar, and the Teutonic Knights; Philip Augustus, King of France; and King Richard the Lion-Hearted of England. Their crusade failed. In 1187 Saladin shocked the western world when he captured Jerusalem with a mighty Turkish army. A historian described Saladin as "a short man, with a roundish face, a trim black beard, and keen, alert black eyes." The gate to the stables was blocked shut by Saladin as the Muslims took over. Although unable to recapture the holy city, Richard, the only one of the three kings to continue the campaign, finally obtained a three-year treaty in which Saladin agreed to permit Christians to visit the Holy Sepulchre without being disturbed. Support for the Templars Order faded when the holy land was lost.

KING SOLOMON'S MINES: How did those stonemasons in Solomon's day, early Iron Age, cut and shape these huge building stones? How did they even get them out of this underground cave? Our guide explained the workers grooved the stone, then placed a wood piece in the groove and wet the wood to expand, repeating until they created a crack in the stone. Just imagine the noise.

The book of Kings describes it this way. *King Solomon had a labor force of thirty thousand men. He sent ten thousand at a time to work cutting cedar for a month in Lebanon.* The cedar trees of Lebanon were legendary for their excellent timber. *At the end of the month, the crew would rotate to Jerusalem to work on building the temple for two months before returning to Lebanon.*

Also, he hired seventy thousand who "carried burdens" and eighty thousand who quarried stone, plus more than three thousand supervisors. Adoniram was his superintendent in charge of the labor force. 1 Kings 5:13 says, *And the king commanded them to quarry large stones, costly stones, and hewn stones, to lay the foundation of Solomon's builders, Hiram's builders, and the Gebalites quarried them; and they prepared timber and stones to build the temple.*

AUTHOR'S PRIVATE COLLECTION

FIGURE 20: INSIDE THE MINE
Tourists observe where slabs of stone were carved out of the cave.

So, who is Hiram?

King Solomon sent to Tyre and brought Hiram, whose mother was a widow from the tribe of Naphtali and whose father was a man of Tyre and a craftsman in bronze. Hiram was highly skilled and experienced in all kinds of bronze work. He came to King Solomon and did all the work assigned to him. Hiram was extremely skillful and talented in any work in bronze, and he came to do all the metalwork for King Solomon, (1 Kings 7:13-1 NIV). Hiram also built the huge bronze basin supported by twelve bronze oxen pictured in chapter seven (1Kings 7:15 NLT).

After all that effort the Babylonians destroyed the glorious temple in just a few hundred years. What a disappointment.

AUTHOR'S PRIVATE COLLECTION

FIGURE 21: WINDOW FLOWER BOX
The Jewish Quarter of Jerusalem has many beautiful gardens and historic buildings. The quarter has been rebuilt since being recaptured by Israeli paratroopers in the 1967 Six-Day War.

And all the articles from the house of God, great and small, the treasures of the house of the Lord, and the treasures of the king and of his leaders, all these he took to Babylon. Then they burned the house of God, broke down Jerusalem's protective wall, burned all its palaces, and destroyed all precious possessions, (2 Chronicles 36:18–19 NLV)

KING ZEDEKIAH'S END AT THE CAVE: The Israel Tourism Department says Zedekiah, Jerusalem's last biblical king, a puppet deposed during the final siege on the city, attempted to flee Jerusalem to Jericho through this cave. He was captured and brought before King Nebuchadnezzar, where they killed his sons in front of him, and put out his eyes in one of the old Testament's most grisly scenes. The website www.JewishHistory.org describes King Zedekiah this way, *"Even though he did wrong things, he was a very idealistic, moral, and ultimately righteous person. Nebuchadnezzar killed the sons and then blinded Zedekiah. The last thing the Judaean king ever saw with his eyes was the terrible, horrendous image of his sons being executed (2 Kings 25:7 NIV).*

MOVING FROM THE CAVE TO THE JEWISH QUARTER: From the mosque in the Dome of the Rock, we walk to the Jewish Quarter for a visit to the recently restored Cardo, a covered marketplace from Jesus's time. A double-columned main thoroughfare traversing many Roman cities from north to south, this one starts at Damascus Gate in the north, crossing southward to the Zion Gate.

Jerusalem's main street from fifteen hundred years ago is today a fascinating blend of history and modern shopping, featuring an open central passageway for use by carriages and animals, with portico footpaths on each side. In another section, pillars separate the open section near the main square in the Jewish quarter. Part of the Cardo shows how stalls and shops would have looked in Roman times. Mr. Aaron tells us it is possible today to stroll through the Cardo in the same manner as did Jerusalem's residents in the sixth-century.

GARDENS IN THE JEWISH QUARTER: Entering through the Jaffa Gate and traveling to David Street places the Christian quarter on the left. On the right, as you continue down David Street, you'll enter the Armenian section. To the left of Jews Street is the Muslim area, and to the right is the Jewish quarter. During the nineteen years of Jordanian rule after the 1948 War, they demolished most of the Jewish buildings. However, since the 1967 Six-Day War, the quarter is fresh and new, completely rebuilt.

When Roman Emperor Hadrian came to rebuild Jerusalem in AD 130, he had the Tenth Legion set up their camp on land now the Jewish quarter. He changed the name of the city to *Aelia Capitolina* and dedicated it to the pagan god Jupiter. The Romans allowed Christians to stay but forbid any Jew ever to set foot in the city again. Hadrian didn't care for either ethnic group, so to encourage both Jews and Christians to leave, he changed the name of the province of Judea to Palestine, a derivative of the Greek word for Philistines, particularly distasteful to Jewish people. Above the eastern entrance gate, you can still see a fragmentary inscription in Latin, *"... by the decree of the decurions of Aelia Capitolina."*

EXPLORING THE JEWISH QUARTER: The Jewish Quarter incorporates many holy and historical sites and is an excellent starting point for any Jerusalem tour. Interestingly the Herodian quarter is located **inside** the Jewish quarter, along with the western wall. The Herodian quarter comprises only six houses built close together on a hillside facing the Temple Mount, attesting to their owners' wealth. The archeological discoveries come mainly from the cellars of these six remaining two-story houses, formerly the homes of the Jerusalem aristocracy and priesthood.

We toured the Burnt House, destroyed by Romans in the first century. You can almost smell the smoke two thousand years later. Household utensils and pottery remain untouched by fire, and you find them displayed along with a carefully constructed scale model of the original structure. Old wine jugs stack in the wine cellar, and beautiful mosaic tiles still carpet the floor in places.

FIGURE 22: THE GIHON SPRING
Buy a ticket to Hezekiah's Tunnel at the entrance to the Gihon Spring in the City of David.

THE LIFE-SAVING GIHON SPRING: The word Gihon means "bursting forth" because the spring waters sometimes burst unexpectedly with energy and flow more rapidly for a time. Centuries earlier at the base of the stairs in this same Gihon Spring, Nathan the prophet and Zadok the priest crowned Solomon as king of Israel. *There Zadok the priest took the horn of oil from the tent, and anointed Solomon. Then they blew the trumpet and all the people said, Long live King Solomon!* (1 Kings 1:38-39 RSV).

Gihon Spring provided water for the city of David, but it was outside the safety of city gates. In the eighth-century before Christ, King Hezekiah built a tunnel aqueduct allowing his people access to water in relative safety. Close to the old city wall there once was a "water gate" where people could go down into the spring of Gihon to get pure water. The spring is just outside the gate. Two teams dug this amazing tunnel, one team starting at each end, carving through rock the length of six football fields with twists and turns. The tunnel rats met in the middle, digging with picks from opposite ends of the tunnel with no modern communication or electronic tools to guide them. An inscription commemorates this dramatic moment. The plaque is now on display in the Istanbul Archeological Museum.

WHO WAS KING HEZEKIAH? He built a wall to enclose the western part of Jerusalem including the Pools of Siloam, in preparation for Judah/ Judea's rebellion against Assyria. We did not understand the importance of Hezekiah's wall until we returned five years later to climb and crawl through Hezekiah's

FIGURE 23: HEZEKIAH'S TUNNEL
We crawled through the dark, wet, narrow maze of Hezekiah's Tunnel.

Tunnel. One of the greatest kings of ancient Israel, Hezekiah directed this tunnel chiseled through almost two-thousand feet of solid rock some twenty-five hundred years ago for a very good reason (2 Chronicles 32:2–4).

HEZEKIAH'S TUNNEL AND THE POOL OF SILOAM: Our guide decided we should each experience sloshing through Hezekiah's tunnel to qualify as pilgrims. We had no warning of what lay ahead in one of the most unforgettable events we experienced in all of Israel. We walked through the door at Gihon Spring and stepped down a very steep stone stairway. The rock ceiling is so low we must stoop to enter the tunnel. That small opening should have been our first red flag. We got a surprise when we stepped down off the last step … into … water! We should not have been surprised; after all the name of the place is Gihon Spring, and that usually means water is coming in.

We soon learn it is very dark and sometimes even windy in the tunnel. With our ticket receipt, we each received an eight-inch lighted candle (another hint). Wind drafts often blew out our candle, and we had to locate someone in the dark to re-light our wick from their flame.

Most of the way, my shoulders could touch on both sides, which is a little uncomfortable for near-claustrophobics like me. Sometimes the ceiling dropped so low we had to crouch down to walk, and other times it seemed fifteen-foot high. We never knew what to expect around the next dark corner as the tunnel twisted and turned. The floor was not smooth. There were sharp edges and holes that we stumbled over in my tennis shoes. I felt sorry for Susan, who left her shoes on the bus.

IT IS VERY WET IN HEZEKIAH'S TUNNEL! Sometimes we sloshed through ankle-deep water and occasionally into a hole where water reached to our knees. Moisture sometimes dropped on our heads. We found ourselves at the back of our group in line, with more groups following us so we could not turn around and go back the way we came. Thankful not to be alone in this dark, wet, narrow passageway, we continued trudging through to find the way out. We often needed to re-light our candles. We wandered in the wilderness of Hezekiah's Tunnel some ninety-five minutes and were the last of our group to make it out. We all earned our T-shirts that said, "I made it through Hezekiah's tunnel!" *Tip: Take a small flashlight with you.*

We will never forget that experience in Hezekiah's Tunnel. When we read or hear something about Hezekiah, we will know about whom they are speaking. At the end of the tunnel, Gihon Spring empties into the pool of Siloam, where Jesus healed a blind man by smearing mud on the man's eyes. Jesus told the man to wash his face in the Siloam pool. Once the man did that, he could see again.

Our trip through Hezekiah's Tunnel parallels life. You can't go back when you get scared, or the going gets rough, you have to push on through. Sometimes you need to allow other travelers on your life's journey to re-light your candle. Siloam pool is located on the southern slope of the city of David and is just outside the Old City walls. Archaeologists discovered a much larger pool of Siloam recently. *Tip: Anyone with a walking disability probably should not try the tunnel.*

OPHEL ARCHAEOLOGICAL PARK: Located near the western wall plaza at the foot of Temple Mount, the Ophel Park features archaeological finds spanning more than two thousand years. The name *Ophel* in Hebrew means "to climb" or "ascend," and this was the way up to the complex. Highlights of this dig include the remains of dwellings from the Bronze Age, stairs to the second temple, a partial Byzantine residence, and a series of monumental buildings that archaeologists identify as royal palaces from the early Islamic period. The Ophel, fully opened in 2011, is located below the southern wall between the City of David and Temple Mount. Aaron described one stone weighing four hundred tons. Most weigh at least one hundred ton, and the wall of rock in Jesus's day was more than 120 feet tall. How did they do it? No one knows. As we climb up, down, and around the ruins, our guide moves a barrier and urges us to continue clambering around those massive walls.

BEWARE OF GREEKS AND HASMONEANS: Following Alexander the Great's conquest of much of the ancient world, this place came under Greek control. At least a hundred fifty years before the birth of Christ, the troops of Antiochus IV, a Greek king, sacked Jerusalem and removed sacred objects from the Jerusalem temple again. They took the golden altar, the candlestick of light, and all the vessels thereof, but there is no mention of the Ark (1 Maccabees 1:20–25). During Greek rule Judaism was effectively outlawed, the temple in Jerusalem looted, and all religious services stopped. The Greeks wanted the Jews to dress, eat, and think like them. They tried to root out all Jewish beliefs.

SADDUCEES AND PHARISEES: Next came the Hasmoneans, under the leadership of Simon Maccabaeus, when two conflicting religious factions, the Sadducees and the Pharisees, took over Jerusalem. The **Sadducees,** members of the upper strata of Jerusalem society, including most of the priestly families, focused on rituals and the temple orders. By contrast, more educated sages led the **Pharisees**. Their primary interest lay with Torah law and its practical application in daily life. Hasmoneans ruled for close to a century. The website www.JewishHistory.org says the Hasmonean era is among the most glorious in Jewish history, yet it also contained self-destructive seeds that almost destroyed everything.

HERE COME THE ROMANS AGAIN: The Hasmonean era came to an end, brought to submission under Roman client Herod the Great around 37 BC. The installation of Herod as King of Israel, even though he was only a puppet controlled by Rome, ended the Hasmonean dynasty. The legacy of the powerful Hasmoneans was so great, however, that Herod decided to marry a Hasmonean princess, Mariamne I, to strengthen his power and increase support for his reign. *Note: He murdered her later.*

TO THE VICTOR GO THE SPOILS: (Skipping forward about two thousand years.) Following the First Arab-Israeli War of 1948–1949, this land was divided into three parts: The State of Israel, the West Bank (of the Jordan River) and the Gaza Strip. *Note: See the Greenline map on page 89.* Israel held the western part of Jerusalem while Jordan captured East Jerusalem, including the Old City. The Jordanians immediately expelled all Jewish residents of the Jewish Quarter, destroyed more than fifty synagogues, and desecrated the ancient Jewish cemetery on Mount of Olives by using the tombstones for construction and paving roads. For almost twenty years, Jews were not allowed at the Wall, and neither Muslims nor Christians could visit the shrines of their faiths across the armistice line. The Old City remained under Jordanian control until 1967, which almost wiped out the Jewish quarter during these eighteen years.

THE SIX-DAY WAR EVERYTHING CHANGES AGAIN: Israel captured the West Bank in 1967 and eventually incorporated East Jerusalem and surroundings into the municipality of Jerusalem. Under **Israeli** rule, all religions had access to their holy sites, except that area controlled by Muslims, namely the Temple Mount and Muslim sacred sites.

- The rules change all the time. On our first visit to Israel, we were not allowed at the Dome. When we came to Jerusalem in 1998, as gentiles, we were permitted to tour inside the Dome, but that is no longer allowed.
- Israel captured the Gaza Strip from Egypt in 1967, but Israel pulled out troops and settlers in 2005, and soon the strip came under the control of Palestinians.
- Sinai, to the south of Gaza, returned to Egypt after the 1979 peace accord.
- Up north, in 1981, Israel annexed the Golan Heights, which they captured from Syria. The annexation is not internationally recognized.

- West Bank and East Jerusalem, captured from Jordan in 1967, continue to be controlled by Israel, but support of settlements on occupied land has complicated peace negotiations.
- In 1980, Israel took control of the entire city and officially proclaimed Jerusalem the capital of Israel. The Arabs resent this action, and many nations still refuse to recognize Israel's claim to sovereignty.
- Israel and Jordan signed a peace pact in 1994.
- For almost half a century, a bewildering array of organizations, programs, strategies, and leaders have struggled for control of this place.

SO MUCH TO LEARN, SO LITTLE TIME: There is so much to learn, such massive information assaults our ears constantly, all this knowledge is a little overwhelming. Others in the group agree only in years to come will we be able to sit down with books and notes to sort things out, and only on additional trips can we begin to comprehend it all. At the moment, the mission seems impossible. By studying this book before you go, perhaps the information will be more easily assimilated.

RIDING A CAMEL AND GETTING KISSED: At one stop, several of us tried a ride on a "Ship of the Desert." Once we mastered the climb aboard, this camel was so gentle that even when chased by a yapping dog, he continued his rocking, rolling meander down the street. The gait was not a trot, a gallop, or a canter, and certainly not at all like riding a horse. The ride was more like straddling a loose-wheeled roller coaster. We were drawn by that rare novelty, which gave us a fresh new exhilarating sensation.

A dark-skinned turbaned animal trainer led the hump-backed beast down the street, around the corner, and back to the starting line where the old camel would then obediently kneel for an easy dismount. Unexpectedly, when our friend Jeanna crawled off, the awkward but lovable animal gave Jeanna a big kiss.

A visit to Israel would not be complete without riding a camel. All the "camels" in the Holy Land are dromedaries. The dromedary or one-humped camel is mentioned in the Bible many times. Bedouins joke about a woman's value based on the price of camels, and camel racing is a very popular

AUTHOR'S PRIVATE COLLECTION
FIGURE 24: A CAMEL AND A PRETTY GIRL

FIGURE 25: THE MODEL CITY
A popular tourist destination at the Israel museum shows Jerusalem as it was in AD 66.

sport in some parts. Like floating in the Dead Sea, the memory of riding a camel is like a souvenir or relic you can haul out of the country to keep forever.

JERUSALEM'S AMAZING MODEL CITY: On the campus of the Israel Museum is an extensive outdoor second temple model of Jerusalem in AD 66, before destruction by the Romans. This model, formerly at the Holyland Hotel, moved to the Israel Museum's sculpture garden next to the Shrine of the Book. The move alone cost three and a half million dollars. Covering almost one full acre, the model scale 1:50 is complete down to the most minute detail, using the same building materials employed in the year AD 70.

Initially built in 1966, Holyland Hotel owner Hans Kroch dedicated the model in memory of his son Jacob who fell in Israel's War of Independence. Kroch argued that Israel, in general, and Jerusalem lacked a historical monument that could compare with the antiquities of Athens and Rome. He commissioned a professor of archaeology at the Hebrew University, *Avi-Yonah*, to create the model and provide architectural design.

The model of Solomon's Temple is most impressive. It reveals the sanctuary, the court of women, and the court of gentiles. Although a caste lower than men, the Jewish women were considered a cut above gentile women. *Note: There's that word gentile again.*

Now a cultural landmark, the model remains a popular and educational tourist attraction. Visitors may walk around the outdoor model, but there is no protection from sun or rain. On the day of our visit, the usual blazing ball of fire burned out our enjoyment much too soon.

*Tip: *Tip: Don't miss seeing the model city that puts all the ancient puzzle pieces together, but choose a moderate day to visit this outdoor exhibit.

CELEBRATING ISRAEL'S INDEPENDENCE DAY: In Jerusalem, the Israelis are celebrating Independence Day with dancing in the street, music, and fireworks. Israel is a young country, and the citizens feel joy at their independence. Like a phoenix, Jerusalem has risen from the dust and ashes after being conquered thirty-six times. Destroyed and rebuilt ten times, the city lives on.

Political life in this democracy carries on in the imposing Knesset building. We noticed a patent lack of deference to authority, for every Israeli appears to believe he could run the country better himself. However, the citizens seem unanimous in their respect for the mayor.

COMMAND PERFORMANCE: One night, each hotel guest received a special invitation to hear the President of Israel speak at the hotel. Our bunch excitedly made plans to attend. However, he couldn't come at the last minute, so hotel personnel quietly passed the word that the beloved mayor of Jerusalem and his wife would preside. That was even bet-ter! Then he didn't show up either, and they did not tell us. *Oy Vey!*

AUTHOR'S PRIVATE COLLECTION

FIGURE 26: ISRAEL CELEBRATES INDEPENDENCE
A handsome Israeli man and a distinguished-looking couple gave a short speech and cut the cake.

ENJOYING SPEECHES AND EATING CAKE: A decorated cake arrived with lots of fanfare and excitement, and the lobby filled with observers clapping and cheering. After a slight delay, a handsome Israeli man we assumed to be a government official standing in for the President, and a distinguished-looking couple, no doubt Mr. and Mrs. Mayor, performed the honors.

They cut the cake while speaking Arabic—or some foreign language.

I snapped many photos of the dignitaries before we learned the mayor and his wife hadn't shown up either. Our "surrogate officials," actually the hotel manager and an elderly couple of guests, enjoyed the event. We felt a little foolish and decided to make a joke of it.

We befriended a dignified couple from Australia and let them in on the secret. Then we introduced them as the mayor and his wife to several persons in our group. Before finally confessing to the hoax, we photographed our stand-in mayor and his wife with our group. Everyone had a good laugh.

ENJOY AN ADVENTURE IN THE OLD CITY: Several of us forged out on our own to ride the city bus downtown late at night for the Israeli Independence Day celebration. To our surprise, we were able to reach the street party by following our city maps and riding city buses. We bragged about not needing to ask for directions. We joined Israelis dancing in the street to celebrate their independence. Many of the participants held little plastic hammers that made a squeaking noise as the revelers tapped others on the head with lots of laughter and singing. The exuberant revelers sprayed everyone with colored confetti, and one youngster decorated us effusively with the pink stuff.

No one took offense. We felt perfectly safe and never had a moment's concern.

We walked back to the hotel around midnight, exhausted but full of joy and proud to have been a part of a fantastic evening, one we'll never forget.

AUTHOR'S PRIVATE COLLECTION

FIGURE 27: BAGEL CART
A cart welcomed us at Damascus Gate filled with Jerusalem's famous bagels.

As we leave the old city through Damascus Gate, cart vendors greet us with the smell of fresh hot bagels topped with sesame seeds. Suddenly aware we are hungry we purchase a bag of the inexpensive stuff and break bread together. The dough is crusty on the outside, soft and flavorful inside. Thinking of it, remembering the taste months and even years later, still makes us drool. Boiled-and-baked bagels may be traditionally associated with New York Jews, but Israel is awash in Jerusalem Bagels. These have a ring-shape reminiscent of their American cousins but are larger, thinner, more rectangular. They are nearly always covered in sesame seeds and never boiled. *Tip: Jerusalem is famous for their delicious bagels.*

What a day to remember forever!

NINE

DAY OF TRIAL

Tuesday: Last Supper, Tomb of Kings, Emperor Constantine and Queen Helena, Holy Relics, Church of Sepulchre, Golgotha and the Garden Tomb

DAY NINE: Today, we visited the church of Saint Anne. This twelfth-century Crusader church in the Muslim Quarter remains near the grotto believed for centuries to be the birthplace of Mary, mother of Jesus. An ancient tradition, recorded in the Apocryphal Gospel of James dating around AD 150 places the house of Mary's parents, Anne and Joachim, close to the Temple area. This would be the traditional site of the home of Jesus's grandparents. However, we do not recall ever hearing the names of Mary's parents before and do not find any confirmation in the New Testament. Our group toured inside Saint Anne's and sang "Amazing Grace," harmonizing beautifully. That was undoubtedly amazing. Up to this point, we hadn't even been able to carry the tune of "Happy Birthday"! After the Muslim conquest, this Romanesque structure became an Islamic law school, later abandoned. France undertook extensive restoration, returning Saint Anne's to its present appearance.

FIGURE 1: CHURCH OF ST. ANNE
The crusader-era church of Saint Anne, marks the believed site of the home of the Virgin Mary's parents.

WASHING IN THE POOL OF BETHESDA: Next to the church, we walk beside a sizeable confusing dig with strange-looking piles of rocks in an excavation area for the pool of Bethesda, where Christ healed a sick man (John 5:1-9). The rocks did not make much sense until we saw the reconstruction at the scale example at the model city. The pool, actually a reservoir, is beyond Lion's Gate and near the Antonia fortress. The word *Bethesda* means "house of mercy." A nearby spring supplied water. With no piped faucets during biblical times, pools were public facilities where they stored water for later use. The pools were not for swimming. Bethesda had five porches. A significant number of people used to lie on the porches; blind and lame people. They believed an angel might stir the water. If they could be first to climb into the pool, the water would heal them. A man there had been lame for thirty-eight years. Jesus healed him by merely saying, "*Take up your bed and walk.*" And so, he did.

FIGURE 2: SEVERED HEAD
Beheading of John the Baptist, with Antipas and Herodias pictured in an ancient church window in Alsace, France.

GOING THROUGH THE EYE OF THE NEEDLE: Exiting the pool of Bethesda, we walked through an "eye of the needle" opening in Lion's Gate out of the temple area. "*It is easier for a camel to go through the eye of a needle than for a rich man to enter heaven.*" (Matthew 19:24). Most of the gates in the walls and into the churches are very large, perhaps ten feet high and quite wide. Often the large gate remains closed while opening a small gate built into the big gate. The small gate in this type of opening is called the "eye of the needle." We could see it would be impossible for a camel to go through the small gate without removing the saddle and saddlebags. Even pulling an unburdened camel through would be difficult. To get through the "eye," you must unload the camel and have the camel go through the door on his knees, transfer the load to the other side, and then load the camel again. Our guide told us the symbolism of this is that we must be wholly unburdened before we pass through the door into heaven. *Note: Most historians say this is a lovely parable, but there was never an eye-of-the-needle gate in early Jerusalem.*

ABOUT JOHN THE BAPTIST: On Day Four, we visited *Yardenit* on the Jordan River, where John the Baptist baptized Jesus. John was a holy man, a prophet, described as wearing clothes made of camel's hair, living on locusts and wild honey. John, the Baptizer, said another would come after him who will not baptize with water, but with the Holy Spirit. John, called "the forerunner," is believed to be speaking of his cousin, Jesus.

HEROD ANTIPAS LOVED HIS BROTHER'S WIFE: Herodias, the wife of Herod Antipas, did not like the Baptist because he had publicly shamed her. She wanted him dead. Antipas, son of the now-deceased Herod the Great, had taken Herodias as a concubine, although Herodias was already married to Antipas' quiet half-brother Philip. Historian Josephus supplements the gospel story: "It all began when Herod Antipas lusted after his brother's wife, Herodias. Antipas persuaded Herodias to divorce her husband and marry him. John the Baptist denounced this union as unlawful, naturally making Herodias his enemy."

MACHAERUS PALACE: Machaerus, the easternmost of Antipas' renovated magnificent fortresses, rises majestically above the Dead Sea. His contacts could see smoke signals from the citadel from as far north as Alexandrium and as far south as Masada. They were even visible in Jerusalem. That is how the officials communicated with smoke signals. Protected on three sides by deep ravines that afforded seclusion and safety, Antipas turned the initially defensive center into a lavish palace, setting the stage for this (deadly) Herodian birthday party. In the dungeons of Machaerus fortress, John the Baptizer was under lock and key in one of those gloomy holds. His crime was that he rebuked Herod for stealing another man's wife (Herodias).

SALOME AND DANCE OF SEVEN VEILS: During her first marriage to Philip, Herodias had borne a daughter named Salome, a dancer. Herodias asked Salome to dance for her new stepfather, Herod Antipas, at his infamous birthday party at Machaerus Palace (now Madaba, Jordan) on the east side of the Dead Sea. Herodias' beautiful daughter Salome danced, swayed, and twirled to the music in front of Antipas and his birthday party guests. After her performance, Antipas and the guests applauded. What a performance, he said! Inflamed by the mood of the moment, Antipas told Salome, "*Ask me what you want up to half my kingdom and it is yours!*" (Mark 6:22 NASB).

BEHEADING OF JOHN THE BAPTIST: Antipas probably expected Salome to ask for some jewelry or at most a house. He could well afford either one. Uncertain what to ask for, Salome whispered with her mother. Then she announced: "*We want the head of John the Baptizer on a platter!*" Even that reckless, hardened lot present at the party must have drawn sharp breaths at such a gruesome request. John had a multitude of followers; why make them mad and risk rebellion? Antipas feared and respected "John the Baptizer." Nevertheless, to save face, he must fulfill his promise. According to Josephus, Antipas ordered the Baptist brought from the dungeon in chains, and Antipas ordered John beheaded. A guard brought the Baptizer's head in on a platter and handed it to the girl who carried it to her mother. *Note: It is hard to imagine such a barbaric act today. It must have been scandalous, even then.*

FIVE LOAVES AND TWO FISH: John's friends came and claimed his body. After the burial, they went to find Jesus. When Jesus heard what had happened, it hit him as hard as any of us when we lose a dear friend. John, the son of Elizabeth, Jesus's beloved cousin, had been murdered in the prime of his life. Jesus mourned for his cousin, who was living a just life. Sadly, he withdrew by boat alone to a solitary place, now known as Tabgha, the same place we visited on Day Four. Still, the crowds followed Jesus on foot from nearby towns. Matthew says a large crowd gathered, and Jesus felt compassion for them. By evening the worshipers were hungry. All the disciples could find to feed them was some bread and a few fish. Jesus took the five loaves and two fish, looked up toward heaven and blessed them. Then, breaking the loaves into pieces, he gave the bread to the disciples, who distributed it to the people. They all ate as much as they wanted, and afterward, the disciples picked up twelve baskets of leftovers (Matthew 14:19-20 NLT). Researchers believe only six months after John the Baptist died at Machaerus, Herod Antipas ordered Jesus crucified at Jerusalem.

JOHN'S SEVERED HEAD: John's severed head was claimed as one of the religious relics preserved in Constantinople. And then, on April 13, 1204, during the Fourth Crusade, an army of knights from Western Europe seized the capital of the Roman Empire at Constantinople. The city was looted and decimated. After being moved several places, the preserved relic was believed placed in the cathedral in Amiens, France. In mid-2012 Pope Benedict XVI commemorated the transfer of this relic to be enshrined in the Basilica of San Silvestro at Rome. So, perhaps if we were so inclined, we could go there to see it.

ANTONIA, GUARDING THE TEMPLE AREA: From the ruins of the Pool of Bethesda, we walked to Antonia Fortress, a military barracks and citadel built by Herod the Great to guard the temple. The Roman army completely destroyed Antonia in AD 70 when the attackers leveled the fortress to allow passage of siege materials into the temple. The courtyard of Antonia, once open to the sky, now supports a convent above, the Convent of the Sisters of Zion. Inscribed on one of the stones in the pavement inside the convent is a pattern for a Roman game. Previously many believed the pavement was from the floor of Fort Antonia where Jesus stood trial before Pilate. Perhaps Roman soldiers could have played such a game as they waited for Jesus's trial and execution. However, recent and more accurate archaeology places this pavement on the street of the open market from around AD 135, a century after the death of Christ. The brutal game called "kill the king," that we saw etched into the paving stone was most likely cut and played by Roman soldiers, not at Christ's trial but by soldiers waiting in the streets at the market.

HIS LAST DAYS: Jesus's last week on earth is as follows:

- **Sunday:** Triumphant entry into Jerusalem of Jesus on a donkey with many followers.
- **Monday and Tuesday:** Jesus returns to the city and confronts the moneychangers.
- **Wednesday:** Jesus goes into the wilderness.
- **Thursday:** Jesus goes to Bethany, home of Mary, Martha, and Lazarus (Luke 10:38-42). The Lord's Prayer is first spoken in the evening when Jesus goes to the home of John Mark, called the Cenacle or Upper Room. He is there to share the Passover meal with his disciples and

friends. In the evening, he and his friends go to the Garden of Gethsemane, where soldiers arrest Jesus as he prays. The soldiers take him to the house of High Priest Caiaphas in the upper city.

- **Friday:** Guards take Jesus to Pontius Pilate at the Praetorium in Herod's Jerusalem palace. The trial is held outside before Pilate and the Sanhedrin judges, who find him guilty of treason and condemn him to die. That same afternoon guards take him to Calvary for the crucifixion. He dies before sundown. Joseph of Arimathea, a wealthy Jewish follower of Jesus, claimed the body and laid it in his new tomb. He rolled a large stone against the door and departed (Matthew 27:57-60). No work could occur on the Jewish Sabbath (*Shabbat*), so the task of preparing Jesus's body for burial had to wait. In the Gospel of Peter: the scribes, Pharisees, and elders go on Friday to Pilate, who gives them a Roman guard. They all proceed to the place of burial. They roll the great stone across the entrance of the tomb, seal it seven times, and keep watch.
- **Saturday:** Disciples and followers mourn.
- **Sunday:** Early Sunday morning, Mary Magdalene and several other women go to the tomb. They bring spices to anoint the body. When they arrive, they find the tomb open. Going in, they do not find Jesus's body, and they wonder what happened. Suddenly two angels in dazzling white clothing appear. The women are frightened. The angels speak, *"Why do you look for the living among the dead? He is not here; He has risen!"* (Luke 24:5 NIV).

SUBSEQUENT APPEARANCES: Reports vary on Jesus's appearances after that; some of the gospels say he returned as a traveler to Emmaus, as a gardener, to Mary Magdalene, to the disciples, and other people in many places. Although some reports are a little sketchy and second-hand, the disciples sin-cerely are convinced they saw him. They rejoice that Jesus is alive, resurrected from the dead.

FOLLOWING THE VIA DOLOROSA: We journey down the Via Dolorosa, the allegorical way of the cross. For many Catholics and other Christian pilgrims, this trip is the most meaningful thing they will do in Jerusalem. The event is televised each Easter. Traditionally Jesus followed this path from the Judgment to Golgotha, touching fourteen 'stations of the cross,' marked on the stones of the Via Dolorosa. Our guide confesses he has serious doubt about this tradition being authentic. Many author-ities feel the same. The legend, like the prayers on a rosary, gives participants comfort in the tradition. Every Friday afternoon, Franciscans, a Catholic order founded by Francis of Assisi, lead a procession along the way, with thousands of pilgrims joining the parade during Holy Week on the Friday before Easter Sunday. For most pilgrims, the exact location of each event along the path is not of prime impor-tance. They care about the symbolism, meaning, and reflection along the way. We soon discover prayer and contemplation an uneasy task with all the busy streets, many snack bars, and interesting touristy shops.

THE MYSTERIOUS LEGEND OF VERONICA: At Station Six on the via Dolorosa, we heard the story of a young girl named Veronica, whom Jesus may have cured. She saw Jesus's suffering, rushed to him,

FIGURE 3: VERONICA'S VEIL
*Station Six on the Via Dolorosa, Veronica's Legend.
Behind the blue door is the "Little Sisters of Jesus" workshop.*

and wiped his face with her veil. When Veronica looked at the cloth, she noticed the image of Jesus's face imprinted on the veil. The story is found in Catholic literature.

Mark Twain says: *"No tradition is so amply verified as this of St. Veronica and her handkerchief. We saw this handkerchief in a cathedral in Paris, in another [cathedral] in Spain, and in two other [cathedrals] in Italy. It costs five francs to see in the Milan Cathedral, and at St. Peter's in Rome, it is almost impossible to see it at any price."*

A small workshop at Station Six presents nuns painting and selling icons. A small Greek Catholic chapel is also located here, named "The Holy Face," because of the legend. The front door to the Holy Face chapel, located on the left, is usually closed. The shop called Little Sisters of Jesus is behind the blue door on the right, where the icons are for sale. Many people find meaning in different religious icons. Peggy, my Catholic friend collects them.

STATIONS OF THE CROSS: The fourteen stations, marked with small, difficult-to-find plaques, are as follows:

1) Condemned by Pilate,
2) Receives the cross,
3) Falls for the first time,
4) Encounters his mother,
5) Helped by Simon of Cyrene,
6) Veronica wipes the face of Jesus,
7) Falls for the second time,
8) Speaks to the daughters of Jerusalem,
9) Falls for the third time,
10) Is stripped of his garments,
11) Is crucified,
12) Dies on the cross,
13) His body lowered from the cross,
14) Laid in the tomb of Joseph of Arimathea.

JUST WALKING IN THE RAIN IN OLD JERUSALEM: A colorful conglomeration of old city markets near the Temple tempt us with brightly embroidered dresses, hand-woven intricate rugs, straw baskets of every shape and size, leather goods, jewelry in all price ranges. Open-air shops offer fresh fish, luscious- looking fruits, spices, appetite-enticing fresh vegetables, and even a carcass of raw beef hanging over the walk. As we stroll through the narrow cobblestone streets in the old city area admiring the colorful goods and good-smelling foods, rain begins to fall. They say the rain only comes

AUTHOR'S PRIVATE COLLECTION

FIGURE 4: STEPPING DOWN
Many long steps lead down to the "Tomb of the Kings" at the end of Nablus Road.

twice a year, the early rain and the late rain. If that is true, Jerusalem's late rain arrived just in time for us to experience it in the Old City markets. We scurry for cover, hurrying through the old marketplace. Jerusalem natives are thankful for the rain because it washes all the dirt from the streets. However, the wet cobblestone streets create a dangerous situation. A new 35mm Olympus landed with a thud on the cobblestones. Lens cover and hand grip clatter down the walk. Several previously stoic Israeli people express sympathy with loud "Oohs!" They graciously helped pick up the pieces. Luckily the camera continues to operate. We caught only a glimpse of all the numerous shop fronts and delectable items as we ran out of the rain. One of our group, a dear lady named Lois suffering from painful sciatica, said if it had not been for a fellow traveler helping her along, she would never have made her way along that slippery cobblestone street.

THE QUEEN OF ADIABENE: Starting at Damascus Gate, we take the ancient road North on Nablus Road, one of the traditional routes into Jerusalem's walled city. At the end of the road, we reach a gate with a sign: "Tomb of the Kings." In Medieval times they believed the site to contain burials of King David and King Solomon. Although disproved, the name did not change. There is an entry fee, of course. Some still attribute the tomb complex to Herod Agrippa, grandson of Herod the Great. Most believe the so-called "Tomb of the Kings" actually held the final resting place of the family of Queen Helena of Adiabene in the first century AD. She is not Helena, the mother of

Constantine. Occasionally, Jewish merchants visited the country of Adiabene, now located in northern Iraq, on business. Through them, Helena became acquainted with and interested in the Jewish religion. Her son Izates took the throne as king at his father's death. Both mother and son were impressed by all they learned, and they abandoned the pagan faith of their land. Helena, the Queen of Adiabene, converted to Judaism along with her sons, Izates and Monbaz, and their families. The royal house of Adiabene helped the Jewish state in many ways. For instance, Queen Helena arrived in Jerusalem during a famine one year. She imported food from Cyprus and Egypt. She also built magnificent palaces in the former City of David. Often, Adiabene sent large sums of money to Jerusalem, either to provide for the Temple's needs or to help the poor and came to visit often. Authorities believe Queen Helena built this beautiful mausoleum where she and her sons were to be buried. The Queen died in AD 50.

AUTHOR'S PRIVATE COLLECTION

FIGURE 5: CRAWLNG INTO A TOMB

The tiny doorway opened into a large "mourning room" with stone benches all around.

EXPLORING THE TOMB OF A QUEEN: Josephus, in *The Antiquities of the Jews*, describes this opulent royal necropolis. Some thieves robbed the tomb centuries ago. The basics are still there, but we never saw any of the elaborate items Josephus described. We enter a large courtyard hewn in the rock and descend twenty-three steps, each exactly twenty-nine feet wide. The staircase was paved initially and led to a forecourt with two cisterns and ritual baths. To the right of the stairs, a gutter sent rainwater into the cisterns located below, necessary for the purification ceremonies. The cisterns are blocked, but the baths are visible through the bars. At the bottom of the staircase, we turn left to reach an enormous vaulted opening. Three pyramids once crowned the ninety-foot-wide façade. The obelisks no longer exist but are described by Josephus and other ancient sources. Archaeologists found fragments of two pillars that supported the large opening. Josephus describes the necropolis of Queen Helena. "*The main beam is ornamented with a wreath and a tablet, a carved bunch of grapes and acanthus leaves.*" He also described the three stone pyramids above the center of the facade. We didn't see any of that. Some remains recovered from the excavations of this tomb may be at the Louvre in Paris. A Greek geographer described the tomb as the second most beautiful

FIGURE 6: TOMB OF THE KINGS
Artist's concept of the entrance to the tomb of the kings a hundred years ago or more.

in the world after the tomb of Mausolus, one of the seven wonders of the ancient world. *(NOTE: Not recommended for those with walking difficulty.)*

INSIDE THE TOMB: To the left of the platform and down a few steps more, we find a cave with a small opening previously sealed with a large rolling stone. The stone, set in a deep channel, could be pushed back and held in place with a smaller stone. In Josephus' book, an ingenious mechanism opened the door of the crypt once a year at a specified hour and closed itself again, to stay closed for another twelve months. The rolling stone is rolled back today and held in place by a smaller stone, so Mr. Aaron urged us to go inside the tomb and look around. The idea seemed more than a little creepy, but our guide urged us on, and an adventurous partner crawled through immediately. Like Alice in Wonderland's rabbit hole, the tiny doorway opened into a large "mourning room" with stone benches all around, allowing room for about fifteen members of our group to be seated at one time. From this room, at least three more large doorways open into a labyrinth of burial chambers, all carved from solid rock. *Note:*

FIGURE 7: THE TOMB ENTRANCE
The tomb entrance as it was for our visit in the late 20th century.

Visits inside the tomb are no longer permitted. The experience helped prepare us to visit the Garden Tomb when we visited there later on this day.

KOKHIM AND *ARCOSOLIUM*: In that period, our guide explained, the people customarily buried a body for a year and kept that chamber sealed. After the year of grieving ended, the family would open the sealed door, collect the bones and place them in an ossuary or box. Some of the rooms leading off the mourning room had table height shelves to hold ossuaries. The guide said both of the two most common types of first-century tombs, *kokhim* and *arcosolia*, are found in this complex. First, *kokhim*, long narrow shafts in which they placed the deceased. They closed the shaft with a stone slab. An inscription probably identified each shaft, but we felt a little uncomfortable being there and did not look close enough to see. Second, *arcosolia*, resting places containing a bench with an arch over it, included triangular niches for oil lamps to give light during the burial preparation process. No bones remain, so we are not desecrating anything. Being in a burial chamber felt kind of weird. Walking in the empty tomb of a Queen is an unforgettable, unique, and educational observation, a once in a lifetime experience. When curiosity was satisfied, we crawl out of the tomb, exit the outer courtyard, climb the massive stairway, and follow the leader to our next adventure.

THE EMPEROR CONSTANTINE: Constantine became emperor of the Roman Empire in AD 307, and five years later, he issued the Edict of Milan, making Christianity legal. The cross eventually became his battle symbol, and Christianity began to receive favored treatment among religions in the empire. Perhaps it was a political move in the beginning because Constantine himself was not baptized until shortly before he died. With the ascent of Constantine as Emperor, the days of bloody Christian persecutions came to an end. He founded his capital, Constantinople, on the site of an existing city, Byzantium, now called Istanbul. He made other favorable changes, in addition to encouraging Christianity. Where previously Roman women had no legal rights, Constantine held them in high regard and he seemed to especially revere and respect his mother, Queen Helena.

COMMONS
FIGURE 8: CONSTANTINE

ANOTHER QUEEN HELENA: At Constantine's direction, his mother, Queen Helena of Constantinople, at the age of almost eighty gathered a crew of monks and traveled to the holy land. A prominent churchman, Rufinus of Aquileia, wrote a full account of Helena's discovery when he returned to Italy in AD 397. Rufinus said Helena came to Jerusalem and asked people there about the crucifixion site, and they told her it was under the pagan Temple of Venus. Even though more than three hundred years had passed, the legends came down through generations. Queen Helena immediately ordered the pagan Temple demolished. Saint Ambrose of Milan (AD 395) said ... *she opened up the earth, scattered the dust, and found three crosses in disarray.* Queen Helena and Constantine proclaimed Christianity to be the official religion of the Roman Empire. Soon, through Helena's influence, all forms of heathen sacrifice were forbidden. Helena called for constructing at least two basilicas or churches of ancient building design; first, a basilica over the discovered tomb in Jerusalem; a second one over the cave of the nativity in Bethlehem. They still stand. The Church of the Sepulchre in Jerusalem has three naves with four columns supporting the dome and dates back to the twelfth century. Perhaps these same columns saw the coronation of Melisende, Queen of Jerusalem in AD 1131, as told on Day One.

A CONFUSING ARRANGEMENT OF CHAPELS, SPACES: The basilica contains a bewildering conglomeration of more than thirty chapels and worship spaces, but no direction signs. Immediately inside the main door is the Stone of Anointing, with responsibility for care belonging jointly to Greek Orthodox, Catholic, and Armenian Orthodox. Next, the Armenian Station of the Holy Women commemorates Jesus's mother and her companions at the crucifixion. Turn left to see the Tomb of Christ. ... and so on. To visit the Chapel of the Finding of the Cross inside the church, first, find Helena's Chapel, then descend twenty-one steps from the right side of the chapel. Visitors through the centuries carved crosses into the rock walls on both sides of the stairs down to the chapel. Everywhere are candlesticks and those gaudy hanging lamps typical to the Middle Eastern religious shrines. We visited one of

Helena's basilicas, the Church of Nativity in Bethlehem, but only viewed the Church of the Sepulchre in Jerusalem from afar.

BITING THE TRUE CROSS: The Chapel of the True Cross is now property of the Armenians. Catholic legend is that the Queen and her escorts came to visit the holy places more than three hundred years after the fact. Helena reportedly discovered the hiding place of three crosses used at the crucifixion of Jesus and the two thieves, Saint Dismas and Saint Gestas, who were executed with him. Helena's escorts pressured an aged Jew to guide them to the site of the crucifixion. The mysterious unnamed Jewish man was said to have inherited traditional knowledge of the crucifixion hidden in a location under Hadrian's temple of Venus. Constantine's aged mother ordered the idolatrous temple destroyed and the Sepulchre uncovered, whereupon three crosses and the inscription from Jesus's crucifixion were reportedly found in a dry abandoned cistern. Guards had to be posted around the reputed "true cross" discovered by Helena, to prevent pilgrims who kissed it from biting off splinters to take back home with them. In Socrates' version of the story, the three crosses were placed in turn on a deathly ill woman. This woman recovered at the touch of the third cross, which was taken as a sign this was the "True Cross." Socrates also reports Helena found the nails with which Christ had been fastened to the cross. She sent these to Constantinople, where they were incorporated into the emperor's helmet and the bridle of his horse.

When the Persians captured Jerusalem in AD 614, they stole the legendary "true cross" hidden at the Sanctuary Church. The cross, later recovered and restored to the church, eventually disappeared again due to Christian pilgrims picking pieces of wood from the sacred object and taking them home. No authentic trace of the relic is believed to exist today. By the end of the Middle Ages in the fifteenth-century so many churches claimed to possess a piece of the "True Cross" that John Calvin remarked enough of the wood existed to fill a ship. We did not visit the chapel of the finding of the cross inside the cathedral in Jerusalem, but you might.

FIGURE 9: HELENA OF CONSTANTINOPLE
The mother of Constantine, is always pictured with a cross.

THE QUEEN LOVED RELIGIOUS RELICS: Helena also identified numerous holy objects and took many of them back to Constantinople. Nothing seemed too inconsequential so long as it had some religious connection. The veneration of holy objects grew. Some churches claimed many relics, which meant much more to them and their congregations than mementos or souvenirs. Medieval Christians had a strong belief in the power of relics for healing and as a point of contact. Monasteries and cathedrals vied for possession of the prestigious relics, and these treasures were often found far away from their reported beginning. Some of the stories might make an objective reader raise an eyebrow, but for those soldiers who took up the cause of the Crusades, the relics were real enough to stake their life on. Some relics, like physical remains of a holy site or holy person, might be stolen from one church to find a new home in another. That is what we found at Saint Mark's Basilica in Venice. The cathedral, built in the ninth century, housed some sacred relics—stolen sacred relics! In AD 828, some merchants from Venice stole from Alexandria, Egypt, the body of Saint Mark the Evangelist, one of the apostles. They slipped the bones past Muslim guards by hiding the body (surely only bones by then) in barrels under layers of pork. While at sea on the way to Venice, a storm almost drowned the grave robbers and their precious cargo. They claimed Saint Mark himself appeared to the captain and told him to lower the sails. That saved the ship, and the merchants said they owed their safety to the miracle. Saint Mark's body (if it is his) remains in Venice at the famous basilica named for him. The entire story is pictured on the early day mosaic above the entry door at Saint Mark's.

RELIGIOUS RELICS THROUGH THE AGES: Rome's Lateran basilica, created under the orders of Constantine in the fourth century, boasted many religious relics. For instance, the tablets of Moses, the Ark of the Covenant, a tunic of Mary, the hair shirt worn by John the Baptist, some fish and loaves leftover from the feeding of the five thousand, and more. According to tradition, the staircase that Jesus ascended to Pontius Pilate's palace in Jerusalem was brought to Rome by St. Helena of Constantinople. The Basilica of Saint John Lateran remains the cathedral of Rome and the Pope's official residence. Within that Basilica today are listed the following relics and many more:

AUTHOR'S COLLECTION

FIGURE 10: THE BAPTIZER'S ARM
Religious relics became so popular that monasteries and cathedrals vied for possession. We saw "John the Baptist's arm and a piece of his skull" so labeled in the Topkapi Palace in Istanbul, Turkey.

- Two gilded silver busts containing the heads of Saints Peter and Paul;
- A wooden altar, supposedly used by the first popes, from Saint Peter to Saint Sylvester I (AD 314-355);
- A bronze relief of the Last Supper, behind which is a fragment of wood thought to be from the table the disciples used at the Last Supper.

CONSTANTINOPLE FALLS: Constantinople remained an imperial capital, the center of the Roman Empire, from AD 330 through the following eleven centuries. The city had been besieged many times but was captured only once, during the Fourth Crusade in 1204. When Constantinople fell to the crusaders, extensive collections of relics disappeared. In the twelfth century, Constantinople achieved fame for architectural masterpieces such as the phenomenal church of Hagia Sophia, Topkapi, the sacred palace of the Sultans, the hippodrome, the gates of gold lining the arcaded avenues, and more. Constantinople contained numerous artistic and literary treasures before the Ottoman Turks sacked it in 1453. After the Turks conquered the city, this capital of Christian civilization became transformed into the capital of Islamic concerns. The Turks changed the name from Constantinople to Istanbul.

DAVID SHANKBONE, WWW.WIKIPEDIACOMMONS.ORG

FIGURE 11: MAIN ENTRANCE OF THE CHURCH OF THE HOLY SEPULCHRE

MORE RELIGIOUS RELICS: Topkapi Palace is the treasure house of the Ottoman Turks, who added in the sixteenth century the adjoining Turkish Harem with more than a hundred rooms. In the Palace, now a museum in Istanbul, we viewed a relic marked "John the Baptist's arm and a piece of his skull." The alleged hand, arm, and skull bones of John the Baptist encased in jeweled metal cases, are in the display case. A gold-embellished silver reliquary holds the fabled arm. Inscribed on the forefinger is: "The beloved of God," on the wrist: "This is the hand of the Baptist." The skull rests on a golden plate decorated with gold bands with inset gems and old Serbian inscriptions. The plate itself is inside a sixteenth-century rock crystal box. We saw documents at the Topkapi that say the relics became a bar-gaining tool to rescue the Sultan's son from the Knights of Rhodes.

And now it is time for our guide to lead us to a new adventure.

THE CONFUSING CHURCH: In Jerusalem, most Catholics identify the site of the crucifixion and the tomb of Jesus as inside the Church of the Holy Sepulchre. Although we did not go there due to time constraints, our guide pointed out a rooftop mish-mash of towers, buildings, and domes. They built this confusing structure over the revered sites. Mark Twain remarked on his visit, somewhat sacrilegiously (sic), *"The Sepulchre is near the Western Gate; the place of the crucifixion, and every other place intimately connected with that great event ingeniously massed together and covered by one roof the dome of the Church. A marble slab covers the Stone of Unction, where the leader's body is laid to prepare it for burial. It was necessary to conceal the real stone in order to save it from destruction. Pilgrims got caught chipping off pieces of it to carry home.* Twain continues his description. *Over the slab hang some fifty gold and silver lamps, kept always burning, and the place fills with trumpery, gewgaws, and tawdry ornamentation. All sects, except Protestants, have chapels under the roof, and each must keep to itself and not venture upon another's ground. They cannot worship together around the grave of the leader of the world in peace.* (paraphrased.) That has not changed in hundreds of years. Today, the church serves as headquarters of the Greek Orthodox Patriarch of Jerusalem. Several Christian churches and secular entities share control of the building, in complicated arrangements unchanged for centuries. The arrangement is similar at the Church of the Nativity in Bethlehem. The church is home to branches of Eastern Orthodoxy and Oriental Orthodoxy as well as to Roman Catholicism.

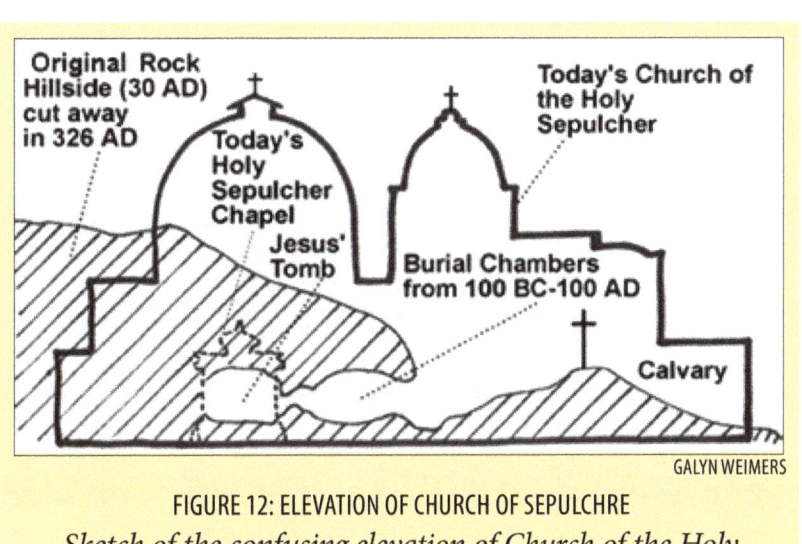

FIGURE 12: ELEVATION OF CHURCH OF SEPULCHRE
Sketch of the confusing elevation of Church of the Holy Sepulchre in Jerusalem. The Church contains a curious conglomeration of altars, chapels, and architectural styles.

FIGURE 13: THE IMMOVABLE LADDER
No one dares to move this ladder for fear of starting another war.

ELEVATION OF THE CHURCH: An edifice built by crusaders over earlier foundations, the remarkable structure contains such a curious conglomeration of altars, chapels, and architectural styles that anyone might become confused. Byzantine, medieval, crusader, and modern elements combine to create an odd mish-mash of styles. Roman Emperor Constantine in AD 326 ordered the building of this place. He wanted *"that it should surpass all the churches of the world in the beauty of its walls, columns, and marbles."* By the time the Crusaders came to Jerusalem more than seven hundred years later, the structure appeared battered by neglect and earthquakes. Wars and conquests drastically damaged it. After Queen Melisende's coronation in 1131, peace reigned, but only until 1187, when a Muslim army under Saladin reconquered the city.

THE IMMOVABLE LADDER ON THE BALCONY: There is an "immovable ladder" on an outside balcony of the Church of the Sepulchre. The wooden ladder leaning against a window ledge has been there since early in the eighteenth-century. No one knows why it is there, but it was apparently in place when the "Status Quo" began in 1757. Therefore, it must remain in place. No one dares touch it, lest they disturb the status quo, and provoke others' wrath. The first evidence of the ladder comes from 1852, and it has not moved since. The various factions residing in the church disagree on almost everything. Therefore, to keep the church and its shrine open, the keys are entrusted to a Muslim.

THE KEEPERS OF THE KEYS: Two Jerusalem Palestinian clans have been custodians of the entrance to the building since the twelfth-century; one man from the Joudeh family and another man from the Nuseibeh family. Every morning, a monk knocks on the main entry door, which is unlocked by a Muslim man. The same family is handed down responsibility for the key until today. According to a 2012 news story by the Inter Press Service (IPS), the two Muslim families became keepers of the keys because of quarrels within the church. *Like brothers, we sometimes fight,* confessed the Very Reverend Father Samuel Aghoyan, Armenian Superior of the place. The churches would not go along with each other, so the key was entrusted to a neutral monotheistic faith that embraces Christ as a prophet. That faith is Islam.

AN EARLY EVERY-MORNING RITUAL: Every morning the alarm goes off at 4:30. Adeeb Joudeh travels from his apartment outside the walls of the Old City to bring the cast-iron key to the church, just as his father and his forebears did before him. The key, a twelve-inch iron wedge, Joudeh entrusts to Wajeeh Nuseibeh, who calls the priests and pilgrims who spent the night praying inside. A wooden ladder is passed through a porthole to Nuseibeh to unlock the upper part of the gigantic door. Then, he unlocks the large lower hatch before handing the precious key back to Joudeh. Every evening at 7:30, after hundreds of tourists and pilgrims have left the church, they perform the ritual in reverse. Each governing Christian community decorates the shrines in their distinctive way. The building is in great disrepair, but there is no hope of getting those in control to agree on a plan for restoration. For more info: search online for the ladder on the balcony of the Church of the Sepulchre.

CHAOTIC HISTORY OF SEPULCHRE: When Roman emperor Constantine converted to Christianity in AD 325, he ordered the pagan Temple of Aphrodite in Jerusalem demolished to make way for a church. In the course of demolition, workers discovered a tomb thought to be the tomb of Jesus. Constantine's mother Helena saw to it the new basilica covered this sacred spot. A few hundred years later the Caliph Hakim destroyed that first structure in 1009. Another hundred years after Hakim, crusaders began renovations. Subsequent centuries have not been kind to this building. According to the New Testament, they crucified Jesus at Golgotha, "the place of the skull," outside the city wall (Matthew 27:33 NKJV). Some researchers believe "The place of the skull" has to be in an area of abandoned stone quarries outside the city. However, the wall moved in antiquity. While inside the current city wall, the sanctuary remains outside the wall of Jesus's day.

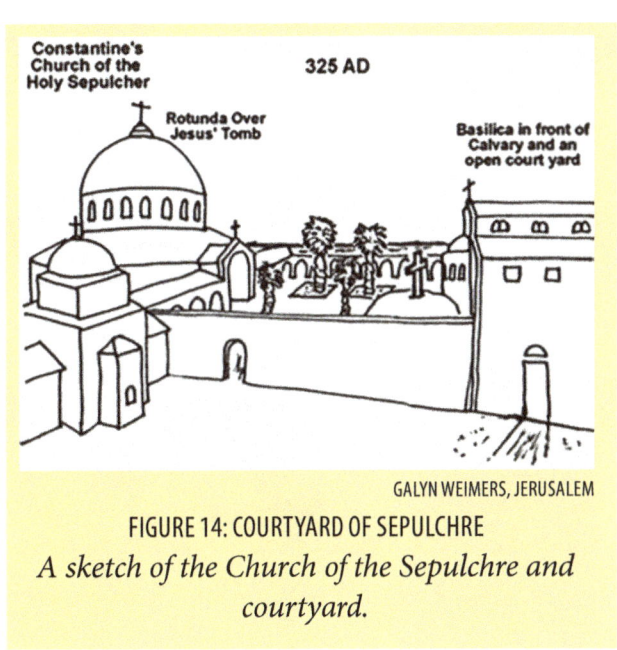

GALYN WEIMERS, JERUSALEM

FIGURE 14: COURTYARD OF SEPULCHRE
A sketch of the Church of the Sepulchre and courtyard.

DINNER IN AN UPPER ROOM IN THE OLD CITY: Our guide led us to a building in the upper part of the old City. This three-story house, called the Upper Room or Cenacle, represents the home where Jesus and his disciples shared their "last supper" or Passover Seder in the house of John Mark (Mark 14:12-16 RSV). This place we are visiting is not the same building but near the same location. On the night before the Romans captured Jesus, he and his disciples met to share the meal at the home of John Mark's parents in an affluent area on Mount Zion in the southwest part of the city. The wars of AD 70 and AD 135 destroyed the buildings in this area. The house of High Priest Caiaphas and the home of John Mark would stand somewhere along the top of the hill where the wealthy could enjoy the view and a cool southwesterly breeze. Coming from a small community where families lived for generations, we

FIGURE 15: THE CENACLE
Room of the Last Supper (Upper Room or Cenaculum) on Mount Zion.

accept that residents might recall names and locations over many years. John Mark, the author of the Gospel of Mark, was an eyewitness to many events in Jesus's life. Later he was a companion of disciples Peter and Paul. His parents, Aaron and Mary, were strong Jesus supporters. From the Cenacle, just up the street north toward the Temple, they could see the house of Caiaphas and further north, the palace of Herod where Roman Governor Pontius Pilate was staying with his wife during the feast.

WHAT HAPPENED AT THE CENACLE THAT NIGHT: Peter and John took the paschal lamb to the temple altar to be sacrificed, and afterward carried it back to the home of John Mark for the meal.

On their return, the young man's parents were expecting them and showed them to a large upper room already furnished and ready for their Passover *seder*. The disciples found wine and cups, cakes of unleavened bread, sauce with bitter herbs, and everything they needed. They would share red wine, the ordinary country liquid mixed with water in the proportion of one-part wine to two parts water. Jesus and the other ten disciples left Bethany, where they were visiting friends. They headed toward Jerusalem. Stars began to appear, and the moon peeked above the eastern horizon. Once inside the city, they quietly followed a short path through the streets to Aaron and Mary's home on Mount Zion. Passing by windows of festively lit houses, Jesus would have seen families sharing their Passover meals. In the approaching darkness, Mark saw their guests coming. He called Peter and John, who quickly led Jesus and the others up the stairway to the upper room where the meal waited. No one noticed them arriving. The disciples did not know this would be their last meal together (Mark 14:13). The Jewish Passover feast they were celebrating is described more fully on Day Ten.

THE UPPER ROOM BUILDING: This structure remains sacred to all three religions:
- Jewish: The ground floor is a Jewish holy site once believed to house the tomb of the biblical King David. A beautiful statue of King David with a harp is just outside.

AUTHOR'S PRIVATE COLLECTION

FIGURE 16: THE CHURCH OF ALL NATIONS
Donations from many countries built The Church of all Nations in the Gethsemane garden.

- Christian: The second floor is the Christian site Upper Room (Cenacle) symbolic of the site of Jesus's Last Supper.
- Muslam/Islam: On the roof, an old minaret marks a Muslim holy site.

We approach the second-story room through an arched entrance from the central lane, past a courtyard that was part of a former Franciscan monastery. We reach the building and climb the stairs in the courtyard. We enter a large rectangular room with graceful pillars, a high-vaulted ceiling, and two-story-tall stained-glass windows with large half-circle transoms. In the sixteenth century, after the Turks captured Jerusalem, the room became a mosque in memory of the prophet David. The stained-glass windows with Arabic inscriptions remain. As if part of the script while Mr. Aaron talked, a white dove flew in through the open door across the crusader arches and perched in a gothic window directly above him. Some found it hard to concentrate because of an irreverent concern the bird might drop "blessings" on our guide's head. A closed staircase leads down to the first floor, the traditional site of King David's tomb. Following Jewish tradition, only men are permitted to enter the room. Women must view the covered box through an opening in the wall. The king's actual burial place is in the City of David.

CELEBRATING THE PASSOVER WITH FRIENDS: Joy and fellowship filled the upper room as he washed his disciples' feet, ate the Passover meal, instituted Communion, sang the Hallel psalms, and prayed the high priestly prayer (John 17 RSV). Within hours, these young people would zoom from the height of rejoicing to the depth of agony in Gethsemane's garden.

JESUS REACHED A DIFFICULT DECISION: After their meal in the upper room, Jesus came to Gethsemane with the disciples on that fateful night, to rest and pray as was their custom during Passover week. Judas certainly knew of this custom because he had been there with Jesus several times. Here in this field of olive trees, Jesus spent the night before his arrest, praying in anguish. He grew despondent and considered seeking a way out, only finally to accept his fate. On the Mount of Olives, we visited the Roman Catholic Church of All Nations, built over the rock on which Jesus might have prayed the night the soldiers arrested him (Matthew 26:39 NLT). We shared a quiet moment of meditation with our group in that solemn place before returning to the bus. Our usual noisy bunch remained subdued for the trip.

VIOLET BLUE ALABASTER WINDOWS: The front of the church, facing the temple mount, features a striking mosaic. Violet blue alabaster windows create a somber mood, and ceiling domes recreate the dark blue of a star-studded night sky. Donations from many countries between 1919 and 1924 built this church, also known as the Basilica of the Agony. The coats-of-arms of these nations appear in the glass ceiling. The current church rests on the foundations of two earlier ones, that of a small twelfth-century crusader chapel abandoned in 1345, and a fourth-century Byzantine basilica, destroyed by an earthquake in the eighth century. In 1920, during work on the foundations, two meters beneath the floor of the medieval crusader chapel, they discovered a column and fragments of a magnificent mosaic.

HOW IT CAME DOWN: Deciphering how the conviction and trial of Jesus happened is a daunting task. Our entire understanding of events come from five different accounts, all written by Christians who recorded the event many years later and did not witness what happened. The accounts do not agree on the time and place sequence, only on the outcome. Judas led the soldiers to Gethsemane, where he knew Jesus would be. Judas identified Jesus to the soldiers by the prearranged signal of a kiss. The chief priests paid Judas thirty pieces of silver for the betrayal, the going price for a slave (Matthew 26:15). Trying to protect Jesus, his disciple Peter took a sword and attacked a man named Malchus, the high priest's servant, cutting off his ear. Jesus said to Peter, *Put your sword back into its place; for all those who take up the sword shall perish by the sword* (John 18:10). Soldiers took hold of Jesus, tied his hands together, and led him back to the upper city. Caiaphas held the High Priest title, but his father-in-law Annas actually performed the duties, so they took Jesus first to Annas for an indictment (John 18:13). The scribes and the elders (the Sanhedrin)) were assembled at Caiaphas' house (John 18:24). Behind Jesus followed Simon Peter and one other disciple (Note: probably the apostle John) known personally to the high priest. The other disciple went with Jesus into the courtyard, but Peter was left standing at the door. Roman rulers appointed the high priests, so the priests had to juggle their Jewish religious interests with Rome's political interests. Following his arrest, Jesus remained quiet in front of the Sanhedrin. He did not mount a defense and rarely responded to the accusations. When Jesus did not deny being the son of God, the Sanhedrin considered it an act of blasphemy.

THE TRIAL OF JESUS: Since Jesus did not deny the charge, the Jewish elders then took Jesus to the palace of Pontius Pilate, governor of Judea. Pilate and Caiaphas had probably worked long and well together, so this arrangement of moving a prisoner from one place to another seems a little odd, but we do not know the customs of that time. The Sanhedrin asked for a death sentence for blasphemy, saying Jesus claimed to be King of the Jews. Pontius Pilate usually maintained and held court at his official residence in Caesarea-by-the-sea in the former palace of Herod. On special occasions such as the Passover festival, Pilate would go to Jerusalem, where he had a second judgment-hall (*Praetorium*), another former palace of Herod. Jesus's accusers did not enter Pilate's residence because by Jewish law, even entering the house of a gentile was a grave offense. Now the sun was coming up, and the Jews did not enter the palace because they wanted to be able to eat the Passover lamb. (John 18: 28).

WHAT WERE THE CHARGES AGAINST JESUS? Pilate considered the charges the Jewish leaders brought against Jesus.

1) He subverts the nation.

2) He opposes the payment of taxes.

3) He claims to be a king.

These were false accusations because Jesus refused the title of king in a political sense, and he did not oppose paying taxes. Jesus criticized the leaders on religious issues, not political (John 18:33-19:12).

PILATE OFFERED A SUBSTITUTE: According to Matthew 27:19, even Pilate's wife spoke to her husband on Jesus's behalf. Pilate wanted to give the responsibility of sentencing to the Jewish authorities. When he learned that Jesus came from Galilee, he sent him to Herod Antipas, ruler of that district who was also in Jerusalem at the time. Antipas also found nothing treasonable in Jesus's actions. Pilate lobbied to invoke the custom of releasing a prisoner in honor of the Jewish Passover and let the multitudes decide, encouraging them to choose Jesus. They chose instead a murderous criminal named Barabbas (John 19: 1-16 RSV). Pilate then went back inside the palace, summoned Jesus, and asked him, "*Are you the king of the Jews?*"

"*Is that your own idea,*" Jesus asked, "*or did others talk to you about me?*"

Pilate tried to avoid judging Jesus and gave his verdict on all three counts, saying: "*I find no case against him.*" Finally, Pilate had Jesus scourged in the hope the Sanhedrin would feel pity. He laid open Jesus's back with a leaded whip, and the soldiers made a crown of thorns and placed it on his head. The Sanhedrin did not waiver. Jewish resentment ran unusually high during national and religious holidays. Pilate did not want to be responsible for the death of Jesus, so he said to the Jews: "*I am going to bring him out to you now, but understand clearly that I find him not guilty,*" (John 19:4).

He knew the Jewish rulers had complained about him to Caesar before, and they threatened to do so again if Pilate did not do what they wanted. He knew Caesar would punish him if they complained. The Jews cried, *Let His blood be upon us and on our children* (Matthew 27:25).

Pilate finally washed his hands of the whole situation in the presence of all the people, and reluctantly turned Jesus over to his soldiers for crucifixion. He ordered a sign posted above Jesus on the cross, "*Jesus of Nazareth, The King of the Jews.*" The sign was to give public notice of the legal charge against him for his crucifixion. Then Pilate delivered him to them to be crucified. So, they took Jesus and led him away. The crucifixion was a common form of execution when the convicted criminal was a slave, Jew, or another foreigner. Jesus was condemned as a violator of Roman law, not Jewish. Roman citizens were exempt from this martyrdom, which was considered the most painful and humiliating punishment possible. A capital sentence under Jewish law would have meant stoning. I will not go further into the gruesome and horrific details of the Roman torture.

A BRIEF OBJECTIVE SUMMARY: A writing by Josephus confirms the life of Jesus. There lived Jesus, a wise man, a performer of marvelous feats, and a teacher. He attracted many Jews and many Greeks. He was called the Christ. Pilate sentenced him to die on the cross, being urged to by the citizens.

FINDING THE TOMB OF JESUS: When we first met our Israel guide, one member of our group asked, "*Will we get to see the tomb of Jesus*?"

"*Certainly,*" our guide replied with a chuckle. "*Which one would you like to see?*" That was the beginning of our learning experience. Several places are proposed as the place for the tomb of Jesus. Three top contenders are:

- Church of the Holy Sepulchre in Jerusalem;
- Garden Tomb discovered in the nineteenth-century outside the old city; and
- The Talpiot Tomb, also in Jerusalem area.

FIGURE 17: ANCIENT OLIVE TREE

In this field of olive trees, Jesus spent the night before his arrest, praying in anguish. Judas led the soldiers to Gethsemane, where he knew Jesus would be.

Another guide told us a standing joke about leading a group of British professors on a tour of the Holy City. He noticed they were all carrying notebooks, and at each site, they noted the letters, "A. B. C." The guide finally got curious enough to ask them what the letters meant. Their answer, "Another Bloody Church." Truthfully, we felt the same disillusionment; that every site was hidden inside a building and guarded by representatives of different religions. While all the trappings and accoutrements sometimes detract from the sights we expected to see, we know these structures did preserve the attraction.

GOLGOTHA AND THE GARDEN TOMB: Our guide takes us outside the city walls to the Garden Tomb, a peaceful place maintained by the British who believe it to be the garden of Joseph of Arimathea. Exiting the old city through Damascus Gate, we come to a hillside where, with an active imagination, the rocks form the shape of a skull on the side of the hill with eye sockets and bridge of the nose. It could have been Golgotha.

THE GARDEN TOMB, MAINTAINED BY THE BRITISH: The British maintain a beautiful two-acre garden oasis just outside the city wall. In the garden area, they uncovered a man-made tomb cut from the solid rock (John 19:41-42). Major General Charles George Gordon, a British army officer detailed to Palestine in the 1880s, discovered this spot. He became convinced this was the historic garden and tomb, for the following reasons that agreed with the prediction:

AUTHOR'S PRIVATE COLLECTION
FIGURE 18: THE EUCHARIST
Communion in the Garden with tiny hand-carved olivewood chalices.

- One of the oldest and largest cisterns for water is on the grounds, as necessary for a garden in the Middle East. The cistern dates to be at least two thousand years old.

- After the crucifixion, a Jewish man by the name of Joseph of Arimathea took the body of Jesus and laid it in his new, unused tomb which was carved out of the solid rock.

- The tomb was in a garden very near the crucifixion site; a pre-Christian-era grape vineyard grew here.

- Logic says it would be near the main road and a trade route ran nearby.

- A great stone was rolled in front of the tomb after they laid Jesus's body inside. A great circular stone disc rolled across a trough in front of the doorway opening.

- Archeologists agree the tomb is ancient.

WALKING INSIDE THE TOMB: We are in a large open area. We decide everything about this location fits the biblical

AUTHOR'S PRIVATE COLLECTION

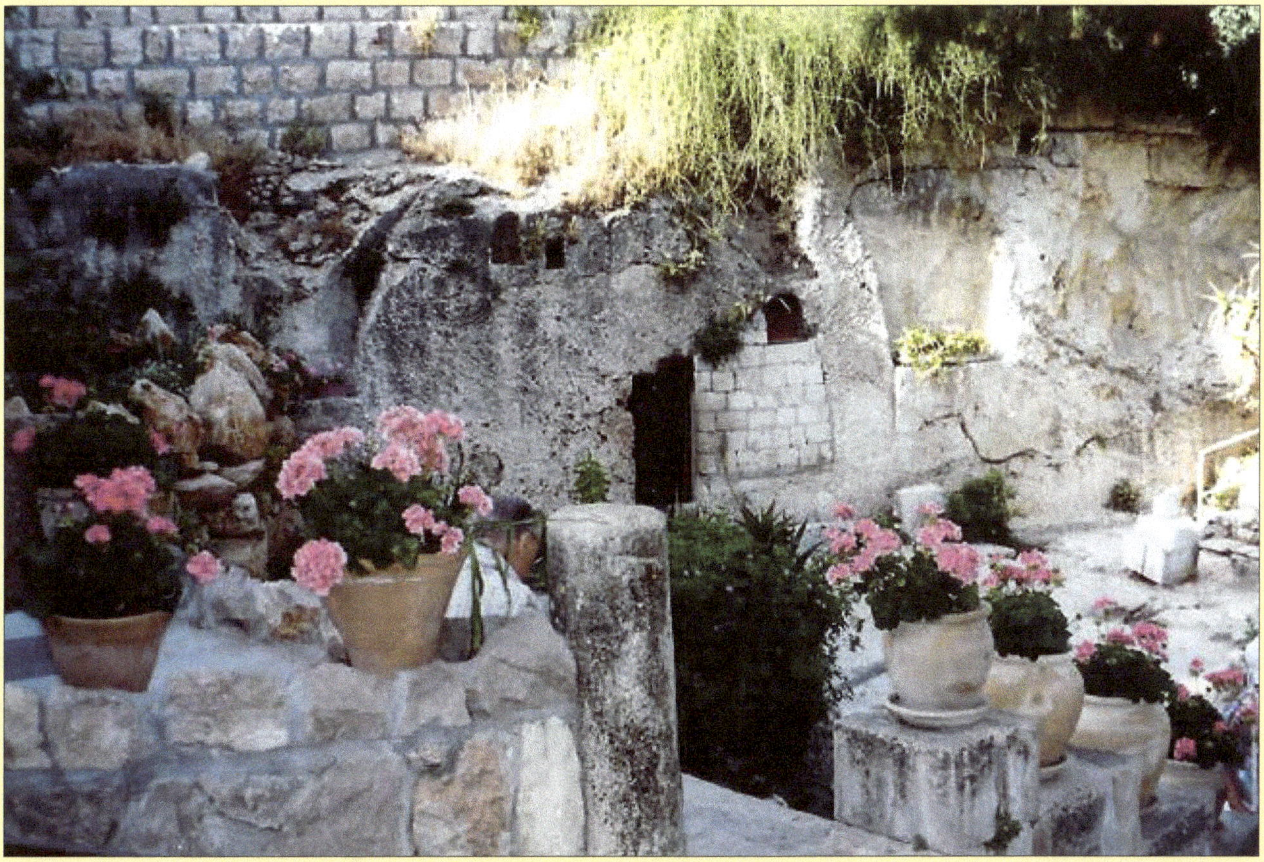

FIGURE 19: THE GARDEN TOMB

The British maintain this beautiful two-acre garden oasis just outside the city wall.

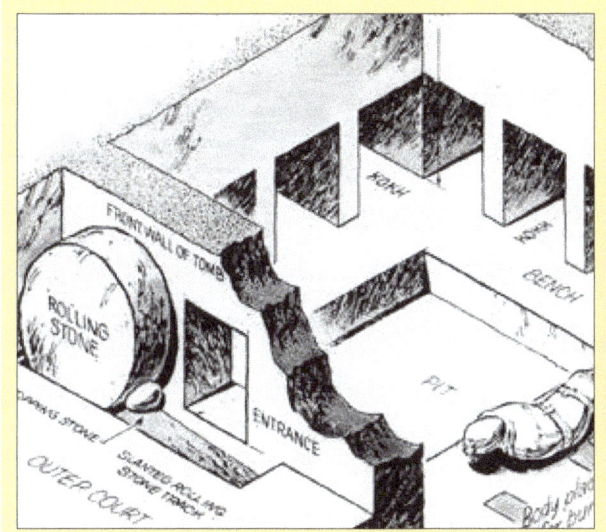

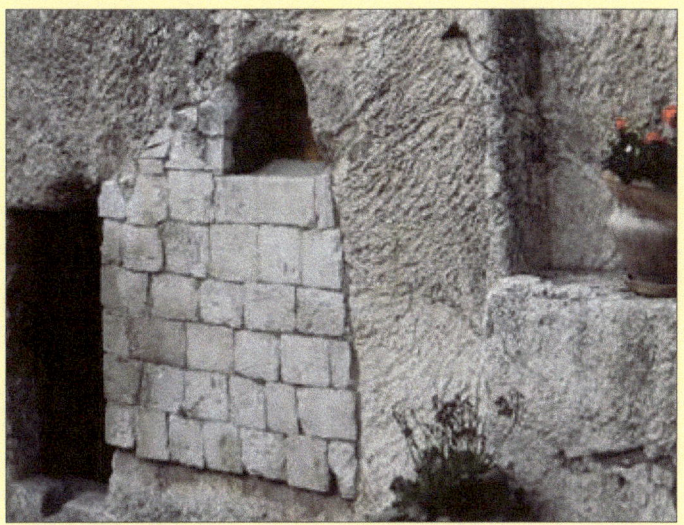

description. For once, something looks like it should, the hillside nearby sports a skull face, sort of. We stand in what once was a huge stone quarry with open space where people might gather to watch an important event. We stepped inside the open tomb to see the burial chamber itself. Two stone benches are evident, both empty of course, where they could lay a corpse. Despite hundreds of pilgrims lined up to inspect the grounds, and although located in a Muslim neighborhood, peacefulness reigns. Several little "chapels in the woods" hideaway just out of the traffic pattern and almost out of view. This feels right.

WHO IS IN CHARGE HERE? The Garden is owned and administered by the Garden Tomb Association, a charitable trust based in the United Kingdom. The Association maintains conservation of the site, such as the work in progress to stabilize the cliffside. The ancient Roman plaster inside the cistern is deteriorating. A substantial vertical crack needs repair to retain rainwater stored there to water the garden in dry summer months. Our guide tells us thousands of visitors from around the world come here to see this unique place every year. Many find peace and renewed hope. There is no entrance fee for places to sit, drinking water and toilet facilities, even wheelchair access. No eating, drinking, or smoking is permitted, and mobile phones are banned.

A SPECIAL EUCHARIST: Our Rev. Brinkworth shared a prayer with us in one of the small gardens and offered communion or Eucharist, the feast of thanksgiving. She served the wine in tiny hand-carved olivewood chalices, a souvenir gift to us from the guide and his wife.

TEN

DAY OF MOSES

Wednesday: Yad Vashem, Joseph, Moses, Egypt, Passover, and the moral of the story

DAY TEN: For our last day in Jerusalem, we will visit the enormous Holocaust Museum in Jerusalem, built by Jewish people to document their heartbreaking experiences in the concentration camps and crematoriums of Nazi Germany before and during World War II. In more than thirty countries, museums and monuments were built as memorials to the Nazi Final Solution, but *Yad Vashem* is special, Israel's official memorial to the victims. The purpose is to keep the Holocaust memory alive while inspiring citizens and leaders to confront hatred, prevent genocide, and promote human dignity in our complex, ever changing world.

Hundreds of life-size photographs and filmstrips and a hundred video screens show survivor testimonies and short films. At the end of the Museum's historical narrative is the Hall of Names, a repository for the personal names of millions of victims, a memorial to every Jew who perished in that persecution. Established in 1953 and located on the western slope in Jerusalem, this memorial is the second most-visited Israeli tourist site. Curators charge no fee for admission and welcome approximately one million visitors a year.

Despite Nazi efforts to keep secret the unfolding state-sponsored persecution and murder of six million people—Jews, Gypsies, men, women, children, and especially handicapped—the horrifying information did leak out. German officials identified who was a Jew, marked them, confiscated property, and deported them. Companies fired Jews and later employed them as slave labor. Universities dismissed Jewish faculty and students. At least seven thousand prisoners endured experiments; most died as a result immediately or later. Without the help of local collaborators, the Germans would not have been able to extend the Holocaust across most of Europe.

How could humans allow such a terrible thing to happen to fellow humans? The German farm people, even those living close to the camps, claim they did not know this was happening. Maybe it is true. Many Germans continue to deny the extermination programs ever happened. Perhaps the atrocities are too difficult to conceive, too horrible to acknowledge.

NAZI GERMANY 1940s: The Holocaust was a top state secret in Nazi Germany. Hitler ordered no mention of the plan in print nor public statements, and the Nazis destroyed most camp documentation before the end of the war. The few documents that survived relating directly to the killing program were classified and stamped *Geheime Reichssache* (Top Secret). Once marked with that stamp, the records required special handling and destruction to prevent capture by the enemy, according to a speech by Nazi Secret Service (SS) General Heinrich Himmler, Reich Leader of the SS and Chief of the German Police. He was a key architect of the Holocaust and commanded the death squads who murdered Jews, Poles, Soviet prisoners-of-war, Roma (Gypsies), and others categorized as "racially inferior." Caught by British soldiers as he was trying to escape after the surrender in 1945, he managed to swallow a cyanide capsule and died quickly by suicide.

UNITED STATES: The United States Holocaust Memorial Museum (USHMM) in Washington, DC, is the official American memorial to the atrocities. Dedicated to helping leaders and citizens of the world confront hatred, prevent genocide, promote human dignity, and strengthen democracy, researchers documented more than forty-two thousand ghettos and concentration camps throughout German-controlled areas of Europe from 1933 to 1945. Nevertheless, the United States museum cannot compare to *Yad Vashem*.

THE CHILDREN'S MEMORIAL: A visit to the adjoining Children's Memorial in Jerusalem is an emotional experience, somewhat like a journey into outer space accompanied by soft electronic background music. This memorial, hollowed out from one of Jerusalem's uncountable underground caverns, is a tribute to the approximately one-and-a-half million Jewish children murdered during the Holocaust. Enormous poster-size pictures of healthy, happy children lead visitors down a long curving hallway that grows progressively darker. Soft music caresses the ear, while mirrored walls and ceiling enlarge the space. Shiny black marble tiles reflect from the floor. The hallway begins to brighten with millions of tiny twinkling stars, reflections from only six candles mirrored a thousand times. Tiny ticks of light on the floor guide footsteps. Like a Star Trek movie, a voice gently speaks the names of hundreds of murdered children, their ages, and countries of origin. All these young, innocent children died in the Holocaust. We want to believe they are now playing happily in their safe outer space freedom. This experience deeply moved us, and hardly a dry eye could be found as we exited the memorial. We needed comforting.

THE SILENT CRY: A bronze statue in the courtyard at first appears to be a sorrowing woman. The base around the statue is piled high with stones. Named "The Silent Cry" by sculptor Leah Michelson, he represents the only surviving member of a family killed in the Holocaust.

The figure is not a woman, but a robed man with a phylactery (*tefillin*) on his forehead. The Jewish National University Library in Jerusalem said, *"It is not against the Jewish law for women to wear the tefillin, so some women have prayed while wearing one."* The library also sent information on the artist Michelson, who described her sculptures as, *Bereavement bursts out from them from time to time, pain cries out from them.* The Museum's comment on the sculpture is: "Silence, restrained in its gravity, is sometimes only hinted at in this connection with the basalt monument, *The Silent Scream.*"

AUTHOR'S PRIVATE COLLECTION

FIGURE 1: STATUE

The Silent Scream by Leah Michelson, only surviving member of a family killed in the Holocaust. (Statue located outside the Children's Memorial at Yad Vashem.)

The silent sculpture indeed cries out quite loud and clear. The base is piled high, with many stones of memory. We added two more.

"THE PASSOVER STORY" — THE BLOOD WILL PASS OVER YOU: It is time to go, and we re-board the bus. After a bit, Mr. Elie pulls into parking, and lets us off for a Lebanese five-course meal, but the dinner is anti-climactic. Our guide used this opportunity to explain the Hebrew Passover meal in remembrance of the Jews' escape from Egypt. However, we must review the Day Two story about Abraham, Isaac, and Jacob to understand why the Jews were in Egypt. This story starts with Joseph, the first son of Jacob and Rachel.

FIGURE 2: JOSEPH
Joseph, son of Rachel and Jacob, shows off his coat of many colors.

JOSEPH'S COAT OF MANY COLORS: Joseph lived in the land of Canaan near Jerusalem with his widowed father, ten half-brothers, one full brother, and one half-sister. Joseph was Rachel's first-born and Jacob's eleventh son. Rachel, the love of Jacob's life, died in childbirth, bringing her second son, Benjamin, into the world. Of all his children, Jacob loved Joseph best because he was Rachel's child and also because Rachel's sons, Joseph and Benjamin, came to him in his old age. Since Rachel's sons were younger than the other boys, they spent more time helping their father at home while the older ones worked in the fields. One day Joseph's father gave him a colorful coat, a long robe with full sleeves. Joseph wore the cloak proudly, but every time the older brothers saw the coat, they only saw one color—red. They felt sibling rivalry. One day when Joseph was about seventeen, Jacob asked Joseph to check on his brothers who were working in the fields several miles away. Obedient Joseph went to find them, wearing his fancy coat. Joseph's reputation as a tattle-tale went with him, and he also tended to act superior. When the brothers saw Joseph in the distance, they started plotting ways to get rid of him.

At first, they planned to kill him. Reuben, Joseph's oldest brother, said, "Let's just give him a good scare. We will throw him in the cistern out here in the field."

When Joseph got there, the brothers pulled off his brightly-colored robe and threw him into a dry well, or cistern. Impossible to escape from, the cisterns were carved out of rock and shaped like a bottle with a small covered hole at the top. Reuben intended to go back and rescue Joseph later in the day, thinking it was just a funny trick to play on a kid brother. Reuben went back to work in the field. *Note: That sounds more like bullying.*

KIDNAPPED TO EGYPT: While Reuben was gone, some Ishmaelite travelers in a camel caravan came by on their way to Egypt. The merchants crossed the Jordan following the caravan road near the site of *Beit*

She'an. Reuben was out in the field, and the other brothers decided to sell Joseph for twenty pieces of silver. When Reuben came back to get Joseph, the well was empty. He was dismayed when he learned what the others had done because he knew his father would hold him responsible. The brothers came up with a lie to hide their wrong-doing. They killed a goat and splattered blood on Joseph's coat. They took the coat to their father and said: *We found this in the field, is it Joseph's coat?* Jacob recognized the colorful cloth immediately and was comfortless. He remained in deepest mourning for many weeks, believing a wild animal had torn his little boy into pieces.

FIGURE 3: CAMEL CARAVAN 1855

So that is how Abraham's great-grandson Joseph came to be sold by his jealous brothers into slavery in Egypt (Genesis 37 TLB).

BECOMING A SLAVE: When Joseph arrived in Egypt as a captive of the Ishmaelite traders, Potiphar, a member of the personal staff of Pharaoh, purchased him. At that time, Egypt was under the control of the Hyksos kings. Potiphar wore many hats. In addition to being on the King's staff, he also served as captain of the bodyguard and as chief executioner. He soon took notice of handsome Joseph and put him in charge of all his business affairs and administration of Potiphar's household.

THE BOSS'S WIFE LONGS FOR JOSEPH: It was not Joseph's fault that Potiphar's lovelorn wife took a shine to him. Islamic tradition says her name is Zuleikha. When Joseph dodged 'Zulu's' attempts to seduce him, she became so angry she falsely accused him of rape (Genesis 39). Potiphar believed his wife's story and threw Joseph into prison.

However, even in prison, Joseph was able to make friends and survive because of his talent at interpreting the meaning of dreams. One night, Pharaoh had a dream about seven fat cows and seven lean cows and another dream about seven heads of grain and seven shriveled heads. One of his servants told the Pharaoh about Joseph, how he could interpret the dreams of other prisoners. Pharaoh called for Joseph, now age thirty, to come before him. Hastily brought from the dungeon and given a quick shave and change of clothes. Pharaoh told Joseph of the dream and asked what he thought. *Both dreams mean the same thing, Joseph said. The seven fat cows mean seven years of prosperity, followed by seven years of famine.* Joseph suggested Pharaoh divide Egypt into districts. Each district should gather all excess crops into storehouses during the good years, so there would be enough food when the famine years came.

PHARAOH TAKES A LIKING TO JOSEPH: The King liked Joseph's idea and made him part of the inner circle. He gave Joseph beautiful clothing, golden neck chains, a chariot, and placed his signet ring on Joseph's finger. The king appointed Joseph as his second in command, and put him in complete charge over all the land of Egypt. He even gave Joseph a wife named Asineth, who may have been the daughter of Potiphar.

For the next seven years, there were bumper crops everywhere. Then the weather changed. The rains did not come in abundance, and the Nile did not overflow. The crops began to fail. Seven years of famine hit Canaan. The famine seemed worldwide. Many people were starving because of the drouth in neighboring countries. In Egypt, all was well because their storehouses were full. Joseph interpreted the king's dream correctly; otherwise, there would have been widespread death in Egypt. Neighboring countries sent emissaries, begging for grain. Pharaoh sent them all to Joseph, who opened up the storehouses and sold grain at a high price requiring bags full of silver. Joseph became one of the most powerful men on earth.

CREATIVE COMMONS
FIGURE 4: EGYPTIAN FEMALE

CANAAN GETS HUNGRY: Jacob heard there was grain available in Egypt, so he said to his sons, Go and buy some grain for us before we all starve to death, but leave Benjamin here. Jacob would not let his youngest go anywhere for fear some harm might come to him as it had to Joseph.

Jacob's ten older sons went down to Egypt to buy grain. Since Joseph, as the Pharaoh's assistant, was in charge of grain sales, the Canaanite brothers came to him. Joseph recognized his brothers instantly, but they did not recognize him. After twenty years, Joseph looked and spoke like an Egyptian. He was clean-shaven, while Hebrews always wore beards. Joseph wore his hair in Egyptian fashion and used the cosmetics that Egyptian royalty applied to their faces.

Joseph accused them of being spies. The brothers knew they were in danger, and they felt extreme fear. They knew they were totally at this ruler's arbitrary mercy. Joseph questioned them about their need for grain and learned that his father and little brother Benjamin were still alive. After holding the Hebrews for three days, Joseph decided to give them an option. Nine brothers could go home with the grain they needed to feed their clan, but one brother, Simeon, must remain hostage. They were to bring back the youngest brother, Benjamin, from Canaan to prove they were not spies.

GOING HOME WITH THE GRAIN: Joseph pretended he required an interpreter during his dealings with the Hebrews, so the brothers discussed their plight in front of Joseph, assuming he could not understand their language. They remarked this was their punishment for what they had done. Joseph told them if they did not bring Benjamin with them next trip, The hostage would die. Secretly, Joseph ordered the money the brothers paid for grain hidden in the necks of their grain sacks. When the nine brothers got home, opened their sacks, and discovered the money, they were even more afraid. They thought the Egyptians would think they were thieves. Jacob would not trust them to take Benjamin to Egypt, and the brothers did not dare return without him. What were they to do?

A RETURN TO EGYPT: Soon, the grain was gone, the drought and famine did not let up, and they were all hungry again. Jacob finally decided there was no other alternative. If he was to lose all of his sons, then so be it. They would all surely starve without the grain from Egypt. He turned the worry over to God. Sending Benjamin as well as gifts, returning the money that had mysteriously found its way into their grain bags and an equal amount to buy new grain, Jacob sent his sons back to Egypt. The brothers hoped to return safely to Canaan with grain as well as both of their younger brothers. They reached Egypt's granaries safely. Joseph was overjoyed when he saw his brothers, but he remained careful not to show his emotion.

FIGURE 5: LIFE IN EGYPT

AN EGYPTIAN BANQUET: He quietly ordered a banquet prepared and served at noon in his own home. The brothers immediately suspect a trap, and think they are in trouble because of the money found in their packs. Joseph's house manager assures them that that is not the case, but they are still suspicious. When Joseph comes home, the brothers present him with gifts from Canaan, including the best fruits of Jericho, balm from Gilead, honey, spices, myrrh, nuts, and almonds. At seeing his little brother Benjamin, Joseph became so emotional he had to leave for a few moments to regain his composure. When he returns, the guests sit at three separate tables.

- Joseph eats alone.
- A servant mysteriously seats the Hebrew brothers in order of birth, and they eat together as one group.
- The Egyptian house servants eat separately from both the brothers and from Joseph.
- This seating is typical for the time and place in Egypt. Jews were typically shepherds. Egyptians considered shepherds the lowest class of people because they raised sheep. An Egyptian would never eat with a shepherd, nor with Jews, nor eat with the servants.

THE REVEAL: After several little twists and turns of the story, Joseph finally revealed himself to his brothers, and they all wept together with joy at the reunion. Joseph told the brothers not to fear because what they meant for evil, God intended for good. Joseph coaches his brothers to tell the Pharaoh they raise livestock and wish to settle in Goshen, a flat, fertile area along the Pelusiac branch of the Nile River. They would be away from the bulk of Egyptian society to herd their sheep and live in peace. Joseph said, *"Five more years of famine are coming, so get my father and your families, and bring them to the land of Goshen. It is the very best territory in Egypt."*

HOME AGAIN, HOME AGAIN: Upon their return to Canaan, the brothers told their father that Joseph was alive and, in fact, a ruler in Egypt. They said Joseph wanted them to come live near him. Jacob and his tribe of seventy gathered up all their livestock and journeyed to Egypt. Joseph settled his father in Goshen, a fertile land suitable for crops and livestock (Genesis 46-50) where he lived out his last years with his sons and their families. When he died, his sons took his bones to lie with his ancestors. The Hebrew people stayed in Egypt and multiplied for more than a hundred years.

LIFE IN EGYPT BECOMES UNBEARABLE: A century later, the friendly Hyksos Kings of Egypt suffered defeat, and many changes took place under more cruel rulers. These new monarchs made slaves of the Hebrew people and put brutal taskmasters over them while using them to build massive structures. The taskmaster continued to make slavery ever more bitter, forcing them to toil long and hard in the fields, and carry heavy loads of mortar and brick. The situation became unbearable. Something had to change.

CREATIVE COMMONS
FIGURE 6: EGYPTIAN MALE

WELCOME THE LEGEND OF MOSES: On Day Two, we learned the genealogy of Abraham, from Isaac to Jacob whose four wives: Leah, Rachel, Bilhah, and Zilpah, presented him with twelve sons. Leah's third son, Levi, gave birth to a son Kohath, who had a son Amran, who became the father of Moses. As an adult, Moses took the responsibility of leading the tribe out of Egypt to the "promised land" of Israel. The story of that exodus is immortalized in the movie, *The Ten Commandments,* and in the Bible's Old Testament book of Exodus. Here's a quick summary.

FINDING A BABY IN A BASKET: As this story begins, Joseph, his brothers and the Pharaoh that Joseph once served have all long since died. More than four centuries passed. Feeling threatened by Jacob's descendants who have multiplied into an enormous tribe, the new leadership in Egypt embarked on a campaign to subdue the Israelites, first forcing them into slavery, and eventually decreeing that all Jewish boys must be killed at birth.

The Hebrew women resisted the decree and one woman named Jochabed opted to save her newborn son by setting him afloat in a papyrus basket on the Nile. Fortunately, the king's daughter, Bithiah, came to the river to bathe and discovered the abandoned child. She unknowingly hired the baby's mother, Jochabed, as his nurse. Bithiah raised the boy in Egyptian royalty, and accepted the name, Moses (*Moshe*).

MOSES BECAME A MURDERER: When he turned forty years old, Moses learned about his Hebrew heritage. Soon after that, while walking by the work projects, he saw an Egyptian slavemaster unmercifully beating a Hebrew. Knowing this was one of his people, Moses became very angry. He struck down the Egyptian and hid the dead body in the sand. However, fearing retribution, Moses ran away. He settled in Midian, where he fell in love with Zipporah, daughter of a priest. She may have been a descendant of Abraham through his third wife, Keturah. Moses had a good life in Midian, but he wanted to return to Egypt eventually.

ANOTHER RETURN TO EGYPT: Moses was tending his father-in-law's flock when he led the sheep to the back of the wilderness and came to Mount Sinai. An angel appeared to Moses in the flames of a burning bush near the mountain, encouraging Moses to return to his brothers in Egypt to see if they are still alive. Moses returned to Jethro and begged. *Please let me return to my brothers in Egypt and see whether they are still alive.* Jethro told his son-in-law to go in peace.

MOSES RETURNS TO THE SCENE OF THE CRIME: Moses, now eighty years old, found the situation no better in Egypt than when he left. His Jewish friends begged him to find a way to return them to Israel. Moses went to the rulers, but they would not agree to let the Hebrews go.

God helped the Israelite Hebrews escape by inflicting ten plagues on the Egyptians before the Pharaoh finally agreed to release them. The tenth and worst of the plagues was the deaths of all the Egyptian first-born, including the death of the Pharaoh's beloved son.

BLOOD ON THE DOORPOSTS: The Hebrews were instructed to mark the doorposts of their homes with the blood of a slaughtered spring lamb and the spirit of the Lord would know to *pass over* the firstborn in these homes. *Note: This is the connection to a mezuzah on modern doorposts as explained on Day One and also to the Passover holiday still celebrated.*

LET MY PEOPLE GO: That night, the Pharaoh, angry and grief-stricken, summoned Moses and told him to leave Egypt. *Get out immediately!* The Jews did not wait for the yeast in bread dough to rise. In commemoration for the duration of Passover, the feast of unleavened bread is celebrated. Today *matzo* (a flat unleavened bread) is a tradition of the Jewish holiday. When Pharaoh calmed down and realized he was losing all of his slave workers, he changed his mind and sent six hundred of his best chariots after Moses to bring back the slaves. Who would do the work without them? However, the Hebrews escaped across the Red Sea.

But their suffering was not over. The people nearly starved to death as Moses led them wandering about in the desert for many years. *Note: The biblical quote is forty years.* They encountered many difficulties. Luckily, they found "quail and manna" which kept them alive during this difficult time. Eventually Moses brought his people out of Egypt back into Israel.

FIGURE 7: MOSES
The marble statue of Moses, by Michelangelo, housed in the church of San Pietro in Vincoli in Rome.

To reach their "promised land," Moses and his followers had to conquer the people living there. Their first military objective was Jericho. The date is around 1250 BC, and Moses' military general was named Joshua, and we told his story of the Battle of Jericho in Chapter Five. According to Jewish tradition, Moses wrote the first five books of the Bible known to the Jews as the Torah. The books of Exodus, Leviticus, Numbers, and Deuteronomy tell the Exodus story, basically Moses' autobiography. The Jewish people honor Moses today as the Lawgiver of Israel.

BUT IS IT TRUE?

Archaeological evidence does not support the escape from Egypt's story told in the book of Exodus. Most researchers abandoned the investigation of Moses and the Exodus as "a fruitless pursuit." The opinion of the overwhelming majority of modern biblical scholars is that the exodus story became shaped into its present form after the exile period.

The story of Moses and the Exodus is a fascinating tale. However, so far there is no confirmation by contemporary extra-biblical references, but neither is the story proven false, according to a 2007 article in *National Geographic*.

BREAKING BREAD AND SHARING THE PASSOVER MEAL: Passover (*Pesach*) usually celebrated in April, marks the 'passing over' or sparing homes of the Israelites from the plague of death in Egypt. The event lasts for seven days in Israel and eight days outside Israel. It begins with the Jewish Seder, a ceremonial feast including symbolic foods such as unleavened bread and bitter herbs in memory of the many harsh years of slavery. It also includes special blessings, songs, and the retelling of the exodus narrative.

Aaron, our Moses, picked up a hefty "cracker" of matzo, tearing it apart to demonstrate how they 'broke bread.' On the subject of food, our guide described how God provided quail and manna to feed the Israelites in the barren desert during their exodus. *There went forth a wind from the Lord and brought quails from the sea and let them fall by the camp. The manna, a flaky, sweet substance, gathered early in the morning to be ground and made into bread* (Numbers 11:31). *Manna* is a secretion exuded by tamarisk trees and bushes. Aaron said to this day, quail migrate across the Mediterranean Sea and drop exhausted in the desert. Bedouins of the Sinai Peninsula still hasten to gather up manna early in the morning before the ants find it first.

THE TEN COMMANDMENTS AND THE ARK: On the way to Israel, Moses climbed Mount Sinai to meditate and pray. God gave him commandments or rules for his people to follow. The rules appeared on stone tablets. Years later, Solomon built an impressive golden chest to house the commandments that became known as the Ark of the Covenant. The book of Exodus gives detailed instructions on construction of the Ark.

The Bible denounces all forms of idolatry; however, all people seem to have a passion for holy relics. The Ark served as the talisman of the Israelites for several centuries. Many people remain fascinated

240   To Isreal with Love

WWW.WIKIPEDIA.COM

FIGURE 8: PRIESTS CARRYING THE ARK
*When the Jewish people traveled, Levite priests always led the procession
with the ark on their shoulders.*

with details about the holy box, and a few people spent their entire lifetimes searching to find it, as told in Chapter Seven.

LEAVING ISRAEL: Unlike the Levites and the Israelites who traveled on foot, we jump on our big blue bus to continue our journey of discovery, but we must travel without the Ark or our Moses. After dinner, Mr. Elie takes us from Jerusalem to our beginning at Ben Gurion Airport in Tel Aviv. It is the middle of the night in America. We pause on the summit of a distant hill to take a final look back and say a sad farewell to this historic and fabled city that gave us such an education. We bid the walls and gates of Jerusalem goodbye, perhaps forever. We do not want to leave, but we do want to go home. We are not just tired. We feel completely drained. Our brains overflow with new information. Our hearts abound with love for our travel group, for Jerusalem and all of Israel. Nevertheless, complete exhaus-tion claims our bodies. As Aaron promised, we earned our title of Pilgrims, with all this climbing on our feet. But… such total fatigue!

AN AIRPORT CALLED TOWER OF BABEL: Ben Gurion Airport this night is a beehive of activity, unbelievably crowded and jammed in mass confusion with travelers of all nationalities speaking different languages and seemingly moving in all directions at once. Jon says it gives new significance to the story of the tower of Babel. *"That is why the place was called Babel, meaning confusion, because it was there Jehovah gave them many languages"* (Genesis 11:9 RSV). The Israel airport scene reminds of round-up time on the ranch with a herd of restless cattle, all moving and stomping and bawling noisily at once in a small corral. These Israelis are impatient people, and they do not tolerate waiting in orderly lines. We recognize those of our group trying to observe little civilities and good manners. We are concerned they may not make it to the plane by liftoff. We decide if there is an opening in the serpentine line, we better move up quickly before someone else does. Uniformed guards scrutinize passengers and bags for a long time before anyone gets even close to an airplane. Those measures improve the safety factor, but it increases pushing, swarming, and stress.

WANDERING AROUND TO CUSTOMS: We are tired and cranky and no longer envious of the dozen people of our group going on for an extended adventure in Egypt. Our group scattered in the crowd, and we see no familiar faces. We are in some kind of line, but it is impossible to tell which ticket counter we are heading to. Aaron—our Moses—is gone. Like the Israelites in the exodus (Exodus 15-18), we wonder if we must spend the rest of our lives wandering in the desert of Ben Gurion Airport. After what seems like hours in the overcrowded confusion, we finally reach the relative peace and safety of the customs desk. Repeating our frustrating experience in New York on the way over, we struggle through customs and security. Finally, we are allowed to board the crowded El Al flight leaving at 1:00 a.m. Israel time.

ANOTHER ALL NIGHTER: Exhausted, this plump American shoehorns into a seat built for slender Israelis. This time I remember to slip on soft socks. It will be another all night and all morning flight, eleven hours in the air, riding in the "cattle car." On the plus side, once we are inspected, approved, baggage-handed, passport-stamped, boarded, and seated, El Al Airline employees are friendly and helpful. We are so tired that sleep comes quickly despite cramped quarters. We are going home, one flight-hour at a time.

MORNING COMES QUICKLY: Before we are ready to leave our sleep world, the El Al stewardess surprises us with a warm wet cloth as they serve breakfast. This meal is delicious—as if we needed any more food. We have eaten our way through many days of bountiful buffets, festive falafel, and numerous roadside fresh fruit with yogurt stands. After landing in New York, we claim our baggage and shuttle from JFK to LaGuardia to change to American Airlines for our flight to Dallas. The returning experience with customs officers is smooth. We move our baggage to the checkout counter, and we will not see it again until we are home. Our adventure is ending, where it began at the airport. We may look the same, but we are different people now. We have come full circle, and this

FIGURE 9: FAREWELL
Saying goodbye to our new Israel friends.

seems like the start of a whole new journey.

At the end of his visit to Israel, Twain ended with: *We do not think in the holy places. We think in bed, afterward when the glare and the noise and the confusion are gone. In our fancy, we revisit alone the solemn monuments of the past and summon the phantom pageants of an age that has passed away.*

AIRPLANE ETIQUETTE: The American Airlines flight attendant warns jet lag is much worse flying west. Good. We can blame it on jet lag and the time change that we no longer know for sure, or even care, what day it is. We feel worn out, washed out, played out, spent, fatigued, dog-tired, wholly emptied of resources. **Tip: Schedule a day of rest on return home. You will need it!* We may be a sad-looking crew, but we have shared an incredible experience, and none of us will ever be the same again. We have learned too much. Traveling is not just seeing something new. It is also leaving behind what you have found. Not just opening doors but closing them behind you, never to return. However, the place you leave is always there for you to go back to in memory. This pilgrimage is not a journey for the infirm or faint of heart. It is a life-changing event. As our guide predicted, when we are home, people will notice we are now different people. Still gentiles, but different in our minds.

WHAT DID WE LEARN? We became acquainted with two bodies of water, the Sea of Galilee and the Dead Sea, both fed by the Jordan river and yet very different, one from the other. The Galilee takes from Jordan and gives it to the Dead Sea. The Galilee has sweet and pleasant water, and the Dead Sea is salty and bitter because it only has an inlet. We should follow the example of the Jordan River by caring for people and giving of ourselves on our journey through life.

We take home with us what we came to Jerusalem to find. We know the treasure of the holy land lives on in the realm of our imagination. We did not solve the mystery of the missing Ark of the Covenant, but we did dig up several new theories.

Shalom chavarim, Shalom chavarim
Shalom. Shalom.
le heet rah oot, le heet rah oot
Shalom. Shalom.

Farewell my friend, farewell my friend
Farewell. Farewell.
Till we meet again, till we meet again
Farewell, Farewell!

O Israel, we love you.
We will never forget you, Jerusalem
—Even if we are gentiles!

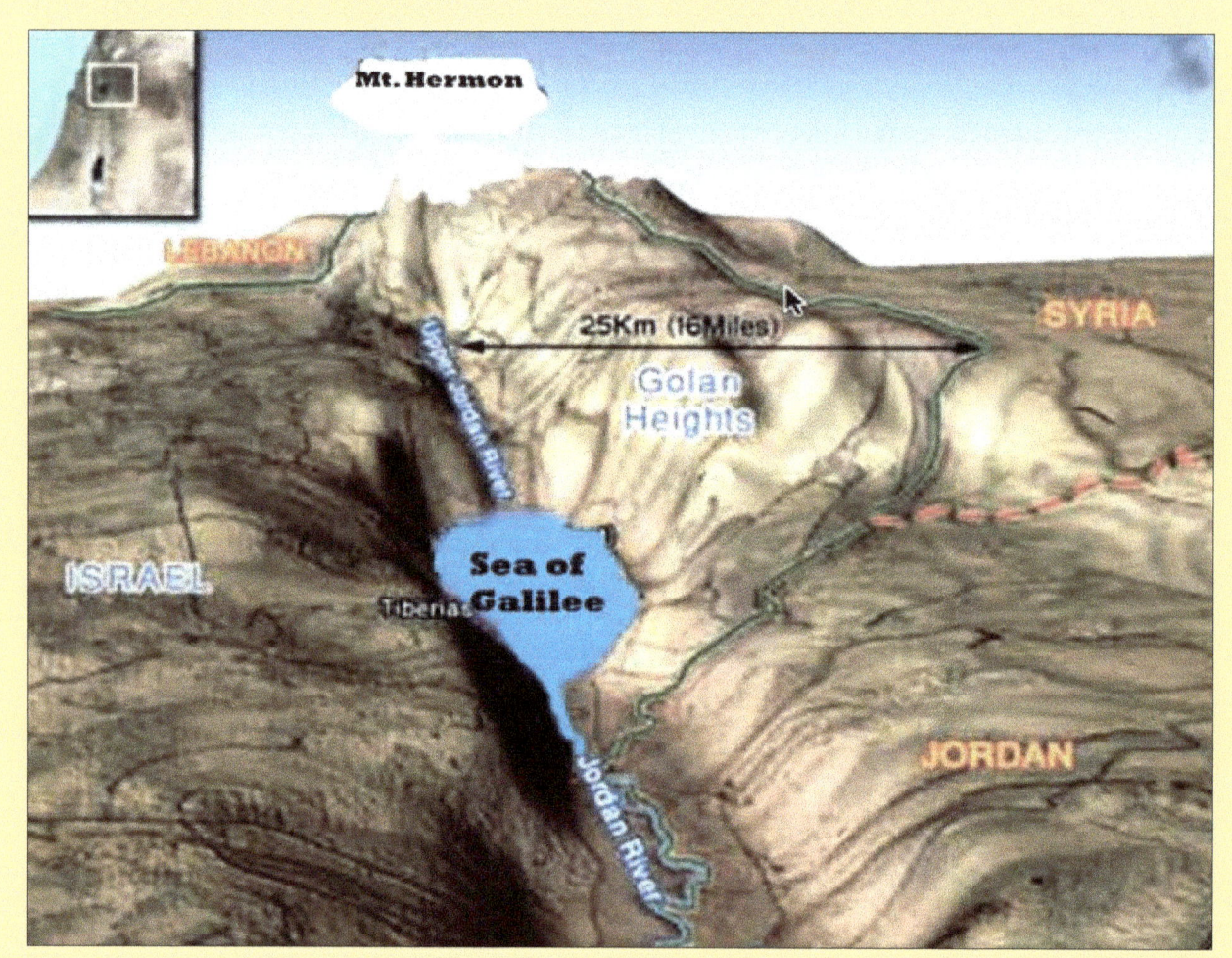

FIGURE 10: TOPOGRAPHIC MAP OF THE GOLAN HEIGHTS.

FIGURE 11: ISRAEL MAP
At the time of Christ, AD 30.

Chart of Biblical History

BC

7000 BC	First walls of Jericho built
2000 BC	Period of the ancestor Abraham
1700 BC	Jacob's family enters Egypt
1260 BC	Moses leads the escape from Egypt
1220 BC	Joshua leads the people into Canaan
1200 BC	Israelites colonize Palestine
1020 BC	King Saul reigns
1000 BC	King David buys rock from Araunah
975 BC	King Solomon begins temple
950 BC	Solomon's temple completed
922 BC	Judea is divided into two kingdoms
869-850 BC	King Ahab rules (Northern Kingdom)
721 BC	Northern Kingdom destroyed
597 BC	Jerusalem falls to Babylon,
586 BC	Solomon's Temple is destroyed,
586 BC	Jews are exiled into Babylon
538 BC	Jews return to Jerusalem
515 BC	2nd Temple (Zerubbabel's) rebuilt
333 BC	Alexander the Great conquers Israel
167 BC	Jews revolt - (Hasmonean period)
63 BC	Romans capture Jerusalem
47 BC	Antipater is procurator of Judea
37 BC	Herod the Great becomes king
31 BC	Caesar Augustus is emperor of Rome
20 BC	Third Temple (Herod's)
4 BC	BIRTH OF JESUS
4 BC	Herod dies,
4 BC	Herod Antipas rules

Chart of Biblical History

AD

AD 26-36	Pontius Pilate governor over Judea
AD 25-26	Jesus's ministry in the Galilee
AD 29-30	Herod Antipas executes John Baptist
AD 30	Jesus is crucified
AD 10	Paul's birth
AD 30-31	Paul's conversion
AD 46	Paul's first journey
AD 60-61	Paul's voyage to Rome
AD 62-64	Temple restoration completed
AD 64	Nero burns Christians
AD 62-68	Paul and Peter are martyred
AD 66-70	Jewish revolt against Rome
AD 70	Temple destroyed again
AD 70	Masada captured,
AD 70	Diaspora (dispersing Jews) begins
AD 81	Domitian is Roman emperor, a tyrant
AD 95/96	John, Christian, writes Revelations
AD 132-135	2nd Jewish revolt against Rome, fails
AD 330	Constantine capitol of Roman Empire
AD 636	Muslims build "Mosque of Omar"
AD 395-637	Byzantine Rule
AD 638-1099	Arab Rule
AD 646	Caesarea falls to the Muslims
AD 1099	Crusaders take Caesarea
AD 1099-129	Crusader Kingdom
AD 1250-1516	Mameluke rule
AD 1291	Caesarea is abandoned
AD 1516-1917	Turkish rule
AD 1917-1919	World War I
AD 1917	British Mandate
AD 1942-1946	World War II
AD 1948	Israel proclaims Independence
AD 1948-1967	Israel is divided into many sectors

Bibliography by Title: (Works Cited)

ARCHAEOLOGY IN THE LAND OF THE BIBLE; Negev, Prof. Avraham;

ASIMOV'S GUIDE TO THE BIBLE; Asimov, Isaac;

ANCIENT WORLD (The); Briquebec, John;

AND THE WALLS CAME TUMBLING DOWN; Dehan, Emmanuel;

ANTIQUITIES OF THE JEWS; Flavius, Josephus

BEDUOIN LIFE IN BIBLE LANDS, Whiting, John D.

BIBLE ALMANAC (THE); Packer, Tenney and White;

BIBLE ARCHAEOLOGY REVIEW, Jan/Feb 2013; May/June 2017

BIBLE AS HISTORY(THE); Keller, Werner;

BIBLE DICTIONARY;

BIBLE THROUGH THE AGES (THE); Reader's Digest Books;

CAESAREA MARITIMA; Hohlfelder, Robert L.;

CONSTANTINOPLE; Young, Geo;

CRADLE OF CIVILIZATION; Time-Life Books

CRUDEN'S CONCORDANCE

DARK AGES (THE); Asimov, Isaac;

DEATHBED CONFESSION OF RON WYATT, online

DISCIPLE; Wilke, Richard Byrd and Wilke, Julia Kitchens;

GREAT CITIES OF THE ANCIENT WORLD; Camp, L. Sprague de;

HISTORY OF ANCIENT ISRAEL (THE); Grant, Michael;

HISTORICAL SITES IN THE HOLY LAND; Pearlman, Moshe and Yannai, Yaacov;

HOLY BIBLE (THE); Old and New Testament in the King James Version

HOLY LAND (THE); Baseman, Bob;

HOLY LAND (THE); Time-Life Books;

INCREDIBLE MYSTERIES OF THE BIBLE; Miller, Stephen M.

INNOCENTS ABROAD (THE); Twain, Mark;

IN SEARCH OF THE HOLY LAND; Morton, H.V. and Burri, Rene;

IN THE STEPS OF JESUS; Illustrated Guide to Places of the Holy Land; Walker, Peter.

JERUSALEM, History, Archaeology, and Apologetic Proof of Scripture; Wiemers, Galyn.

JOSEPHUS, The works of; Complete & Unabridged (First Edition), Translated by Whiston, William.

KING HEROD'S DREAM, CAESAREA ON THE SEA; Holum, Hohlfelder, Bull,

LAND OF JESUS (THE); Bonechi, Casa Editrice;

LIFE OF ANTONY, Flavius, Josephus

LIFE OF CHRIST; Stalker, James;

LIFE OF PAUL; Stalker, James

LIVING BIBLE (THE); Campus Life Magazine editors,

LESSONS OF HISTORY (THE); Durant, Will and Ariel;

LOST CIVILIZATIONS —THE HOLY LAND; Time Life Books of Alexandria, VA;

MAPBOOK, NELSON'S 3-D BIBLE; Jenkins, Simon;

MODEL OF ANCIENT JERUSALEM (THE); Holyland Corp., Inc;

NATIONAL GEOGRAPHIC MAGAZINE (THE); Jan 1937 pp 64,65; John D. Whiting, "Bedouin Life in Bible Lands.

PASSAGES, A BIBLICAL TREASURE TROVE; The Green Collection Exhibit

PEOPLE & PLACES IN THE BIBLE; Farrar, John;

PROMISED LAND; Eban, Abba;

REFORMATION (THE); Durant, Will;

RAIDERS OF THE LOST ARK, Indiana Jones, Adventure film

ROMAN EMPIRE (THE); Nardo, Don

ROMAN EMPIRE (THE); Whittock, Martyn

ROMAN EMPIRE (THE); Salinas, Jose L. Cortes

ROSE GUIDE TO THE TABERNACLE; (no author named)

ROSE GUIDE TO THE TEMPLE; Price, Randall

SEALS OF JEREMIAH'S CAPTORS DISCOVERED; Armstrong Foundation

STEPPING UP: A journey through the Psalms of Ascent; Moore, Beth

STORY OF THE BIBLE WORLD; Keyes, Nelson Beecher;

THIS IS ISRAEL; Mann, Sylfia;

THE HOLY LAND, TIME-LIFE BOOK 1992

TOPICAL JOSEPHUS (THE); Rogers, Cleon L. Jr;

UNPUBLISHED MANUSCRIPT; Glass, Neil;

UNPUBLISHED MANUSCRIPT; Simpson, Laveta;

WAY (THE); The Living Bible, Illustrated

WORLD'S BIGGEST SANDBOX (THE); Waters, Michael, Sooner Magazine, 1994

WASHINGTON POST (THE); 14 July 2012 The Six-Day War

VERSIONS OF THE HOLY BIBLE:
NIV New International Version
NLT New Living Translation
KJV King James Version
NKJV New King James Version
ESV English Standard Version
NASB New American Standard Bible
TLB The Living Bible
NRSV New Revised Standard Version
CEV Contemporary English Version

Bibliography by Author:

Asimov, Isaac; ASIMOV'S GUIDE TO THE BIBLE; Doubleday & Co Inc; ©1968 by Isaac Asimov; Library of Congress card number 68-23566 (no ISBN). Also the reprint by Avenel Books; ISBN 0-517-34582-x. Pages: 1,295.

Asimov, Isaac; THE DARK AGES; Houghton Mifflin Company of Boston 1968; © 1968 by Isaac Asimov; Library of Congress card number 68-28051 (no ISBN).

Author not listed; ROSE GUIDE TO THE TABERNACLE; © 2008 Bristol Works, Inc; www.rose-publishing.com; ISBN 1-59636-276-6.

Author unknown; MODEL OF ANCIENT JERUSALEM (THE) at the time of the Second Temple, Pictorial Guide; (small booklet); ©Holyland Corp Inc. Produced by Palphot Ltd, Printed in Israel.

Barkey, Gabriel; *"Who was Buried in the Tomb of Pharaoh's Daughter,"* Bible Archaeology Review, Jan/Feb 2013.

Baseman, Bob; THE HOLY LAND; Produced by Palphot Ltd; Copyright 1992 by Palphot Ltd., Holy Views, POB 2497, Jerusalem.

Biblical Archaeology Review; several short articles, Jan/Feb 2017; May/June 2017.

Bonechi, Casa Editrice; THE LAND OF JESUS, English Edition, Copyright 1991 by Bonechi, Via Cairoli, 18/b, 50131 Florence, Italy. Pub by Bonechi & Steimatzky. ISBN 88-7009-729-3.

Briquebec, John; ANCIENT WORLD (The), From the Earliest Civilizations to the Roman Empire; © 1990, Warwick Press of New York; ISBN 0-531-19073-0.

Camp, L. Sprague de; GREAT CITIES OF THE ANCIENT WORLD; Published by Barnes & Noble Books; © 1972 by L. Sprague de Camp; ISBN 0-88029-482-5.

Campus Life Magazine editors, THE LIVING BIBLE, Published by Tyndale House Publishers of Wheaton, Illinois; © 1971 by Tyndale House Publishers; © 1972 by Youth for Christ International; ISBN 8423-7820-0.

Cruden's CONCORDANCE; Published by Barbour and Company, Inc. PO Box 719, Uhrichsville, OH 44683; © 1987 by Barbour and Company, Inc. ISBN 1-55748-015-X.

Di Berardino; Fr. Angelo; HISTORICAL ATLAS OF ANCIENT CHRISTIANITY; Published by ICCS Press, 1300 Eagle Road, St Davids, PA 19087; Copyright 2013 Angelo Di Berardino. Coffee table size Pages: 478. ISBN 978-1-62428-000-9.

Dehan, Emmanuel; AND THE WALLS CAME TUMBLING DOWN; ©1984 by Dehan, free-lance guide, POD 3238, Tel Aviv 61031,

Durant, Will and Ariel; THE LESSONS OF HISTORY; Published by Simon and Schuster of New York; © 1968 by Will and Ariel Durant; Library of Congress Catalog Number 68-19949; (no ISBN).

Durant, Will; THE REFORMATION, The Story of Civilization Part VI, A History of European Civilization from Wyclif to Calvin: 1300 - 1564; © 1957 by Will Durant; Published by Simon and Schuster of New York; ISBN 0-671-61050-3.

Eban, Abba; PROMISED LAND; © 1978 Thomas Nelson Inc., Publishers and Gordon Wetmore; ISBN 0-8407-4061-1.

Farrar, John; PEOPLE & PLACES IN THE BIBLE; Copyright MCMXXCVII by Barbour and Company, Inc.ISBN 1-55748-030-3.

Glass, Neil; UNPUBLISHED MANUSCRIPT of transcribed tape of the tour of Israel.

Grant, Michael; THE HISTORY OF ANCIENT ISRAEL; Published by Charles Scribner's Sons of New York; Copyright 1984 Michael Grant Publications Ltd; Printed in USA; ISBN 0-684-18084-7.

Hohlfelder, Robert L.; "Caesarea Maritima, Herod the Great's City on the Sea"; *National Geographic Magazine*, Vol 171 No2, February 1987.

Holum, Kenneth G.; Hohlfelder, Robert L.; Bull, Robert J.; Raban, Avner; et al; KING HEROD'S DREAM, CAESAREA ON THE SEA; Published by W.W. Norton & Co of New York and London (500 5th Ave,,NY 10110); Copyright 1988 by Kenneth G. Holum and Robert Hohlfelder. Printed in Hong Kong. ISBN 0-393-02493-8.

HOLY BIBLE (THE); Old and New Testament in the King James Version, translated out of the original tongues and with previous translations diligently compared and revised; Copyright 1976 by Thomas Nelson, Inc of Nashville, Tenn.

Holyland Corp., Inc; THE MODEL OF ANCIENT JERUSALEM, Pictorial Guide, at the Time of the Second Temple, in the grounds of the Holyland Hotels Jerusalem Israel; Copyright by Holyland Corp; Produced by Paiphot Ltd, printed in Israel (no date).

Jenkins, Simon; NELSON'S 3-D BIBLE MAPBOOK; © 1985 Lion Publishing; ISBN 0-8407-1964-7 Published by Lion Publishing PLC, Sandy Lane West, Oxford, England.

Keller, Werner; THE BIBLE AS HISTORY, 2nd revised edition translated from the German by William Neil; Published by William Morrow and Co, NY 1981; ©1980 by Hodder and Stoughton; ISBN 0-688-03724-0.

Keyes, Nelson Beecher; STORY OF THE BIBLE WORLD, in Map, Word and Picture; pub by the Readers Digest Association, Inc; Pleasantville, NY; © 1962 by The Readers Digest Association, Inc; Library of Congress Card Number 62-17861; (no ISBN).

Mann, Sylfia; THIS IS ISRAEL, Pictorial Guide and Souvenir; Produced by Palphot Ltd; Copyright 1992 by Palphot Ltd., POB 2, Herzlia, Israel. Printed in Israel. ISBN 965-280-000-7.

Mazar, Eilat; DISCOVERING THE SOLOMONIC WALL IN JERUSALEM; a Remarkable Archaeological Adventure; ©2011 by Dr. Eilat Mazar and Shoham Academic Research and Publication; Printed in Israel 2011; ISBN: 978-965-90299-69.

Mazar, Eilat; SEALS OF JEREMIAH'S CAPTORS DISCOVERED; Armstrong International Cultural Foundation; ©2012 by Dr. Eilat Mazar and Armstrong Auditorium; Printed in USA 2012.

Mazar, Eilat; THE PALACE OF KING DAVID, Excavations at the Summit of the City of David; ©2009 by Dr. Eilat Mazar; Shoham Academic Research and Publication of Jerusalem and New York; Printed in Israel by The Old City Press of Jerusalem; ISBN: 978-965-90299-5-2.

Miller, Stephen M; INCREDIBLE MYSTERIES OF THE BIBLE, A Visual Exploration; ©2008 by Stephen M. Miller; Zondervan, Grand Rapids, Michigan; ISBN 978=0-310-25594-9.

Moore, Beth; Stepping Up: A JOURNEY THROUGH THE PSALMS OF ASCENT; Lifeway / 2007 ISBN-13: 9781415857434.

Morton, H.V. and Burri, Rene; IN SEARCH OF THE HOLY LAND; © 1979 by H. V. Morton; First published in the USA by Dodd, Mead & Co, Inc; designed and produced in Great Britain by London Editions Ltd, 30 Uxbridge Road, London W128ND; ISBN 0-396-07691-2.

Negev, Prof. Avraham (Professor of Classical Archaeology at the Hebrew University of Jerusalem); ARCHAEOLOGY IN THE LAND OF THE BIBLE; pub by Schocken Books of NY, 200 Madison Ave, 10016; First pub 1977; ©1976.

Nardo, Don; ROMAN EMPIRE (THE); Lucent Books; © 1994 by Lucent; ISBN 1-56006-231-2.

Packer, Tenney and White; THE BIBLE ALMANAC, A comprehensive handbook of the people of the Bible and how they lived; Guideposts; Carmel, New York 10512; © 1980 by Thomas Nelson Publishers, Nashville, Tennessee; ISBN 0-8407-5162-1.

Pearlman, Moshe and Yannai, Yaacov; HISTORICAL SITES IN THE HOLY LAND; © held by authors; 4th edition 1985, Judson Press of Valley Forge PA; ISBN: 0-8170-1086-6.

Price, Randall; ROSE GUIDE TO THE TEMPLE; © 2012 Bristol Works, Inc; Rose Publishing, Inc, 4733 Torrance Blvd, #259, Torrance, CA 90503; www.rose-publishing.com; ISBN 978-1-59636-468-4.

Plutarch, Greek historian AD 46-120; LIFE OF ANTONY.

Reader's Digest Books; BIBLE THROUGH THE AGES (THE); Published by Reader's Digest General Books; ©1996; ISBN 0-89577-872-6.

Rogers, Cleon L. Jr; TOPICAL JOSEPHUS (THE), Historical accounts that shed light on the Bible; © 1992 by Cleon L. Rogers, Jr; Requests for info to: Zondervan Publishing House, Academic and Professional Books, Grand Rapids, Michigan 49530; ISBN 0-310-57440-4.

Salinas, Jose L. Cortes; ROMAN EMPIRE (THE); Published by Children's Press, Chicago; © 1990 UNESCO; ISBN 0-516-08382-1.

Simpson, Laveta; UNPUBLISHED MANUSCRIPT, transcribed tape of David Assael's remarks about Jerusalem.

Smith's BIBLE DICTIONARY; ©1987 by Barbour and Company, Inc.ISBN 1-55748-017-6.

Stalker, James; LIFE OF CHRIST; © MCMXCIV by Barbour and Company, Inc.; ISBN 1-55748-592-5. Barbour and Company.

Stalker, James; LIFE OF PAUL; © MCMXCIV by Barbour and Company, Inc.; ISBN 1-55748-592-5. Barbour and Company,

Time-Life Books; CRADLE OF CIVILIZATION; © 1967 Time Inc.; Library of Congress catalogue card number 67-29528.

Time-Life Books; THE HOLY LAND; ©1992 Time-Life Books; ISBN 0-8094-9866-9.

Time Life Books of Alexandria, Virginia; LOST CIVILIZATIONS—THE HOLY LAND; first printing 1992; Published simultaneously in Canada; Time Life is trademark of Time Warner, Inc. USA. ISBN 0-8094-9867-7.

Twain, Mark; THE INNOCENTS ABROAD; Published by the Penguin Group of New York; written in 1867 "Being some account of the steamship Quaker City's pleasure excursion to Europe and the Holy Land; with descriptions of countries, nations, incidents and adventures, as they appeared to the author." Signet Classic 0451-515889.

Walker, Peter; IN THE STEPS OF JESUS, An Illustrated Guide to The Places of the Holy Land; ©2006 by Peter Walker; Published by Zondervan, Lion Hudson Publishing plc, Mayfield House, 256 Banbury road Oxford OX27DH, England. www.lionhudson,com. ISBN-13; 978-0l-310-27647-0; isbn-10; 0-310-27647-0.

Waters, Michael in the *Sooner Magazine*, Vol. 14, Number 2, pg. 23-29, 1994 Winter; "The World's Biggest Sandbox".

WAY (THE); The Living Bible, Illustrated; Tyndale House Publishers, Wheaton, Illinois; Copyright 1972; ISBN 8423-7820-0.

Wiemers, Galyn; JERUSALEM, History, Archaeology and Apologetic Proof Scripture; ©2010 by Galyn Wiemers; Printed in United States of America by Signature Book Printing. www.sbpbooks.com, Last Hope Books and Publications; ISBN-13: 978-0-9794382-3-3. Pages: 252.

Whiting, John D; "Bedouin Life in Bible Lands," *The National Geographic Magazine*, January 1937, pp. 64,65.

Whiston, William; JOSEPHUS, The works of; Complete & Unabridged (First Edition), ©1905; includes his important work, "The Antiquities of the Jews." The complete works of Josephus (1,000 pages) is available from Amazon.com or at large libraries. Kregel Publications, Green Rapids, MI. ISBN 0-824-2952-8; LC 60-15405.

Whittock, Martyn; ROMAN EMPIRE (THE); Published by Peter Bedrick Books; © 1991, 1993 Whittok; ISBN 0-87226-118-2.

Wilke, Richard Byrd and Wilke, Julia Kitchens; DISCIPLE: Becoming Disciples through Bible Study; Study Manual, 2nd Edition; ©1993 Abingdon Press; 1-800-251-8591 or 672-1789.

Wyatt, Ron Eldon, amateur archaeologist, (1933-1999), SEARCHING FOR THE ARK OF THE COVENANT, http://ronwyatt.com.

Young, George; CONSTANTINOPLE; 1997 edition published by Barnes and Noble Books; 310 pp, ISBN 1-56619-084-3.

Some Interesting facts about Israel

IMPORTANT JEWISH HOLIDAYS
- New Year (*Rosh Hashanah*), the festival of trumpets at the beginning of the religious calendar in September - October.

- Day of Atonement (*Yom Kippur*) ten days after New Year, most solemn of all Jewish holy days.

- Feast of Booths (*Succoth*), five days after Yom Kippur, a time of joy, thanksgiving and celebration, open to all including gentiles.

- Passover (*Pesach*), eight days in the spring commemorating the Israelites escape from Egypt, explained more fully in Chapter Ten.

- Pentecost (*Shavuot*), also called the Feast of Weeks. This feast day falls on the fiftieth day after Passover and celebrates completion of the wheat harvest.

MORE ABOUT DAY OF ATONEMENT (Yom Kippur)

One day a year, designated as the Day of Atonement, the Jews fast and spend the day reflecting on the type of person they are and the kind of life they live. They do not work or do anything else on that day. It is a day to get right with God and fellow man. Under Jewish law, when a person sins against another person, to atone for it, the offender had to do three things:
- They must confess to the person sinned against,

- They must confess publicly, and

- They must ask for God's forgiveness.

SCAPEGOAT
- Want to know the origin of the term "scapegoat"? As part of the traditional Jewish observance of *Yom Kippur*, two goats are chosen as scapegoats to bear the sins of the people symbolically. They kill the first goat as a sacrifice for atonement. The second goat becomes a scapegoat to free the people from their guilt and shame. A priest would tie red wool yarn on the goat's horns, place his hands on the goat (a symbol of the sins of the people), bless the animal, and set it free in an uninhabited area.

FIGURE 11: BOARDING A BOAT ON THE GALILEE.

WWW.GOISRAEL.COM

Dedication

Dedicated to our "family" of pilgrims on Mount Scopus on our first trip in 1993 with the city of Jerusalem and Dome of the Rock in the background: Beginning on the back row left across to the right, then the next row right to left, and the front row left to right again.

AUTHOR'S PRIVATE COLLECTION

Back row: *Jon Heavener, Carolyn Leonard Heavener, Neil Glass, Paula Glass, Delbert Carman, Colleen Carman, Jean Burke, Joe Burke, Herb Wein, Lois Crooks, Ray Crooks, Norman Neaves, Kipp Neaves, Pat King, Art King, Mary Ann Wray, Ben Wray, Bobbie Davidson, Dave Davidson, Mattie Haynie, Dick Haynie, Susan Dickerson.*

Second row: *Kay Sandburg, Letha McMurtry, Phyllis Bennett, Renee Upp, Melba Howard, Bill Howard, Sherman Huff, Andrea Huff, Gayle Dekker, Dana Baze, Danny Baze, Lois Wein, Shirley Foutz.*

Front row: *Sherri Boyd, Linda Brinkworth, Mary Ellen Renshaw, Laveta Simpson, Dixie Fowler, Jeanna Smith, Donna Sanson, Owen Bennett, David Assael.*

Index of Illustrations

Every attempt has been made to identify photographers and secure permission to reprint. Any photo not specified with a credit or owners name is a part of the author's private collection. Public domain photos are photos to which the author has given up all rights and on which nobody is able to enforce any rights. Works of the United States Government and various other governments are excluded from copyright law. Copyright in photos expires after 50 or 70 years as of January 1 following the death of the author. Wikimedia Commons is part of the **non-profit**, multilingual, **free-content Wikimedia** family. Creative Commons is a non-profit organization that has released several copyright-licenses known as Creative Commons (CC) licenses. The Ministry of Tourism in Israel have generously offered the use of the many photos in this book labeled, "www.GoIsrael.com" to share the beauty and diversity of the country.

IMAGE NUMBER, PHOTO OWNER, PAGE NUNBER

COVER	CHARLIE WESTERFIELD	0
FIGURE 1: MARK TWAIN	AUTHOR	viii
FIGURE 3: A DOOR IN THE WADI QELT MONASTERY	VIIIAUTHOR	ix
FIGURE 2: MAP OF ISRAEL IN JESUS'S TIME	AUTHOR	X
FIGURE 4: COME ALONG AND JOIN OUR ADVENTURE!	AUTHOR	x
FIGURE 5: DR. NORMAN NEAVES	PROVIDED	xi
FIGURE 6: A CITY ON A HILL	AUTHOR	xiii

CHAPTER 1

FIGURE 1: TIME FOR A CHALLENGE	WWW.GOISRAEL.COM	6
FIGURE 2: BOYS IN BLACK SUITS	CREATIVE COMMONS	7
FIGURE 3: RELIGIONS	THE BRITISH LIBRARY	9
FIGURE 4: PRAYER BOOK	WIKIPEDIA.COM	10
FIGURE 5: QUEEN MELISENDE		10
FIGURE 6: JOSEPHUS	AUTHOR	13
FIGURE 7: TORAH SCROLL	PINTEREST.COM	14
FIGURE 8: QUILLS	PINTEREST.COM	15
FIGURE 9: GUTENBERG	WIKIPEDIA.COM	16
FIGURE 10: QUEEN MARY TUDOR	WIKIPEDIA.COM	17
FIGURE 11: QUEEN ELIZABETH I	AUTHOR	19
FIGURE 12: LIFE AMONG THE ESSENES	AUTHOR	20
FIGURE 13: THE SHRINE OF THE BOOK	AUTHOR	22
FIGURE 14: BREAKFAST IN ISRAEL	AUTHOR	24

CHAPTER 2

FIGURE 1: FLAGS AND LAUNDRY	NOAM CHEM, WWW.GOISRAEL.COM	26
FIGURE 2: MEZUZAH	LINDA MATHESON, ARTIST	28
FIGURE 3, MAP OF ABRAHAM'S JOURNEY	WWW.FREEBIBLEIMAGES.ORG	29
FIGURE 4: ABRAHAM'S SONS	JON HEAVENER	31
FIGURE 5: ABRAHAM'S DESCENDANTS	JON HEAVENER	31
FIGURE 6: LOVE STORY		32
FIGURE 7: JACOB'S DESCENDANTS	WIKIPEDIA.ORG	33
FIGURE 8: TWELVE TRIBES	DANA FRIEDLANDER, WWW.GOISRAEL.COM	35
FIGURE 9: MEDITERRANEAN BEACH	AUTHOR	37
FIGURE 10: HEADLESS STATUES	WWW.GOISRAEL.COM	38
FIGURE 11: GATE TO THE CITY	AUTHOR	40

CHAPTER 3

FIGURE 1: GATE TO THE CITY	MIKE CABA	40
FIGURE 2: THE DISCIPLE PAUL	CREATIVE COMMONS	41
FIGURE 3: KING AGRIPPA II AT TRIAL OF ST PAUL	CREATIVE COMMONS	43
FIGURE 4: THE ROMAN EMPIRE	JON HEAVENER	45
FIGURE 5: KING HEROD'S FAMILY	AUTHOR	46
FIGURE 6: CAESAREA-ON-THE-SEA	CREATIVE COMMONS	47
FIGURE 7: CLEOPATRA'S LOVERS	CREATIVE COMMONS	49
FIGURE 8: MARK ANTONY	PINTEREST.COM	50
FIGURE 9: EGYPTIAN FEMALE	CREATIVE COMMONS	51
FIGURE 10: CAESARION	CREATIVE COMMONS	52
FIGURE 11: HEROD THE GREAT	WIKIMEDIA COMMONS	53
FIGURE 12: AQUEDUCT	AUTHOR	54
FIGURE 13: SOLDIERS	CREATIVE COMMONS	54
FIGURE 14: OCTAVIAN	WIKIMEDIA COMMONS	55
FIGURE 15: TIBERIUS	CREATIVE COMMONS	56
FIGURE 16: ROMAN EMPEROR NERO		57
FIGURE 17: GEN. VESPASIAN	WWW.WIKIPEDIA.COM	58
FIGURE 18: TITUS, ROMAN EMPEROR		59
FIGURE 19: JERUSALEM TEMPLE SPOILS		60
FIGURE 20: HERODIUM	AUTHOR	61
FIGURE 21: RESTING ON HERODIUM	AUTHOR	62
FIGURE 22: ELIJAH	AUTHOR	63
FIGURE 23: STONE MANGER	JAMES DOBSON	64
FIGURE 24: PAGAN STATUE	NEW WORLD ENCYCLOPEDIA, CREATIVE COMMONS	65
FIGURE 25: KING AHAB AND QUEEN JEZEBEL	WWW.BIBLEWALKS.COM	66
FIGURE 26: ROMAN ROAD	AUTHOR	67
FIGURE 27: HAIFA	AUTHOR	70
FIGURE 28: THE GALILEE	AUTHOR	71
FIGURE 29: MARY'S WELL	AUTHOR	72

CHAPTER 4

FIGURE 1: NAZARETH	ITAMAR GRINBERG, WWW.GOISRAEL.COM	74

FIGURE 2: THE GALILEE BOAT .... AUTHOR 76
FIGURE 3: VIA MARIS .... AUTHOR 77
FIGURE 4: MILLSTONES .... WWW.GOISRAEL.COM 78
FIGURE 5: INSIDE THE CHURCH .... AUTHOR 79
FIGURE 6: RUINS AND THE CHURCH .... AUTHOR 79
FIGURE 6: CAPERNAUM .... WWW.GOISRAEL.COM 80
FIGURE 7: OLIVE OIL PRESS .... GOISRAEL.COM 81
FIGURE 8: BAPTISM .... TAI GLICK, WWW.GOISRAEL.COM 82
FIGURE 9: MOUNT OF BEATITUDES .... AUTHOR 86
FIGURE 10: WALKING TO GALILEE .... WIKIMEDIA COMMONS 88
FIGURE 11: GREENLINE .... WWW.GOISRAEL.COM 89
FIGURE 12: PRAYING AT THE WALL .... CREATIVE COMMONS 90

CHAPTER 5

FIGURE 1: THE WITCH OF ENDOR .... AUTHOR 92
FIGURE 2: BEIT SHE'AN RUIINS .... ITAMAR GRINBERG, WWW.GOISRAEL.COM 93
FIGURE 3: BLOODY AMPHITHEATRE .... AUTHOR 94
FIGURE 4: PUBLIC TOILETS .... AUTHOR 95
FIGURE 5: GIDEON'S SPRING .... AUTHOR 96
FIGURE 6: SWIMMING IN THE SPRING .... AUTHOR 96
FIGURE 7: ON THE JERICHO ROAD .... AUTHOR 98
FIGURE 8: BLOWING THE SHOFAR .... AUTHOR 99
FIGURE 9: CAMELS .... AUTHOR 100
FIGURE 10: FRESH FRUITS .... AUTHOR 101
FIGURE 11: A KICKING DONKEY .... AUTHOR 104
FIGURE 12: THE MONASTERY OF ST GEORGE .... AUTHOR 105
FIGURE 13: THE PATH AROUND THE MOUNTAIN .... AUTHOR 106
FIGURE 14: CAMERA DISCUSSION .... AUTHOR 107
FIGURE 15: ST. JOHN'S CRYPT .... AUTHOR 108
FIGURE 16: WELCOME TO JERUSALEM! .... AUTHOR 110
FIGURE 17: CLIMBING UP .... AUTHOR 112

CHAPTER 6

FIGURE 1: THE GREAT RIFT VALLEY .... AUTHOR 115
FIGURE 2: SWIMMING IN THE DEAD SEA .... WWW.GOISRAEL.COM 116
FIGURE 3: THE CABLE CAR .... WWW.WIKIPEDIA.COM 118
FIGURE 4: A TRIPLE-TIERED PALACE .... GOISRAEL.COM 119
FIGURE 5: RUINS OF MASADA .... WWW.ALLTHINGSCLIPART.COM 120
FIGURE 6: BOY VS. GIANT .... CREATIVE COMMONS 121
FIGURE 7: THE YOUNG DAVID .... WIKIPEDIA COMMONS 123
FIGURE 8: KING DAVID .... LINDA MATHESON 124
FIGURE 9: THE DIVIDED KINGDOM .... LINDA MATHESON 125
FIGURE 10: THE JEBUSITE CITY .... WWW.WIKIPEDIA.COM 127
FIGURE 11: THE TABERNACLE .... WWW.GROWINGKIDSINGRACE.BLOGSPOT.COM 128
FIGURE 12: THE KING'S DANCE .... AUTHOR 130
FIGURE 13: DAVID AND BATHSHEBA .... AUTHOR 131
FIGURE 14: ABSALOM'S TOMB .... NOAM CHEN, WWW.GOISRAEL.COM 135
FIGURE 15: MOUNT OLIVET .... AUTHOR 136
FIGURE 16: DOWN IN THE KIDRON VALLEY: .... ALBERT PERAL, WWW.GOISRAEL.COM 137
FIGURE 17: DAVID THE MUSICIAN .... NOAM CHEN, WWW.GOISRAEL.COM 139
FIGURE 18: EAST JERUSALEM .... GALYN WIEMERS 140

CHAPTER 7

FIGURE 1: SOLOMON'S TEMPLE LAYOUT .... WWW.THEBIBLEREVIEWED.COM 141
FIGURE 2: KING SOLOMON'S WEDDING .... WWW.GOISRAEL.COM 142
FIGURE 3: THE OPHEL STEPS .... AUTHOR 143
FIGURE 4: THE MOLTEN SEA .... WWW.WIKIPEDIA.ORG 144
FIGURE 5: INTERIOR OF THE TEMPLE .... WATCHJERUSALEM.CO.IL 146
FIGURE 6: CITY OF DAVID .... AUTHOR 147
FIGURE 7: SILWAN VILLAGE .... AUTHOR 148
FIGURE 8: TOMB OF THE PHAROAH'S DAUGHTER .... STOCK.ADOBE.COM 149
FIGURE 9: SOLOMON AND SHEBA .... LINDA MATHESON 150
FIGURE 10: JOURNEY TO BETHLEHEM .... AUTHOR 151
FIGURE 11: AN INNOCENT CHILD .... AUTHOR 155
FIGURE 12: THE SHEPHERD CHILD AND HER MOTHER .... AUTHOR 155
FIGURE 13: BETHLEHEM MANGER SQUARE .... JON HEAVENER 156
FIGURE 14: CHOOSING SOUVENIRS .... AUTHOR 158
FIGURE 15: THE DOOR OF HUMILITY .... AUTHOR 159
FIGURE 16: THE BIRTH GROTTO .... STOCK.ADOBE.COM 161
FIGURE 17: THE CHURCH OF THE NATIVITY .... AUTHOR 162
FIGURE 18: WEDDING CEREMONY .... GALYN WIEMERS 164
FIGURE 19: JERUSALEM IN AD 635 .... WWW.GOISRAEL.COM 165

CHAPTER 8

FIGURE 1: MACHICOLATION .... AUTHOR 167
FIGURE 2: SHOPPING .... WWW.GOISRAEL.COM 168
FIGURE 3: DAMASCUS GATE .... WWW.GOISRAEL.COM 170
FIGURE 4: GOLDEN GATE .... AUTHOR 172
FIGURE 5: HULDAH GATES .... ISRAELANDYOU.COM 173
FIGURE 6: MAP FROM JERUSALEM TO BETHANY .... AUTHOR 174
FIGURE 7: STONES OF MEMORY .... GALYN WIEMERS 175
FIGURE 8: TEMPLE MOUNT ELEVATION .... CREATIVE COMMONS 177
FIGURE 9: TEMPLE RECONSTRUCTION .... WWW.GOISRAEL.COM 178
FIGURE 10: WEEPING AND WAILING AT THE WALL .... WWW.GOISRAEL.COM 179
FIGURE 11: PRAYERS FOR PEACE .... AUTHOR 180
FIGURE 12: DOME OF THE ROCK .... WWW.GOISRAEL.COM 182
FIGURE 13: THE JOY OF A BAR MITZVAH CEREMONY .... AUTHOR 183
FIGURE 14: DOME OF THE ROCK .... PINTEREST.COM 184
FIGURE 15: DOME CROSS-SECTION .... PINTEREST.COM 185
FIGURE 16: ARK OF THE COVENANT .... AUTHOR 187
FIGURE 17: THE SACRED ROCK .... AUTHOR 189
FIGURE 18: MASONIC EMBLEM .... AUTHOR 190
FIGURE 19: KING SOLOMON'S MINES .... AUTHOR 191
FIGURE 20: INSIDE THE MINE .... AUTHOR 192
FIGURE 21: WINDOW FLOWER BOX .... AUTHOR 193
FIGURE 22: THE GIHON SPRING .... WWW.GOISRAEL.COM 195
FIGURE 23: HEZEKIAH'S TUNNEL .... AUTHOR 196
FIGURE 24: A CAMEL AND A PRETTY GIRL .... AUTHOR 199
FIGURE 25: THE MODEL CITY .... AUTHOR 200
FIGURE 26: ISRAEL CELEBRATES INDEPENDENCE .... AUTHOR 201
FIGURE 27: BAGEL CART .... WWW.GOISRAEL.COM 202

CHAPTER 9

FIGURE 1: CHURCH OF ST. ANNE .... WWW.GOISRAEL.COM 203
FIGURE 2: SEVERED HEAD .... WWW.BIBLEWALKS.COM 204
FIGURE 3: VERONICA'S VEIL .... AUTHOR 208
FIGURE 4: STEPPING DOWN .... AUTHOR 209
FIGURE 5: CRAWLNG INTO A TOMB .... AUTHOR 210
FIGURE 6: TOMB OF THE KINGS .... AUTHOR 211
FIGURE 7: THE TOMB ENTRANCE .... COMMONS 212

FIGURE 8: CONSTANTINE ................................WWW.CATHOLICCULTURE.COM ...213	FIGURE 3: CAMEL CARAVAN 1855 ....CREATIVE COMMONS 233
FIGURE 9: HELENA OF CONSTANTINOPLE ....AUTHOR.............................214	FIGURE 4: EGYPTIAN FEMALE...WWW.WIKIPEDIA.ORG 234
FIGURE 10: THE BAPTIZER'S ARM............................ WWW.WIKIPEDIACOMMONS.ORG ...215	FIGURE 5: LIFE IN EGYPT ....CREATIVE COMMONS 235
FIGURE 11: CHURCH OF THE HOLY SEPULCHRE ....GALYN WEIMERS 216	FIGURE 6: EGYPTIAN MALE ....WWW.WIKIPEDIA.COM 236
FIGURE 12: ELEVATION OF CHURCH OF SEPULCHRE.......CREATIVE COMMONS 217	FIGURE 7: MOSES...WWW.WIKIPEDIA.COM 238
FIGURE 13: THE IMMOVABLE LADDER ....GALYN WEIMERS 218	FIGURE 8: PRIESTS CARRYING THE ARK.........................AUTHOR....................................240
FIGURE 14: COURTYARD OF SEPULCHRE.......................WWW.GOISRAEL.COM 219	FIGURE 9: FAREWELL......................JCPA, JERUSALEM CENTER FOR PUBLIC AFFAIRS 242
FIGURE 15: THE CENACLE...AUTHOR.....................................220	FIGURE 10: TOPOGRAPHIC MAP OF THE GOLAN HEIGHTS...244
FIGURE 16: THE CHURCH OF ALL NATIONS 221	FIGURE 11: ISRAEL MAP ....WWW.GOISRAEL.COM 245
FIGURE 17: ANCIENT OLIVE TREE...................................AUTHOR.....................................225	FIGURE 11: BOARDING A BOAT ON THE GALILEE. ....AUTHOR....................................253
FIGURE 18: THE EUCHARIST ....AUTHOR.....................................226	
FIGURE 19: THE GARDEN TOMB ....AUTHOR.....................................227	

CHAPTER 10

FIGURE 1: STATUE... WWW.POTTERSPUBLISHING.COM 231	
FIGURE 2: JOSEPH...WWW.WIKIPEDIA.ORG 232	

Index

A

Aaron, Daniel, 23
Abiathar, 123-124
Abraham, vii, xiv, 7, 23, 26-31, 33, 39, 46, 99, 125-126, 154, 163, 175-176, 181, 185, 232-233, 236-237, 246, 255
Absalom, vii, 113, 132-135, 137-138, 256
Adonijah, 132, 137-138, 143
Agrippa, 42-43, 57-58, 209, 255
Agrippina, 56-57
Ahab, 35, 61-63, 65-66, 246, 255
Alexander, 45-46, 48, 50, 197, 246
Amnon, 132-133, 137
Aninoam the Jezreelite, 126
Antipas, 52-53, 55, 75, 98, 204-206, 224, 246
Antipater, 46-47, 246
Antonia Fortress, 58, 204, 206
Apocrypha, 14
Apollodorus, 48
aqueduct, 20, 44, 53-54, 107, 195, 255
Arab, 10, 27, 31, 73, 84-85, 89, 97, 109, 190, 246
Arabian wedding, 141, 164
Aramaic, 73, 153
Araunah, 128, 143, 176, 184, 246
Arch of Titus, 58, 60, 187
Archelaus, 52
Aristobulus, 46, 48, 53, 102
Ark of the Covenant, xii, xiv, 6, 58, 60, 92, 99, 129-130, 143-144, 146, 151, 153, 176, 186-187, 189-190, 215, 239, 243, 251
Armageddon, 62
Armenian Quarter, 168

B

Baal, 8, 60-63, 65, 97
bar mitzvah, 26, 181, 183
bat mitzvah, 26, 181
Bathsheba, 35, 130-132, 137, 149, 256
Battle of Actium, 51
beautiful wife, 125
Bedouin, 154-155, 157, 164, 247, 251
Beit She'an, vii, 43, 91-95, 99, 126, 256
Benaiah, 143
Benjamin, 8, 32-34, 232, 234-235
Berenice, 43, 57-59
Bethany, 10, 82, 135, 171, 174, 206, 221
Bethlehem, vii, 33-35, 48, 52-53, 55, 59-60, 63, 67, 75, 104, 121, 128, 141, 151, 153-158, 160-161, 163-165, 213-214, 217, 256
Bethsaida, 75, 132
Bilhah, 30, 32-33, 236
black mud, 117
Bloody Mary, 17
boat
    (the Jesus boat), 71
Boaz, 121, 153-154, 158
Boleyn, Anne, 16, 17
Branch-Davidian compound, 2
Burnt House, 195
burqa, 8
Byzantium, 213

C

Caesarea-by-the-Sea, 39-43, 46, 54, 223
Caesarion, 49, 52
Caiaphas, 207, 219-220, 223
Caligula, 56
camel, 102, 125, 154, 199-200, 204, 232-233, 256-257
Capernaum, vii, 53, 73, 75-80, 86, 256
Cardo, 168, 194

Catherine of Aragon, 16-17
Cenicle, 203, 214
Children's Memorial, 230-231
Chileab, 132
Church of the Nativity, 34, 157-162, 164, 217
Church of the sepulchre, 8-10, 158, 213-214, 218-219
City of David, 5, 127-131, 134, 141, 144, 147, 149, 152, 175, 195, 197, 210, 222, 249, 256
Claudia, 49, 57
Claudius, 41, 56
Claudius Lysias, 41
Cleopatra, 35, 48-52, 98, 100, 102, 255
Cleopatra Selene, 50
Constantinople, 10, 44-45, 206, 213-216, 247, 251, 257
Cornelia Cinnilla, 48
Cornelius, 41
Crusader, 8-10, 203, 218, 222, 246
Crusaders, 6, 8-9, 39, 107, 157, 164, 168, 190, 216, 218-219, 246

D

Damascus gate, 168-170, 190, 194, 202, 209, 226, 256
Damascus Gate, 168-170, 190, 194, 202, 209, 226, 256
David, vii, xiv, 5, 29, 35, 58-60, 91, 93, 102, 113, 121-134, 136-139, 141, 143-145, 147, 149, 152-154, 157-158, 163, 171, 174-176, 181, 186, 194-195, 197, 209-210, 216, 221-222, 246, 249-250, 254, 256-257
Dead Sea, vii, 11, 18-21, 30, 51, 60-61, 82, 93, 104, 113-120, 134, 200, 205, 243, 256
Dead Sea Scrolls, 18, 21
Diaspora, 67, 179-180, 246
Dickerson, Susan, 254
Dome of the Rock, vii, 29, 85, 152, 167, 176, 180-182, 184-185, 194, 254, 256
Druze, 85
Dung Gate, 171, 175

E

El Al (Israel) Airlines, 1, 3, 4, 23, 39, 241, 242
Eleazar ben Yair, 119
Elie, 23, 67, 83, 98, 102-103, 107, 158, 232, 241

Elijah, 60-63, 102, 104, 107-108, 112, 255
the Tishbite, 60
Elizabeth I, 17, 255
Engedi, vii, 113, 125-126
Esau, 30-31, 33, 46
Essenes, 11, 19

F

falafel, 67-68, 169, 242
Father Antonios, 107-109
Felix, 42
Fulvia, 49-50

G

Galilee, vii, ix, 11, 39, 46, 52-53, 55, 57, 66, 68-71, 73, 75-78, 80, 82-83, 85-86, 88, 91, 93, 115, 224, 243, 246, 253, 255-256
Gallim, 124, 126
Garden of Gethsemane, xii, 82, 134-136, 141, 172, 207
gatehouse, 39-40
gates of Jerusalem, vii, 9, 152, 167, 169, 241
Gaza Strip, 83-84, 98, 198
gentile, 26, 41, 69, 172, 180, 201, 223
Gideon's Spring, vii, 91, 96-97, 256
Gihon Spring, 195-197, 256
Glass, Neil, 254
Golan Heights, 76, 80, 83-84, 98, 198, 244
Golden (or Eastern) Gate, 141, 172, 256
Goliath, 121-122
Great Rift, 115, 117
Greek, 14-15, 44-45, 73, 101, 104, 107-108, 158, 163-164, 194, 197, 208, 210, 213, 217, 250
Gregorian calendar, 25
Gutenberg, Johann, 15
gvil, 12-13

H

Hadrian, 161, 169-170, 180, 194, 214
Hagar, 28-31
Haifa, vii, 39, 67, 70, 255

Hasidic Jews, 5
Hasmoneans, 197-198
Hebron, 30, 126-128, 132-133
Helena, vii, 161, 163, 203, 209-210, 213-215, 219, 257
Herod, vii, xiv, 11, 25, 30, 39, 42, 44, 46-48, 50-55, 57-59, 61, 75, 98, 100, 102, 118-120, 129, 154, 168-171, 176-180, 187, 190, 198, 205-207, 209, 220, 223-224, 246-247, 249, 255
Herod the Great, 25, 46, 50, 52-53, 58, 75, 98, 102, 168, 170, 176, 198, 205-206, 209, 246, 249, 255
Herodian Quarter, 194-195
Herodium, vii, 39, 48, 52, 59-62, 102, 154, 255
hijab, 8
Holocaust Museum, 229
Holy of Holies, 146, 152, 176, 181, 186
Huldah gates, 173, 256

I

Indiana Jones, 186, 189, 247
Isaac, 28-31, 33, 62, 99, 157, 176, 232, 236, 247-248
Ishbaal, 126
Ishmael, 28-31, 157
Ishtar Gate, 152
Israel Museum, 20-21, 119, 200
Israel's Independence Day, 201,202
Istanbul, 10, 44-45, 195, 213, 215-217

J

Jacob, xiv, 30-35, 107-108, 200, 232-236, 246, 255
Jaffa Gate, 129, 168, 171, 194
James and John, 77-78, 132
Jebus, vii, 113, 126-129, 141, 175
Jericho, vii, 48, 50, 82, 91, 97-104, 107, 109, 171, 174, 187, 190, 194, 235, 239, 246, 256
Jesse, 121-122, 153
Jewish calendar, 25
Jewish Cemetery, 75, 175, 198
Jewish Quarter, 171, 193-195, 198
Jezebel, 35, 61-62, 66, 104, 255
Jezreel, 62-63, 91
Joab, 127-128, 131, 133-134, 137-138, 143
John Mark, 206, 219-220

John the Baptist, 52, 82, 102, 107, 204-206, 215, 217
John the Baptizer, 205
Jonathan, 21, 92-93, 122-124
Jordan River, vii, 73, 83-84, 91, 93, 97-98, 101, 103, 198, 204, 243
Joseph, vii, 32-35, 52, 55, 73, 104, 207-208, 226, 229, 232-236, 257
Josephus, 11-12, 30, 46, 52, 57-58, 92, 102, 120-121, 135, 178, 205, 210-211, 224, 247, 250-251, 255
Joshua, 63, 83, 98-99, 187, 239, 246
Julia, 55-56, 247, 251
Julius Caesar, 45-46, 48-49, 51, 55
Justinian, 161

K

Keturah, 30, 237
kibbutz, vii, 39, 68-69, 75-77, 83, 86-88
Kidron Valley, xi-xii, 134, 136-138, 145, 148-149, 152
King Agrippa, 42-43, 255
King David, vii, 5, 29, 91, 102, 113, 124, 128-134, 136-137, 139, 143, 154, 158, 174, 176, 181, 186, 221-222, 246, 249, 256
King Henry VIII, 16-17
King Herod, vii, 39, 42, 46, 51-52, 118, 120, 154, 247, 249, 255
King Hezekiah, 195
King Hussein, 184
King James Bible, 11, 18
King Nebuchadnezzar, 27, 152, 194
King of France, 191
King Saul, vii, 91-92, 121-126, 129, 246
King Talmai, 132-133
King Zedekiah, 194
King's dance (the), 129-130
Kiriath-Jearim, 129
Knights Templar, 190-191
kosher, 12-13, 26, 69
Kursi, 80-81, 87

L

Laban, 30-33

ladder (the immovable), 218, 257
LaGuardia, 1-2, 242
Large Stone Structure, 129
Leah, 30, 32-33, 230-231, 236
Lion's Gate, 168, 171, 172, 204
Little Sisters of Jesus, 208
Livia, 55
Livia Drusilla, 55
Lot's wife, 117
Luther, Martin, 15

M

Maacah, 132, 134
Maccabee, 161
Mameluke, 246
manger, 63-64, 156, 160, 163-164, 255-256
Manger Square, 156, 160, 256
Mariamne I, 46, 198
Mark Antony, 46, 48-51, 55, 102, 255
Mark Twain, v, 74, 92, 168-169, 176, 208, 217, 255
Mary Magdalene, 207
Mary, Queen of Scots, 18
Mary's Well, 72-73, 255
Masada, vii, 2, 48, 58, 102, 113-114, 118-121, 205, 246, 256
Masada Fortress, 2
Masonic Lodges, 190
Megiddo, vii, 39, 62-65, 77, 99
Menelik, 151
mezuzah, 26-27, 237, 255
Michal, 122-124, 126, 129-130, 132
Michelson, Leah, 230-231
mikveh, 19, 26, 177
military service, 53
millstones, 78, 256
model city, vii, xiv, 167, 178, 200-201, 204, 256
Muhammed, 7, 185, 186
Molten Sea (the), 144, 146, 256
Moses, vii, 7, 14, 30, 99, 129, 145, 186, 188, 215, 229, 236-239, 241, 246, 257
Mosque of Omar, 85, 160, 185, 246

Mount Carmel, 53, 60-63
Mount Gilboa, 91, 94
Mount Hermon, 82-84
Mount Moriah, 5, 29, 128, 141, 143, 147, 175-176, 181, 185, 188-189
Mount Nebo, 187
Mount of Beatitudes, vii, 85-86, 88, 256
Mount of Olives, xi-xii, 134-135, 137-138, 141, 152, 171, 174-175, 180, 198, 222
Mount of Temptation, 101
Mount Scopus, xii, 134, 172, 254
Mount Sinai, 129, 145, 237, 239
Mount Zion, 141, 147, 175, 219-221
Murrah Federal Building, 2
Museum of the Bible, 12-13
Muslim, 8, 10, 27, 73, 85, 113, 167-168, 170-171, 186, 188, 190, 194, 198, 203, 215, 218, 222, 228

N

Nabal, 124-126
Naomi, 153-154
Nazareth, vii, 52-53, 55, 73-75, 77, 86, 158, 224, 255
Kipp Neaves, 1, 254
Norman Neaves, iii, vi-vii, xi-xii, 107, 254-255
Nebuchadnezzar, 27, 152, 176, 194
Nero, 42, 56-57, 246, 255
New Gate, 169, 171

O

Obed-edom, 129
Octavia, 50-52, 57
Octavian, 49-53, 55-56, 98, 100, 255
olive press, 80, 135
Oodi, 113-114, 117, 121
Ophel, 141, 197, 256

P

Pagans, 6, 8
Palm Sunday, 135, 172, 174-176
Palm Sunday Road, 135

Paltiel, 124, 126

Paul, 7, 26, 30, 41-43, 47, 57, 59, 215, 220, 246-247, 250, 255

Pentateuch, 12, 14

Peter, 41, 77-80, 83, 85, 176, 207-208, 215, 220-221, 223, 246-247, 250-251, 256

Pharaoh, 28, 35, 51, 91, 142, 145-146, 148-149, 151, 233-237, 248, 257

Pharaoh Shishak, 91

Pharaoh's daughter, 142, 145, 148-149, 151, 248

Pharisees, 74, 198, 207

philactery (phylactery), 230

Philip, 17, 52-53, 55, 98, 191, 205

Philistines, 91-92, 121-122, 129, 187, 194

phylacteries, 26

Plutarch, 48, 52, 250

Pontius Pilate, xii, 44, 55, 207, 215, 220, 223, 246

Potiphar, 233-234

Praetorian Guard, 56

Prince Philip of Spain, 17

Ptolemy, 48

public water closets, 95

Q

Queen Helena of Adiabene, 209

Queen of Sheba, 151

Qumran, vii, 1, 10-11, 18-20, 255

Dead Sea Scrolls, 18, 21

R

Rachel, vii, 23, 30-35, 153, 157-158, 232, 236

Ramallah, 84

Rebekah, 30-31

Red Beard, 191

Rehoboam, 152

religious relics, 158, 163, 206, 214-215, 217

Reuben, 33-34, 232-233

Richard the Lion-Hearted, 191

road system, 65

Robinson's Arch, 177

Ruth, 121, 153-154, 158

S

Sadducees, 198

Saint Mark's Basilica in Venice, 215

Saint Peter's fish, 83

Saladin, 191, 218

Salome, 35, 46-47, 52-53, 205

Samaritan, 103

Samuel, v, 91-93, 121-129, 131, 133-134, 136, 138, 153, 158, 187, 218

the prophet, 7, 60, 92, 102, 121, 124, 153, 187, 195, 222

Sarah, vi, 28-31

Saudi Arabia, 7-8, 10

Scribonia, 55

Septuagint, 14

Shabbat, vii, 113-114, 207

Sharia law, 8

Sheep Gate, 171

shofar, 99, 187, 256

Shrine of the Book, vii, 1, 20-21, 200

Silent Cry, 230

Simeon, 33-34, 234

Simpson, Laveta, 247, 250

Six-Day War, 83, 193-194, 198, 247

Sodom, 117

Solomon, vii, xii, xiv, 5-6, 9, 14, 29, 35, 48, 63, 85, 91, 125, 131-132, 137-138, 141-152, 175-178, 186-192, 195, 201, 209, 239, 246, 256

Solomon's Temple, xiv, 6, 9, 85, 141, 144, 146-147, 151-152, 176, 187-188, 190, 201, 246, 256

Solomon's Stables, 63, 191

Solomons palace, 141

Sons of Thunder, 78

Stepped Stone Structure, 129

Suleiman the Magnificent, 10, 181

T

Tabgha, 78, 80, 83, 86, 206

Tamar, 132-134

Tel (mound or hill), 64
Temple Mount, xii, xiv, 9, 85, 128-129, 134, 141, 167, 170, 173, 175, 177, 181, 185-186, 188-191, 195, 197-198, 222, 256
Terah, 28
The Living Bible, 18, 247-248, 251
Tiberias, 75, 86
(the city), 75, 86
Tiberius, 44, 53, 55-56, 255
tilapia, 83
Titus, 11, 43, 57-60, 187, 255
Tomb of the Kings, 209, 211, 256
Topkapi Palace, 215, 217
Tyndale, William, 15-16

U

Upper Room, 139, 206, 219-222
Uriah the Hittite, 130

V

Veronica, 207-208, 256
Vespasian, 11, 57-59, 255
Via Dolorosa, 168, 171, 207-208
Via Maris, 63, 66, 77, 256
Vipsania, 56
virgin queen, 17-18

W

Waco, Texas, 2
Wadi Qelt, vii-viii, 61, 91, 104-105, 107-109, 255
wailing wall, 6, 168, 180
Well of Souls, 185-186
West Bank,
    (of the Jordan), vii, 18, 34, 73, 83-84, 98, 104, 153, 157, 198-199
Wicked Bible, 16
Witch of Endor, 92, 256
World Trade Center, 2
Wyatt, Ron, 187-190, 247
Wycliff, John, 15

Y

Yad Vashem, vii, 229-231
Yardenit, 82, 204
Yarmulke, 5, 114

Z

Zacchaeus, 100
Zachariah, 137-138
zealot, 2, 118-120, 174
Zebedee, 78
Zerubbabel, 176-178, 246
Zerubbabel's temple, 176-178
Zilpah, 30, 32-33, 236
Zion gate, 168, 171, 194

About the Author

Carolyn B. Leonard

Author of this volume, as well as *Who's Your Daddy? A Guide to Genealogy from Start to Finish,* and *The First Hundred Years {in America},* Leonard is a popular speaker at organizations, fairs, and festivals, especially when talking about her favorite subjects, genealogy and writing.

A former rural newspaper editor, Leonard remained for many years a commissioned writer for *Persimmon Hill,* the award-winning magazine of the National Cowboy and Western Heritage Museum. Hobbies include flower gardening, photography, genealogy, travel, history, computer networking, writer meetings, friends, family and grandchildren (not necessarily in that order). She is especially excited about this book, having recently learned from a DNA test that she is actually 5% Jewish and believes that is one reason why she has always been fascinated with Israel.

I want to thank the many fellow writers who have critiqued my manuscript and offered suggestions over the years of research, but most of all Sandra Soli, poet extraordinaire and the queen of editing, who turned the first edition into an exacting book. There are those for whom my gratitude goes deeper than words can express, my children who have been my biggest supporters in my research and writing, and filled my world with excitement and the joyfulness of life, and my husband Jon who has been my greatest friend, fellow traveler, and my eternal love.

For more information and to learn about her current travels and projects, visit her webpage:
www.CarolynBLeonard.com

You can pick up tips and notes about Israel at:
www.ToIsraelBook.com

Check out her book on genealogy and download free stuff at:
www.WhosYourDaddyBook.com

Let her know how you liked this book about Israel. Email her: **CarolynLeonard@me.com**
Sign up for Carolyn's free monthly newsletter, *Writers Reminder.*

Books by Carolyn B. Leonard, available in bookstores and from Amazon.com.

Who's your Daddy? (2nd Edition)
A Guide to Genealogy from Start to Finish
(Hardback) ISBN 978-1-883852-19-1
(softcover) ISBN 13: 978-1-883852-08-5
(e-book)ISBN 13: 978-1-883852-11-5
Library of Congress Control Number: 2018906060
Size 6x9, 272 pages, 60 illustrations
Spine width 0.614 inches weight 0.891 lb

To Israel, With Love: (2nd Edition)
A Journey of Discovery in History,
Mystery, Travel, and Relationships
Hardback ISBN 13: 978-1883852-18-4
Softcover ISBN 13: 978-1883852-09-2
E-book ISBN 13: 978-883852-10-8
Library of Congress control number 2018902864
Size 8x10, 280 pages, 202 illustrations

The First Hundred Years
The US Presidents, the Federal Census, and Current Events
that Influenced the Lives of your Ancestors 1790-1890
Hardback ISBN: 978-1-883852-14-6
Softcover ISBN 13: 978-1-883852-12-2
E-book ISBN: 13: 978-1-883852-13-9
Library of Congress control number: 2019901259
Size 6x9, 336 pages, 76 illustrations

Coming soon:
The Second Century
The US Presidents, the Federal Census, and Current Events
that Influenced the Lives of your Ancestors 1900-1970
Hardback ISBN 13: 978-1-883852- 17-7
Softcover ISBN 13: 978-1-883852-15-3
E-book ISBN 13: 978-1-883852-16-0

Books by Carolyn B. Leonard, available in bookstores and from Amazon.com.

www.ingramcontent.com/pod-product-compliance
Lightning Source LLC
Chambersburg PA
CBHW051246110526
44588CB00025B/2896